CHAPTER 1
INTRODUCTION

There are many reasons why people choose to grow vegetables at home or on an allotment — exercise, fresh air, an escape from workaday worries, the joy of actually eating your own produce, and so on. There is no need to dwell on these points as you are already beginning or continuing to be a member of the grow-your-own society.

For many years the various editions of the *Vegetable & Herb Expert* have provided information and guidance to millions of people, and now it is time for a new edition. The reason is quite simple — gardening does not stand still. Since the last edition many new varieties of standard vegetables have appeared, and some old favourites are no longer listed in the popular catalogues. There are also non-standard vegetables such as the Oriental and the salad leaf types, and also new products such as grafted vegetables.

Many new vegetables and varieties have appeared, and many established pesticides have disappeared. The purpose of this updated and enlarged *Vegetable & Herb Expert* is to provide you with an up-to-date guide to Britain's favourite outdoor activity.

GETTING STARTED

Seeds were once bought only in packets, but there are now seed tapes, mats and discs to make the job easier. Seedlings were once bought in trays, but roots were damaged when separating the young plants. Plugs in modules have now taken over. Some seedlings such as tomatoes are sold in pots, and so are rooted cuttings of perennials. Finally there are some vegetables where bare plant material is the starting point.

SEED PACKETS

PLUGS IN MODULES

SEEDLINGS IN POTS

PLANTS IN POTS

SEED TAPES

SEED MATS

PLANT MATERIAL

CROP ROTATION

You should not grow a vegetable in the same spot year after year. If you do then soil troubles are likely to build up, and the level of nutrients will become unbalanced. Crop rotation is the answer, and the standard 3 year plan is shown below. A strip of land at one end of the plot is sometimes used for permanent crops (rhubarb, asparagus etc) and is left out of the plan. Not everyone is willing to follow this rotation plan, and regrettably all idea of a rotation is abandoned. It would be much better to follow a very simple rotation which is shown on the right — above ground crops this year, roots next year and then back to above ground crops.

SIMPLE ROTATION

YEAR 1
ABOVE GROUND CROPS

YEAR 2
ROOTS

YEAR 3
SAME AS YEAR 1

TRADITIONAL ROTATION

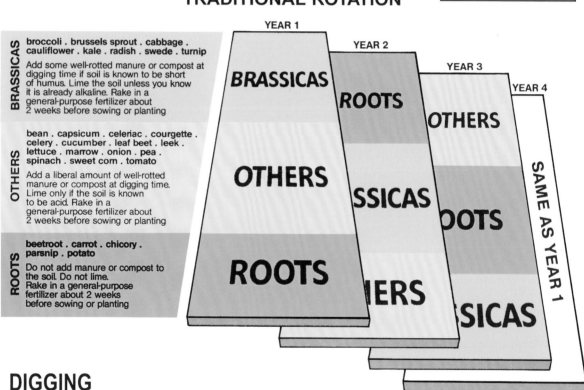

BRASSICAS
broccoli . brussels sprout . cabbage . cauliflower . kale . radish . swede . turnip

Add some well-rotted manure or compost at digging time if soil is known to be short of humus. Lime the soil unless you know it is already alkaline. Rake in a general-purpose fertilizer about 2 weeks before sowing or planting

OTHERS
bean . capsicum . celeriac . courgette . celery . cucumber . leaf beet . leek . lettuce . marrow . onion . pea . spinach . sweet corn . tomato

Add a liberal amount of well-rotted manure or compost at digging time. Lime only if the soil is known to be acid. Rake in a general-purpose fertilizer about 2 weeks before sowing or planting

ROOTS
beetroot . carrot . chicory . parsnip . potato

Do not add manure or compost to the soil. Do not lime. Rake in a general-purpose fertilizer about 2 weeks before sowing or planting

YEAR 1 BRASSICAS / OTHERS / ROOTS
YEAR 2 ROOTS / BRASSICAS / OTHERS
YEAR 3 OTHERS / ROOTS / BRASSICAS
YEAR 4 SAME AS YEAR 1

DIGGING

- Choose a spade which is suited to your height and strength. Keep the blade clean.
- Choose the right day. The ground must be neither frozen nor saturated. If possible pick a time of settled weather.
- Begin slowly. About 30 minutes is quite enough for the first day if you are not used to strenuous exercise.
- Insert the blade vertically, not at an angle. Annual weeds can be turned in but roots of perennial weeds should be removed.
- Leave the soil in lumps — frost will break down the clods during winter.
- Never bring subsoil to the surface — raw clay, chalk or sand will ruin the fertility.

The time for digging is during a dry spell in late autumn or early winter if you plan to sow or plant in spring. Dig out a trench about 45 cm (1½ ft) wide and 1 spit (spade-depth) deep at the front of the plot and transport the soil to the back. Spread compost over the surface of the area to be enriched with humus (see 'crop rotation' above). Now begin to dig the plot — invert a 10-15 cm (4-6 in.) wide strip of soil into the trench in front. Move back, turning over each successive strip until a final trench is formed. Fill this with the soil brought over from the first trench. Once every 3 years some keen vegetable growers still carry out double digging in order to break up the compacted layer below the depth of digging.

The *NEW* VEGETABLE & HERB EXPERT

Dr. D. G. Hessayon

All Editions & Reprints: 6,100,000 copies

Published by Expert Books
a division of Transworld Publishers

Copyright © Expert Publications Ltd 2014

The right of Dr. D. G. Hessayon to be identified
as author of this work has been asserted in accordance with sections
77 and 78 of the Copyright Designs and Patents Act 1988.

A catalogue record for this book is available from the British Library

TRANSWORLD PUBLISHERS
61-63 Uxbridge Road, London W5 5SA
a division of the Random House Group Ltd

Contents

The Random House Group Limited supports the Forest Stewardship Council (FSC®), the leading international forest certification organisation. Our books carrying the FSC label are printed on FSC® certified paper. FSC is the only forest certification scheme endorsed by the leading environmental organisations, including Greenpeace. Our paper procurement policy can be found at www.randomhouse.co.uk/environment

MIX
Paper from responsible sources
FSC
www.fsc.org
FSC® C016897

Reproduction by Spot On Digital Imaging Ltd, Gomm Road, High Wycombe, Bucks HP13 7DJ
Printed and bound in Great Britain by Butler, Tanner & Dennis Ltd, Frome

CHAPTER 2
STANDARD VEGETABLES

This chapter is an A-Z guide to standard vegetables, which raises a question .... what is a standard vegetable? It is not the same thing as a popular vegetable — lettuce, carrots, beetroot, cabbage and the rest of the universal favourites. They are included, of course, but so is celeriac, kohl rabi and aubergine which you will not find growing on the average plot.

The definition is quite simple — a standard vegetable is one you can expect to find in all the popular catalogues, and has been there for many years. No doubt the major part or all of your seed list is drawn from this list, and that is the way it should be. This does not mean that you should grow the same varieties year after year. New varieties continue to appear, and it is worth considering a change if the description offers a worthwhile benefit.

When making up your seed list from the standard vegetable group your first consideration should be the likes and dislikes of the family. It is a waste of time to grow a vegetable which the family will leave on their plate. Once you have this acceptable list, read the notes in this chapter on each of these vegetables. Can you give it a suitable home?

You now have a list of old friends and perhaps some new varieties from the range of standard vegetables. It is now time to look through the chapters on novelty varieties and non-standard vegetables. A plot made up of the top 10 varieties plus potatoes, or a plot full of vegetables your neighbour doesn't have — it is entirely up to you.

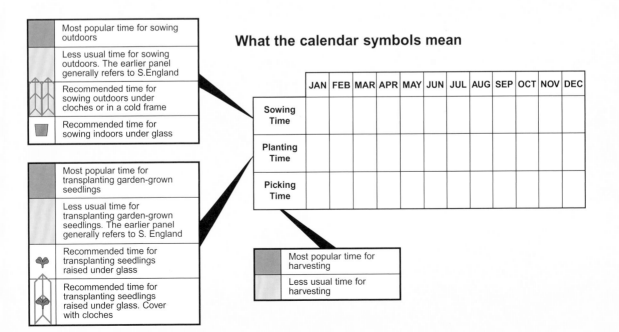

	Most popular time for sowing outdoors
	Less usual time for sowing outdoors. The earlier panel generally refers to S.England
	Recommended time for sowing outdoors under cloches or in a cold frame
	Recommended time for sowing indoors under glass

	Most popular time for transplanting garden-grown seedlings
	Less usual time for transplanting garden-grown seedlings. The earlier panel generally refers to S. England
	Recommended time for transplanting seedlings raised under glass
	Recommended time for transplanting seedlings raised under glass. Cover with cloches

What the calendar symbols mean

	JAN	FEB	MAR	APR	MAY	JUN	JUL	AUG	SEP	OCT	NOV	DEC
Sowing Time												
Planting Time												
Picking Time												

| | Most popular time for harvesting |
| | Less usual time for harvesting |

Artichoke, Globe

Globe artichoke is more at home in the herbaceous border than growing in a small vegetable plot. It is a handsome, thistle-like plant which grows about 1 m (3 ft) high. The leaves provide an attractive feature, but do not let it bloom — the ball-like heads are removed for cooking just before the fleshy scales open. It needs good soil, regular watering and feeding, plus frost protection in winter. Plant rooted suckers each spring so that mature specimens can be disposed of after a few years.

IN A NUTSHELL

Use offsets (rooted suckers) taken either from high-yielding plants in your own garden or bought from a garden centre. These offsets should be about 25 cm (10 in.) high and must have roots attached. Raising plants from seed is possible, but is not advisable.

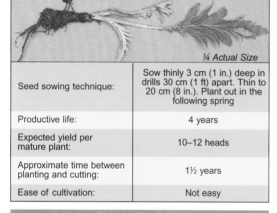

¼ Actual Size

Seed sowing technique:	Sow thinly 3 cm (1 in.) deep in drills 30 cm (1 ft) apart. Thin to 20 cm (8 in.). Plant out in the following spring
Productive life:	4 years
Expected yield per mature plant:	10–12 heads
Approximate time between planting and cutting:	1½ years
Ease of cultivation:	Not easy

SOIL FACTS

- Light or loamy soil in a sunny, sheltered location is needed — it is a waste of time to grow this crop in heavy clay. Good drainage is essential.
- Dig the soil in autumn and incorporate a liberal amount of compost or well-rotted manure. Rake in a compound fertilizer shortly before planting.

PLANTING

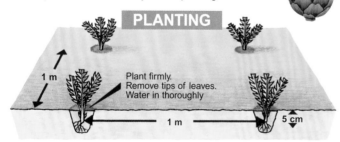

1 m

Plant firmly.
Remove tips of leaves.
Water in thoroughly

1 m

5 cm

CALENDAR

	JAN	FEB	MAR	APR	MAY	JUN	JUL	AUG	SEP	OCT	NOV	DEC
Sowing Time				▓								
Planting Time			▓	▓								
Cutting Time							▓	▓	▓	▓		

LOOKING AFTER THE CROP

- Keep the plants well watered until established. Apply a mulch around the stems in May.
- During the summer months hoe regularly and apply a liquid fertilizer at fortnightly intervals. Water thoroughly when the weather is dry.
- In late autumn cut down the stems and cover the crowns with bracken, leaves or straw. Remove this protective covering in April.

HARVESTING

- A few small heads will begin to form in the first year. Do not let them develop — cut off immediately and discard.
- Regular cropping begins in the season after planting. Remove the terminal bud ('king head') first. It should be large and swollen but still green and unopened. Leave 5–8 cm (2–3 in.) of the stem attached.
- Feed the plants after this initial cropping. Later in the season remove and cook the smaller secondary heads.

IN THE KITCHEN

Eating a globe artichoke may seem inelegant but it is a delicious vegetable, served hot or cold. The fleshy half-moon at the base of each cooked scale is chewed, after which the scale is placed back on the plate. When all the scales have been used in this way, the hairy centre ('choke') is removed. The fleshy heart ('fond') is then eaten with a knife and fork.

STORAGE: Keep in a polythene bag in the refrigerator — heads will stay fresh for up to 1 week.

COOKING: Cut off stalk, remove outer layer of scales and then wash thoroughly to remove insects. Boil in salted water for 30–40 minutes. To eat, remove each scale in turn and dip the base in melted butter, vinaigrette or hollandaise sauce.

VARIETIES

GREEN GLOBE: Large green heads — the variety you are most likely to find in the seed catalogues.

PURPLE GLOBE: Hardier than its green relative, but bottom of the ratings for flavour.

VERT DE LAON: This is the one to buy as offsets from your garden centre. Highly recommended.

VIOLETTA DI CHIOGGIA: An excellent purple variety to raise from seed.

TROUBLES

PETAL BLIGHT

A serious but uncommon disease. Brown spots rapidly join together so that the head is ruined. Remove and burn affected tops.

APHID

Both blackfly and greenfly attack developing flower-heads. Spray with insecticidal soap or pyrethrins as soon as the first attacks are seen.

SLUGS

Young shoots are attacked during wet weather in spring. Sprinkle slug pellets around the plants.

For key to symbols — see page 7

Artichoke, Jerusalem

The knobbly tubers are used as an alternative to potatoes — fine for slimmers but not to everybody's taste. Buy some and try them before planting a row. These grow-anywhere hardy plants will tower up to 3 m (10 ft) or more — an excellent screen or windbreak but a line of them will form a light-robbing shield for lowly vegetables planted below. The name indicates the close relationship to the sunflower and not to the Middle East — it comes from the Italian word *girasole* (sun follower).

IN A NUTSHELL

Tubers bought from the greengrocer or supermarket can be used for planting. Choose roots which are the size of a small hen's egg.

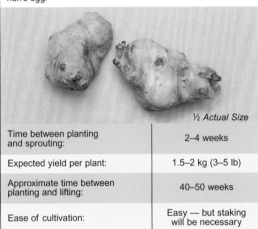

½ Actual Size

Time between planting and sprouting:	2–4 weeks
Expected yield per plant:	1.5–2 kg (3–5 lb)
Approximate time between planting and lifting:	40–50 weeks
Ease of cultivation:	Easy — but staking will be necessary

SOIL FACTS

- Not fussy at all, provided that the soil is neither very acid nor subject to prolonged waterlogging in winter. It is a useful plant for breaking up heavy land.
- Dig the soil in autumn or early winter and incorporate compost if the soil is short of humus.

PLANTING

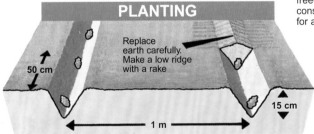

Replace earth carefully. Make a low ridge with a rake

50 cm

15 cm

1 m

CALENDAR

	JAN	FEB	MAR	APR	MAY	JUN	JUL	AUG	SEP	OCT	NOV	DEC
Planting Time												
Lifting Time												

LOOKING AFTER THE CROP

- Use a hoe to earth-up the base of the stems when the plants are about 30 cm (1 ft) high. Water in dry weather.
- Insert a cane at each end of the row and run plastic-coated wire on either side of the plants. In this way they will be protected from the wind.
- During the summer months remove flower buds as they form and feed occasionally with a liquid fertilizer.

HARVESTING

- Cut down the stems to about 30 cm (1 ft) above the ground once the leaves have turned brown in autumn. Lift the tubers as required between October and early spring — cover the stem bases with straw or soil in severe weather.
- At the end of the season reserve some of the tubers for planting purposes. Make sure that all tubers have been removed from the soil — any left in the soil will grow as weeds.

IN THE KITCHEN

Boiled, fried, baked, roasted or stewed — Jerusalem artichokes provide a novel alternative to potatoes. The gourmets praise creamed artichoke soup and also artichoke rissoles made by forming boiled and mashed artichokes into small balls or flat cakes which are then fried in deep fat.

STORAGE: Keep in a polythene bag in the refrigerator — tubers will stay fresh for up to 2 weeks.

COOKING: To prepare artichokes for boiling, scrub the tubers immediately after lifting and then boil in their skins in water containing a teaspoonful of vinegar. Cook for 20–25 minutes — peel before serving.

VARIETIES

The usual planting material is a white-skinned type bought from the greengrocer or supermarket, so the variety is not known. If you can, buy a named variety from your garden centre or nursery.

FUSEAU: This is the one to buy — long, white tubers with a far smoother surface than the ordinary variety. The plant is also more compact, reaching only 1.5 m (5 ft).

DWARF SUNRAY: White skin which does not need peeling. A free-flowering variety with a compact growth habit — worth considering for the flower border, but you will have to search for a supplier.

TROUBLES

SLUGS

Hollowed-out tubers generally indicate attack by slugs — sprinkle slug pellets around the growing plants to prevent trouble later on. Less likely causes of tuber damage are soil-living caterpillars. Non-chemical methods of killing or deterring slugs and snails are using traps filled with beer or placing a ring of sharp grit around the plants.

SCLEROTINIA ROT

The base of stems are attacked, and may show fluffy white mould. Black cyst-like bodies occur inside rotten stems. Lift and burn diseased plants.

For key to symbols — see page 7

Asparagus

Succulent young shoots appear in spring and are cut for the kitchen. Attractive ferny foliage develops later but this should never be cut for flower arranging. Not an easy crop — it needs thorough soil preparation, space and regular hand weeding. Well worth growing, however, if you have free-draining soil, adequate land which can be tied up for a decade or more and also patience — you will have to wait two years for your first hearty meal. Asparagus is a decorative plant — put in a few crowns at the back of a flower border if there is no room in the vegetable plot.

IN A NUTSHELL

Use 1-year-old crowns. You can buy 2- or 3-year-old crowns but they can be temperamental. Asparagus can be raised from seed but it will be 3 years before regular cropping can begin.

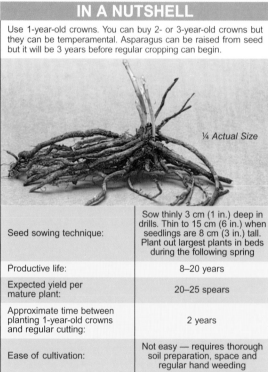

¼ Actual Size

Seed sowing technique:	Sow thinly 3 cm (1 in.) deep in drills. Thin to 15 cm (6 in.) when seedlings are 8 cm (3 in.) tall. Plant out largest plants in beds during the following spring
Productive life:	8–20 years
Expected yield per mature plant:	20–25 spears
Approximate time between planting 1-year-old crowns and regular cutting:	2 years
Ease of cultivation:	Not easy — requires thorough soil preparation, space and regular hand weeding

SOIL FACTS

- Good drainage is essential — the soil type is much less important. Pick a sunny spot, sheltered from strong winds, and dig thoroughly in the autumn — incorporate a liberal dressing of well-rotted manure or compost. Liming will be necessary if the soil is very acid.

- Remove the roots of all perennial weeds during soil preparation. Leave the soil rough after digging — fork over in March and rake in a general-purpose fertilizer.

- Plant crowns in early April if the soil is in good condition — delay for a couple of weeks if the weather is cold and wet. Trenches should be dug about 1 m (3 ft) apart.

- Harvesting of the mature crop takes place over a 6–8 week period. To ensure the maximum harvest period, plant a mixed bed containing an early variety such as Connovers Colossal with a later variety such as Martha Washington.

PLANTING

Keep roots covered under sacking until planting time — never let them dry out

Cover crowns with 5 cm of sifted soil immediately after spreading out roots. Fill in trench gradually as plants grow — bed should be level by autumn

20 cm

8 cm

30 cm

LOOKING AFTER THE CROP

- Keep the bed clean by hand weeding. Provide support for the stems if necessary and water during dry weather. Remove berries before they fall to the ground.

- In autumn cut down the ferny stems once they have turned yellow to 3–5 cm (1–2 in.) above the surface.

- Before the spears appear in spring make a ridge of soil over each row with a draw hoe. Apply a surface dressing of Growmore fertilizer.

HARVESTING

- Soon after planting the first spears will appear. On no account should these be cut — they must be left to develop into bushy fern-like stems.

- In the year after planting little or no cutting should take place. Some experts believe that the removal of a single spear per plant in May will do no harm — others believe that no growth at all should be removed at this stage.

- Cutting can begin in earnest in the second year after planting. As soon as the spears reach a height of 10–15 cm (4–6 in.) they should be severed about 8 cm (3 in.) below the soil surface. Use a long serrated kitchen knife. Cut every day if necessary — never let the spears grow too tall before cutting.

- Stop cutting in early or mid June. All spears must now be allowed to develop into fern in order to build up their reserves for next year's crop.

CALENDAR

	JAN	FEB	MAR	APR	MAY	JUN	JUL	AUG	SEP	OCT	NOV	DEC
Sowing Time												
Planting Time												
Cutting Time												

IN THE KITCHEN

Steaming is the classical method of preparing asparagus — it is then served hot with melted butter or cold with an oil-and-vinegar dressing. The golden rule is to avoid storing or cooking for too long — the cooked heads should be firm (not bending when held from the base) but not so firm as to be crunchy or leathery when eaten. There are other recipes — asparagus soup, asparagus soufflé, etc., but in practice there are usually not enough spears left over for such delights.

FREEZING: Divide the spears into thick and thin stems. Wash thoroughly to remove grit and then tie into small bundles. Blanch (4 minutes for thick stems, 2 minutes for thin ones) and then freeze in a rigid container.

STORAGE: The quality of asparagus deteriorates quickly with age. It should be cooked within an hour of cutting — if this is not possible put the spears in a polythene bag and keep in the refrigerator for up to 3 days.

COOKING: Wash the spears and then use a sharp knife to peel away the skin below the tips. After shaving put the spears into a bowl of cold water until all of them have been prepared. The next step is to tie them into a bundle with soft string, one band close to the base and the other just below the tip. Trim the ends to provide a level base. Place and support the bundle upright in a pan of boiling salted water — the tips must be well above the level of the water. Cover the pan and boil gently for 10–15 minutes — drain carefully and serve. Don't throw the water away — use it for making soup.

VARIETIES

In past years the catalogues were dominated by Connovers Colossal, Giant Mammoth and Martha Washington. These old favourites had their favourite soil types — Connovers Colossal for sandy soil and Giant Mammoth for heavy land. In both cases male plants were sought after as they are more productive than the berry-bearing female plants.

Things have changed in recent years. There are now all-male hybrids available which do not waste energy in seed production. Gjinlim is the new star which is present in the catalogues and is the experts' choice — you can expect to cut your first crop in the spring after planting. Franklim is now hard to find.

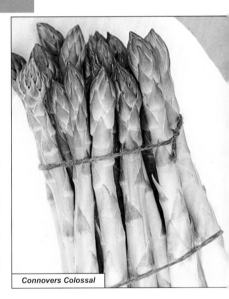

Connovers Colossal

CONNOVERS COLOSSAL: Still the most popular of the mixed male/female varieties. It is grown for its early season production of thick stalks which are excellent for freezing.

ARIANE: The spears are long and thin with heads of tightly-packed buds. Ariane is one to grow if you wish to raise asparagus from seed — it is claimed that some summer spears can be cut in the year after a March sowing under glass.

MARTHA WASHINGTON: The best-known of the U.S. varieties, this type and Mary Washington are the 'old favourites' in America. A heavy cropper with long spears until early June — it is resistant to rust.

GJINLIM: The main claim to fame of this all-male hybrid is that it has produced the heaviest crops in many trials. It is noted for its earliness. This variety is grown from crowns rather than seeds.

JERSEY KNIGHT: An asparagus to raise from seed. The spears are 2–3 cm (¾–1 in.) thick with good disease resistance.

LUCULLUS: This was the first of the all-male hybrids and it has all the features of the newer varieties. Long and straight spears, but you will have to hunt for a supplier.

TROUBLES

ASPARAGUS BEETLE

Grubs and adult beetles attack both stems and foliage. Stems are eaten — leaves are stripped. Beetle is easily recognised by square orange markings on 1 cm (⅓ in.) long black body. Spray with pyrethrins at first sign of attack.

VIOLET ROOT ROT

Most serious asparagus disease. Roots covered with purplish mould — leaves turn yellow and die. If attack is severe make a new bed on a fresh site. Do not grow root vegetables on the affected area for at least 3 years. If not severe, isolate healthy plants by inserting corrugated plastic sheets vertically into bed.

SPINDLY SPEARS

Thin shoots, about 3 mm (⅛ in.) across, are sometimes produced instead of typical thick spears. The most likely cause is prolonged cutting in the previous season. Spears should not be harvested after mid June. Other possible causes are cutting too soon after planting and failing to feed the bed.

SLUGS

Spears are gnawed, making them unfit for table use. Sprinkle slug pellets sparingly around the shoots.

FROST

Young shoots may turn black and die if a severe frost occurs in late spring. Destroy affected shoots. Cover bed with sacking if a hard frost is expected.

RUST

Reddish-brown spots appear on the leaves during the summer. Spraying is not effective so cut down and burn affected shoots as soon as the first spots are seen.

WIND ROCK

Roots are loosened if stems are left unsupported on an exposed site. This can lead to rotting, so some summer support should be provided if windbreaks are absent.

Aubergine

The aubergine or eggplant was once regarded as an unusual vegetable but now it appears in every supermarket. It can be grown as easily as tomatoes in a greenhouse, but outdoors it is much more of a gamble. In a sunny, sheltered spot it will succeed if the summer is long and hot, but it will fail without glass protection under average conditions. It needs pampering — even in a mild area it requires barn cloches or a cold frame. The attractive flowers are followed by shiny fruits, usually oval but sometimes round.

IN A NUTSHELL

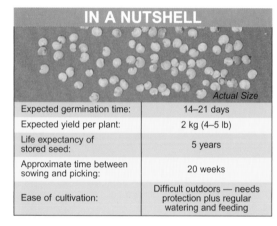

Actual Size

Expected germination time:	14–21 days
Expected yield per plant:	2 kg (4–5 lb)
Life expectancy of stored seed:	5 years
Approximate time between sowing and picking:	20 weeks
Ease of cultivation:	Difficult outdoors — needs protection plus regular watering and feeding

SOIL FACTS

- For outdoor cultivation, well-drained fertile soil in a sunny, sheltered location is necessary. Add a general-purpose fertilizer before planting.
- In the greenhouse grow in pots filled with compost or plant in growing bags — 3 per bag.

SOWING & PLANTING

- Raise seedlings under glass at 15°–21°C (60°–70°F). Sow 2 seeds in a compost-filled fibre pot — remove weaker seedling. Harden off before planting outdoors.

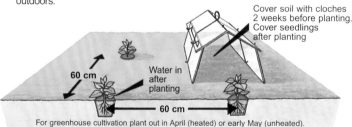

Cover soil with cloches 2 weeks before planting. Cover seedlings after planting

60 cm

Water in after planting

60 cm

For greenhouse cultivation plant out in April (heated) or early May (unheated).

CALENDAR

	JAN	FEB	MAR	APR	MAY	JUN	JUL	AUG	SEP	OCT	NOV	DEC
Sowing & Planting Time (Outdoor crop)			■	■	▮							
Sowing & Planting Time (Greenhouse crop)		■	▼	▼ ▼	▼							
Picking Time												

For key to symbols — see page 7

LOOKING AFTER THE CROP

- Remove growing point when the plant is 30 cm (1 ft) high — stake stems.
- Mist plants regularly to keep down red spider mite and encourage fruit set. When 5 fruits have formed, remove lateral shoots and remaining flowers.
- Water regularly but do not keep the compost sodden. Add a potassium-rich soluble fertilizer with each watering once the fruit have begun to swell.

HARVESTING

- Cut each fruit once it has reached a satisfactory size (usually 15 cm/6 in. long) but before the surface shine has gone. Dull fruit are usually over-ripe and bitter.

IN THE KITCHEN

Aubergines are a basic ingredient for *ratatouille* (French vegetable stew) and *moussaka* (Greek minced lamb stew). They can also be stuffed by cutting in half and filling the scooped-out middles with minced beef, but perhaps the best way to cook them is to fry thin slices, as described below, and serve as a hot vegetable.

STORAGE: Keep in a polythene bag in the refrigerator — aubergines will stay fresh for up to 2 weeks.

COOKING: Slice thinly and sprinkle salt on the cut surfaces to absorb the bitter juices and soften the flesh. Rinse after 20 minutes and then dry with absorbent kitchen paper. Lightly coat the slices with flour and fry until golden-brown.

VARIETIES

LONG PURPLE: The old favourite — no special advantages, but it has stood the test of time.

MONEYMAKER: The most popular aubergine — this F_1 hybrid produces an early crop of good-sized fruits.

BLACK BEAUTY: A century-old variety which is noted for its reliability. The fruits are 10–15 cm (4–6 in.) long.

ORLANDO: This compact F_1 hybrid is used as a patio variety, producing baby dark fruits on compact stems.

TROUBLES

RED SPIDER MITE

Pale mottling occurs on the upper surface of the leaves. Tiny mites can be found on the underside. Spray thoroughly with pyrethrins — mist the leaves regularly with plain water.

APHID

Greenfly can be a nuisance on both the outdoor and greenhouse crop. The answer is to spray with insecticidal soap as soon as the first attacks are seen.

WHITEFLY

A pest of the greenhouse crop — severe enough in some seasons to seriously weaken the plants. Not easy to control with chemical sprays — as an effective alternative hang up several yellow Greenhouse Flycatcher Cards.

Beans

We all know beans when we see them, and yet their classification is bewildering. Words like 'flageolet' and 'haricot' are used to describe both the maturity of the bean at cooking time and also the varieties which are favoured for producing seeds at these stages of maturity. American catalogues contain unfamiliar groupings such as 'snap', 'pole' and 'lima' — it would take a whole chapter to explain all the terms, but the chart below should help to clear up the major misunderstandings. Beans make up an invaluable group for the cook and also for the gatherer of odd facts — beans have been found alongside prehistoric man and yet our old favourite, the runner bean, was grown solely as an ornamental flower and not as a vegetable until late Victorian times.

FRENCH BEAN

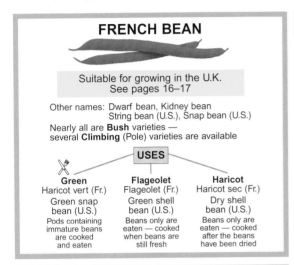

Suitable for growing in the U.K.
See pages 16–17

Other names: Dwarf bean, Kidney bean
String bean (U.S.), Snap bean (U.S.)
Nearly all are **Bush** varieties —
several **Climbing** (Pole) varieties are available

USES

Green
Haricot vert (Fr.)
Green snap
bean (U.S.)
Pods containing
immature beans
are cooked
and eaten

Flageolet
Flageolet (Fr.)
Green shell
bean (U.S.)
Beans only are
eaten — cooked
when beans are
still fresh

Haricot
Haricot sec (Fr.)
Dry shell
bean (U.S.)
Beans only are
eaten — cooked
after the beans
have been dried

BROAD BEAN

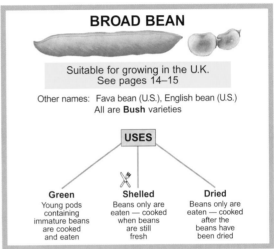

Suitable for growing in the U.K.
See pages 14–15

Other names: Fava bean (U.S.), English bean (U.S.)
All are **Bush** varieties

USES

Green
Young pods
containing
immature beans
are cooked
and eaten

Shelled
Beans only are
eaten — cooked
when beans
are still
fresh

Dried
Beans only are
eaten — cooked
after the
beans have
been dried

RUNNER BEAN

Suitable for growing in the U.K.
See pages 18–19

Other name: Scarlet runner
Nearly all are **Climbing** (Pole or Stick) varieties —
one or two **Bush** varieties are available

USES

Green
Young pods containing
immature beans are
cooked and eaten

Dried
Beans only are eaten —
cooked after the beans
have been dried

BEAN SPROUTS

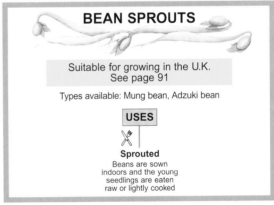

Suitable for growing in the U.K.
See page 91

Types available: Mung bean, Adzuki bean

USES

Sprouted
Beans are sown
indoors and the young
seedlings are eaten
raw or lightly cooked

SOYA BEAN

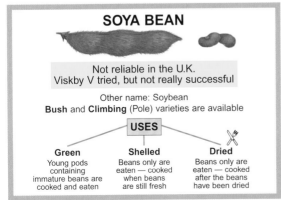

Not reliable in the U.K.
Viskby V tried, but not really successful

Other name: Soybean
Bush and **Climbing** (Pole) varieties are available

USES

Green
Young pods
containing
immature beans are
cooked and eaten

Shelled
Beans only are
eaten — cooked
when beans
are still fresh

Dried
Beans only are
eaten — cooked
after the beans
have been dried

LIMA BEAN

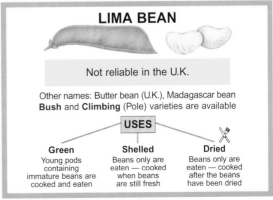

Not reliable in the U.K.

Other names: Butter bean (U.K.), Madagascar bean
Bush and **Climbing** (Pole) varieties are available

USES

Green
Young pods
containing
immature beans are
cooked and eaten

Shelled
Beans only are
eaten — cooked
when beans
are still fresh

Dried
Beans only are
eaten — cooked
after the beans
have been dried

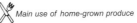 *Main use of home-grown produce*

Bean, Broad

Nearly any soil can produce an adequate crop, although the ideal soil is rich and free-draining. Few vegetables are easier to grow, and these are the first garden beans to grace your table. From each seed about three or four square-sectioned stems appear. The standard varieties grow about 1.2 m (4 ft) high and the dwarf ones reach 30–45 cm (1–1½ ft). Picking can begin as early as the end of May if you have pampered the crop, but even the maincrop sown in early April will be ready in July.

IN A NUTSHELL

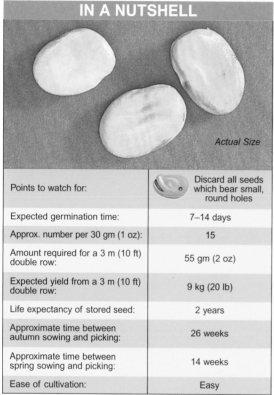

Actual Size

Points to watch for:	Discard all seeds which bear small, round holes
Expected germination time:	7–14 days
Approx. number per 30 gm (1 oz):	15
Amount required for a 3 m (10 ft) double row:	55 gm (2 oz)
Expected yield from a 3 m (10 ft) double row:	9 kg (20 lb)
Life expectancy of stored seed:	2 years
Approximate time between autumn sowing and picking:	26 weeks
Approximate time between spring sowing and picking:	14 weeks
Ease of cultivation:	Easy

SOIL FACTS

- The ideal soil is rich and free-draining, but nearly every soil will produce an adequate crop, provided it is neither very acid nor waterlogged. Lime, if necessary, in winter.
- Pick a reasonably sunny spot which did not grow beans last year. Dig in autumn if the crop is to be sown in spring — add compost or well-rotted manure if the ground was not enriched for the previous crop. Apply a general-purpose fertilizer about 1 week before sowing.

- There are several ways of growing a crop which will be ready for picking in June. November sowing (Aquadulce or The Sutton) will provide beans in early June, but there can be serious losses in a severe winter. Only attempt autumn sowing if your plot is sheltered, free-draining and located in a mild area. It is a better plan to sow under cloches in February.
- Maincrop plantings begin in March and then at monthly intervals until the end of May to provide beans throughout the summer.

SEED SOWING

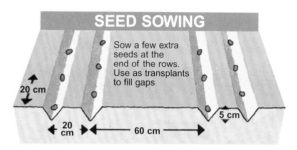

Sow a few extra seeds at the end of the rows. Use as transplants to fill gaps

20 cm

20 cm — 60 cm — 5 cm

LOOKING AFTER THE CROP

- Regular hoeing will probably be necessary to keep down weeds during the early stage of the crop's life, but watering should not be necessary before the flowers appear. If the weather turns dry when the pods are swelling it will be necessary to water copiously.
- Some form of support will probably be necessary for tall-growing varieties. Place a stout stake at each corner of the double row and then string between the posts at 30 cm (1 ft) intervals.
- Pinch off the top 10 cm (4 in.) of stem as soon as the first beans start to form. This will ensure an earlier harvest and also provide some degree of blackfly control. This serious pest *must* be kept down, so spray if attacks persist.
- After cropping has finished, dig the plants into the soil to provide valuable green manure.

HARVESTING

- When growing broad beans for the kitchen, remember that you are not trying to win a prize at the local show. Leaving the pods to reach their maximum size will provide an overwhelming flush of large and tough beans.
- Begin picking when the first pods are 5–8 cm (2–3 in.) long — cook them whole.
- The time to pick beans for shelling is when the beans have begun to show through the pod but before the scar on each shelled bean has become discoloured — it should still be white or green.
- Remove each pod from the plant by applying a sharp downward twist.

Scar not black

CALENDAR

	JAN	FEB	MAR	APR	MAY	JUN	JUL	AUG	SEP	OCT	NOV	DEC
Sowing Time												
Picking Time												

For key to symbols — see page 7

IN THE KITCHEN

The broad beans offered for sale in many shops are well past their prime. The outer surface of the pods has often started to develop black blotches and the skin surrounding the beans has become too tough to be eaten. Do not let your garden crop reach this sorry state — cook the freshly-picked beans or store them for later use by freezing or drying. Salting consists of alternating layers of 1½ kg (3 lb) of beans with 500 gm (1 lb) of salt in a large jar.

FREEZING: An excellent vegetable for freezing — especially the green varieties. Wash the beans thoroughly and then blanch for 3 minutes. Freeze in polythene bags or rigid containers. Use within 12 months.

STORAGE: Keep in a polythene bag in the refrigerator — broad beans will stay fresh for up to 1 week. Stored in a perforated basket in the kitchen they will keep for up to 3 or 4 days.

COOKING: Treat small pods like French beans, cooking them whole and then slicing diagonally. More mature pods should be shelled and the young beans dropped into boiling salted water in a pan. Cook for about 10 minutes. Broad beans, a little melted butter and fried bacon — the combination recommended by the experts! If the beans have become too mature and each one bears a brown or black scar, remove the leathery skins after cooking but before serving. You can either serve them whole in their bright green or white underwear, or turn them into a purée or summer soup. The pods and beans are not the only part of the plant you can eat — the upper leaves can be cooked like spinach (see page 93).

VARIETIES

LONGPOD varieties

The long, narrow pods hang downwards, reaching 40 cm (15 in.) or more in length. There are 8-10 kidney-shaped beans within each pod — both green and white varieties are available. This is the best group for hardiness, early cropping, exhibiting and top yields.

AQUADULCE CLAUDIA (white): The broad bean which is the popular choice for autumn sowing. Tall, prolific, very hardy — an excellent bean for freezing.

IMPERIAL GREEN LONGPOD (green): This tall variety has few rivals for maximum yields and extra-long pods. It is a well-established favourite for the horticultural show bench.

LISTRA (green): The baby vegetable representative among the broad beans. The beans are small but the early-maturing plants produce an abundant easy-to-pick crop.

STEREO (white): A broad bean with a difference — the pods can be picked when they are still small and then cooked whole like mangetout peas.

DREADNOUGHT (white): An exhibition variety bearing extraordinarily long, well-shaped pods. Also a good culinary variety which freezes well.

BUNYARD'S EXHIBITION (white): Not the biggest nor longest nor most delicious. Just a completely reliable old favourite — good yields, good flavour, good for freezing.

MASTERPIECE LONGPOD (green): An early cropper with green beans and a fine flavour — highly recommended for freezing.

EXPRESS (greenish white): One of the fastest maturing of all broad beans — choose it if you intend to sow in early spring. Has earned a high reputation as a heavy cropper.

WITKIEM MANITA (white): Yields are high but the pods are rather small — the one to grow if sowing has to be delayed until late spring.

MONICA (white): It is claimed that this variety is the first one to crop from a spring sowing. Each pod bears 5-6 beans.

Bunyard's Exhibition

WINDSOR varieties

The pods are shorter and broader than the Longpods. There are 4-7 round beans within each pod — both green and white varieties are available. This is the best group for flavour. They are not suitable for autumn sowing and they take longer to mature than Longpods.

GREEN WINDSOR (green): A heavy cropping variety renowned for its flavour. It has given rise to a host of descendants, all claiming to be a little better — Imperial Green Windsor, Unrivalled and so on.

JUBILEE MYSOR (white): This late-maturing variety has taken over from the old favourite White Windsor as the most popular white-seeded type. Excellent flavour and suitable for exhibition.

DWARF varieties

The dwarf, freely-branching bushes grow about 30–45 cm (1–1½ ft) high, making them the ideal choice where tall growth is not required or the site is exposed. These are the broad beans to pick for growing under cloches.

THE SUTTON (white): The most popular of the Dwarf varieties — much praise has been heaped on its small shoulders. 'Ideal for small gardens' is the usual phrase.

ROBIN HOOD (white): Alternatives to The Sutton for growing in containers are hard to find. This patio variety is in at least one of the popular catalogues.

The Sutton

TROUBLES

See pages 20–22

Bean, French

In Britain French beans are a stand-in crop until the scarlet runners are ready, but in Europe it is the *haricot vert* which is queen throughout the summer. The French bean is a half hardy annual which cannot stand frost. It likes warm conditions and hates heavy clay. The standard varieties are bushy plants with 10–15 cm (4–6 in.) green pods which follow the white, pink or red flowers — it is decorative enough to be grown in the flower garden. There are variations — you can buy purple- or yellow-podded varieties and there are climbing types which may grow as tall as runner beans.

IN A NUTSHELL

Actual Size

Points to watch for:	Never plant before the recommended time — seed will rot in cold and wet soil
Expected germination time:	7–14 days
Approx. number per 30 gm (1 oz):	60
Amount required for a 3 m (10 ft) row:	15 gm (½ oz)
Expected yield from a 3 m (10 ft) row (Bush varieties):	3.5 kg (8 lb)
Expected yield from a 3 m (10 ft) row (Climbing varieties):	5.5 kg (12 lb)
Life expectancy of stored seed:	2 years
Approximate time between sowing and picking:	8–12 weeks
Ease of cultivation:	Easy

SOIL FACTS

- French beans will succeed in any soil provided it is neither very heavy nor acid. Lime, if necessary, in winter.
- Pick a reasonably sunny spot which is sheltered from high winds. The site should not have been used for beans last year. Dig in autumn and add compost or well-rotted manure. Prepare the seed bed about 2 weeks before sowing — apply a general-purpose fertilizer at this time.

- For an early crop sow a quick-maturing variety in early May. If you want to pick beans before the end of June then you will have to grow the plants under cloches. Put the cloches in position in early March and sow the seeds in the soil beneath them in early or mid April. Remove the cloches in late May.
- The maincrop is sown during May. Successional sowings up to the end of June will provide pods until early October.
- For a late autumn crop sow in July and cover the plants with cloches in mid September.

SEED SOWING

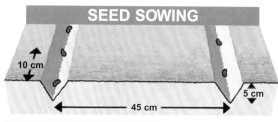

10 cm

45 cm

5 cm

LOOKING AFTER THE CROP

- Protect seedlings from slugs and hoe regularly to keep weeds down during the early stages of the crop's life.
- Support the plants with short twigs or pea sticks to prevent them from toppling over. Use twiggy branches or plastic netting for climbing varieties.
- Spraying the flowers is not necessary in order to ensure that they will set properly. Moisture at the roots, however, is essential to ensure maximum pod development and a long cropping period. Water copiously and regularly if the weather turns dry during or after the flowering period.
- Mulch around the stems in June. Once the pods have all been harvested, feed the plants with a liquid fertilizer. In this way a second crop can be obtained — smaller, of course, but very welcome.

HARVESTING

- Begin picking when the pods are about 10 cm (4 in.) long. A pod is ready if it snaps easily when bent and before the tell-tale bulges of maturity appear along its length. Pick several times a week to prevent any pods maturing — you can then expect to continue cropping for 5–7 weeks. Take care not to loosen the plants when harvesting — hold the stems as you tug away the pods, or play safe and use a pair of scissors.
- Dried beans (haricots) are obtained by leaving the pods on the plant until they turn straw-coloured, then hang the plants indoors to dry. When the pods are brittle and have begun to split, shell the beans and dry them on a sheet of paper for several days. Store the haricot beans in an air-tight container.

CALENDAR

	JAN	FEB	MAR	APR	MAY	JUN	JUL	AUG	SEP	OCT	NOV	DEC
Sowing Time				▨	▨	▨						
Picking Time							▨	▨	▨	▨		

For key to symbols — see page 7

IN THE KITCHEN

To enjoy French beans at their best, pick young pods and cook them whole within an hour of harvesting. Sometimes you will find that the pods are well past this stage, and flat-podded beans are stringy once they have matured. The best plan is to shell them and treat them as flageolets — fresh green beans cooked like peas. You can even wait for a later stage, leaving the pods to mature on the plant and then shelling and drying indoors to produce haricots for winter use.

FREEZING: An excellent vegetable for freezing. Wash and trim young pods and then blanch them for 3 minutes (2 minutes if you have cut the pods into chunks). Freeze in polythene bags or rigid containers. Use within 12 months.

STORAGE: Keep in a polythene bag in the refrigerator — French beans will stay fresh for up to 1 week. Stored in a perforated basket in the kitchen they will keep for up to 3 or 4 days.

COOKING: Whole or cut into pieces — it's a matter of taste. The usual practice is to cook small pencil-podded beans whole but to slice large flat-podded types into 3 cm (1 in.) slices. In either case, wash the pods and remove both tops and tails with a sharp knife. Cook in boiling salted water for 7 minutes (whole beans) or 5 minutes (sliced beans). Serve hot as a vegetable or cold as a salad. If you like haricot beans, grow a suitable variety (see below) and prepare them as described on page 16. To cook, put the beans in cold water and bring to the boil. Switch off the heat and let them stand for an hour. Drain, and then serve as a hot vegetable or in an oil-and-vinegar dressing as a salad.

VARIETIES

Most French bean varieties grow as compact bushes 30–45 cm (12–18 in.) high. There are a few, however, which are climbers and will clamber up supports to a height of 2 m (7 ft).

GREEN varieties

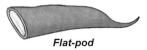

Flat-pod

Pencil-pod

The Prince

These make up the most popular group, with scores of old and new favourites. The well-established ones are generally Flat-podded or 'English' varieties — flat, rather wide and with a tendency to become stringy as they mature. The Pencil-podded types are usually stringless.

HUNTER: Climber. The pods are long, wide, straight and stringless. A high-yielding variety suitable for outdoors or under glass.

ANNABEL: Dwarf. A compact variety which bears masses of thin, stringless pods. It is a good choice if you want to grow the plants in pots.

THE PRINCE: Dwarf. Once the favourite French bean, but not any more. A low-growing Flat-pod which is used for exhibition.

MASTERPIECE: Dwarf. Another old favourite Flat-pod. Suitable for early sowing — an excellent general-purpose variety.

TENDERGREEN: Dwarf. An early-cropping Pencil-pod. It is a prolific cropper and is recommended for freezing. The pods are stringless.

BLUE LAKE: Climber. A popular variety — its 1.5 m (5 ft) stems produce a plentiful supply of white-seeded Pencil-pods.

COBRA: Climber. This climbing variety has taken over from Blue Lake. Mauve flowers.

SAFARI: Dwarf. Low-growing but vigorous — the slender Pencil-pods ('Kenyan beans') are stringless. Excellent disease resistance.

OPERA: Dwarf. A heavy cropper with an upright growth habit. Disease resistance is good. The stringless pods mature early.

ALGARVE: Climber. This variety produces Flat-pods up to 25 cm (10 in.) long. Resistant to virus attack — the pods are stringless.

DELINEL: Dwarf. An RHS Award of Garden Merit winner, noted for the excellent flavour of its straight dark green Flat-pods. Good disease resistance.

YARD LONG: Climber. Not in many catalogues, but worth looking for. Stems up to 2.5 m (8 ft) high bear Pencil-pods up to 45 cm (1½ ft) long. Best under glass.

CROPPER TEEPEE: Dwarf. A white-seeded Pencil-podded variety with just one outstanding feature — the pods are borne well above the leaves for easy picking.

COLOURED varieties

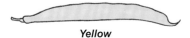

Yellow

Purple

Coloured pods have an obvious novelty value, but they also have practical advantages. The pods can be easily seen at picking time and some have an excellent flavour.

AMETHYST (purple): This dwarf variety is highly regarded for its flowers and for the flavour of its 15 cm (6 in.) long pods.

SUNGOLD (yellow): One of the many yellow varieties of French beans. This variety has long Pencil-pods with a better-than-average flavour.

PURPLE QUEEN (purple): One of the best purple Pencil-pods. Good flavour, high yields — beans turn dark green when cooked.

PURPLE-PODDED CLIMBING (purple): Grows about 1.5 m (5 ft) high. Decorative with its pendent bunches of dark purple beans which turn green when cooked.

Amethyst

TROUBLES

See pages 20–22

Bean, Runner

They can be seen everywhere — clambering up bamboo wigwams, climbing up plastic netting or twining around stout poles. They are both decorative in flower and highly productive — you can expect to harvest 5 kg (11 lb) or more per metre of row between August and the arrival of the first frosts. However you will not achieve this if you treat them as an 'easy' crop. There are several basic needs — thorough soil preparation, strong supports, weekly watering in dry weather once the pods have formed and then picking ripe pods every other day.

IN A NUTSHELL

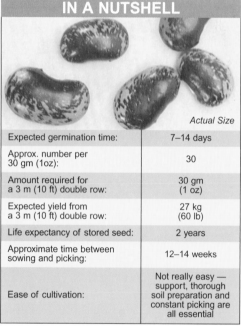

Actual Size

Expected germination time:	7–14 days
Approx. number per 30 gm (1oz):	30
Amount required for a 3 m (10 ft) double row:	30 gm (1 oz)
Expected yield from a 3 m (10 ft) double row:	27 kg (60 lb)
Life expectancy of stored seed:	2 years
Approximate time between sowing and picking:	12–14 weeks
Ease of cultivation:	Not really easy — support, thorough soil preparation and constant picking are all essential

SEED SOWING

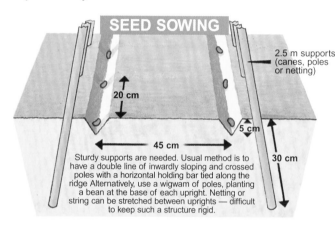

2.5 m supports (canes, poles or netting)

20 cm

5 cm

45 cm

30 cm

Sturdy supports are needed. Usual method is to have a double line of inwardly sloping and crossed poles with a horizontal holding bar tied along the ridge Alternatively, use a wigwam of poles, planting a bean at the base of each upright. Netting or string can be stretched between uprights — difficult to keep such a structure rigid.

LOOKING AFTER THE CROP

- Loosely tie the young plants to the supports, after which they will climb naturally. Protect from slugs.
- Hoe regularly — mulching will help to conserve moisture. Water regularly in dry weather once the first pods have formed. Don't bother misting to help pollination — it's an old wives' tale. Liquid feed occasionally during the cropping season.
- Remove the growing points once the plants reach the tops of the supports. At the end of the season dig in the roots and stem bases.

SOIL FACTS

- Runner beans produce disappointing results in hungry, badly-drained soil. Acid conditions are also undesirable — lime, if necessary, in late winter.
- Pick a sheltered spot where the dense shade cast by the plants will not be a problem. Dig in autumn and add an abundant supply of compost or well-rotted manure. Rake in a general-purpose fertilizer about 2 weeks before sowing or planting.

HARVESTING

- Pick regularly once the pods have reached a decent size (15–20 cm/ 6–8 in.) but before the beans inside have started to swell. If you remove pods as soon as they reach this stage then harvesting should continue for at least 8 weeks. This calls for picking every couple of days — allowing even a small number to ripen will stop production.
- The problem is that you will probably have a glut of beans at some stage — for notes on storage see page 19.

- The standard method of growing runner beans is to sow the seeds outdoors when the danger of frost is past — the end of May in the south or early June in the north. Always sow a few extra seeds at the ends of the rows — use the seedlings as transplants to fill gaps.
- A second sowing in June in mild areas will ensure an October crop.
- Runner beans are often raised by planting out seedlings when the danger of frost is past. These seedlings are either shop-bought (make sure that they have been properly hardened-off) or raised at home from seeds sown under glass in late April. This planting-out method is strongly recommended for the colder areas of the country.

CALENDAR

	JAN	FEB	MAR	APR	MAY	JUN	JUL	AUG	SEP	OCT	NOV	DEC
Sowing Time (outdoors)					▮	▮						
Sowing Time (indoors)				▮	▮							
Picking Time								▮	▮	▮		

For key to symbols — see page 7

IN THE KITCHEN

You will no doubt remember your annoyance when you cooked shop-bought runner beans and then found them to be inedible because of their stringiness. Never let this happen with your home-grown crop — pick them at the stage when the commercial grower would regard the pods as uneconomically small. The best method of coping with the excess is to freeze what you can't use immediately — if you haven't got a freezer then you can shell the beans after drying the pods and treat them as haricots for winter use (see page 17) or you can salt them (alternate layers of 1.5 kg/3 lb of sliced beans with 500 g/1 lb salt).

FREEZING: Wash and trim young pods and then slice them into chunks. Blanch for 2 minutes, cool, drain and then freeze in polythene bags or rigid containers. Use within 12 months.

STORAGE: Keep in a polythene bag in the refrigerator — runner beans will stay fresh for up to 1 week. Stored in a perforated basket in the kitchen they will keep for up to 3 or 4 days.

COOKING: The standard method of cooking runner beans is to wash them and then cut off the tops and tails. Pull off the stringy edges. Cut the pods into 5 cm (2 in.) diagonal chunks and boil in salted water for 5–7 minutes. Drain and serve hot — crowned with a knob of butter. The experts tell us that it is better to cook them whole and slice after cooking, to make sure that the water is kept boiling vigorously and to leave off the lid to ensure that there will be no loss of flavour nor colour.

VARIETIES

STICK runner beans

Nearly all runner beans will grow 2–3 m (7–10 ft) high and bear pods which can reach 25–45 cm (10–18 in.) long. They are grown on tall supports and the usual flower colour is red. There is a bi-colour variety (Painted Lady) and the white and pink varieties are self-pollinating — a point to remember if you have been disappointed by lack of pod formation in previous years.

ENORMA: The improved form of Prizewinner — produces the slender shape and size of pod which wins prizes at the horticultural show.

LADY DI: Dark green slender pods up to 30 cm (12 in.) long. Plant growth is vigorous and the flavour is excellent. There is a long cropping season. Recommended for the show bench.

PRIZEWINNER: Pods are medium length — cropping is heavy and the flavour is good. An old favourite, but the pods can be stringy.

AINTREE: A recently-introduced red-flowered variety. The slim pods reach about 30 cm (12 in.) and the flavour is good. A heavy cropper.

KELVEDON MARVEL: Straight pods are produced very freely. An early cropper with rather short pods which appear about 14 days before the standard varieties. Grows well as a Ground bean.

SCARLET EMPEROR: A popular choice — similar to Kelvedon Marvel in many ways. Cropping starts early etc, but pods are longer. Can be grown as a Ground crop — see below.

RED RUM: The outstanding characteristic of this variety is the ability to set seed in unsatisfactory weather conditions. Early. The 20 cm (8 in.) pods are narrow.

DESIREE: White flowers are followed by long and slender pods. Produces well even in dry weather — highly recommended.

POLESTAR: A scarlet-flowered runner — claimed to crop very heavily. The flowers set very easily and the season starts early. Pods are fleshy and stringless.

WHITE LADY: Like Lady Di this variety copes with bad weather better than most. You can expect high yields of fleshy pods.

ST. GEORGE: Bicoloured (red and white) flowers are followed by 25 cm (10 in.) long fleshy pods borne in clusters. Early flowering.

MOONLIGHT: You will find this British-bred variety in many popular catalogues. The white flowers are self-pollinating and the pods can reach up to 30 cm (12 in.).

Prizewinner

GROUND runner beans

A few varieties such as Kelvedon Marvel and Scarlet Emperor which are naturally tall-growing are sometimes sown 60 cm (2 ft) apart and grown as short and bushy plants by pinching out the growing point of the main stems when they are about 30 cm (1 ft) high. Side shoots are pinched out at weekly intervals and the stems are supported by short twigs. The pods appear earlier than on climbing plants and you are spared the work of creating tall supports, but there are disadvantages. The cropping period is short and the yield is low, the pods are curled and their surface soiled.

DWARF runner beans

A few true dwarfs are available — the plants grow about 45 cm (18 in.) high and the pods are 20 cm (8 in.) long. They should be grown about 15 cm (6 in.) apart in rows 60 cm (2 ft) wide. A good choice where space is limited, but yields cannot compare with their climbing relatives.

HESTIA: An excellent Dwarf for a tub or flower garden. Red and white flowers are followed by 20 cm (8 in.) pods.

PICKWICK: A long-established Dwarf which does not need support. Height 30 cm (12 in.) — crops early and for a long period if picked regularly.

Pickwick

TROUBLES

See pages 20–22

BEAN and PEA TROUBLES

Black bean aphid is the main danger to broad beans and chocolate spot is the most serious disease. The chief disorder of runner beans is the failure of the flowers to set, but French beans are rarely attacked by serious complaints if you plant them at the right time. Peas have two big problems — birds and pea moth maggots.

TUNNELLED SEEDS

1 SEED BEETLE

Seeds of peas and beans are sometimes found to bear small, round holes. Within these tunnels are the tiny seed beetle grubs. Affected seeds either fail to germinate or produce weak seedlings.

Treatment: None.

Prevention: Buy good quality seed. Never sow seeds if they are holed.

TUNNELLED SEEDLINGS

2 BEAN SEED FLY

All bean varieties are susceptible to attack by these soil-living grubs. Damaged seeds fail to germinate; tunnelled seedlings wilt and become distorted. Early crops are worst affected.

Treatment: Destroy damaged seedlings.

Prevention: Prepare a good seed bed or plant compost-raised seedlings.

	Symptom	Likely Causes
Seeds & Seedlings	— missing	3 or 16
	— little or no germination	1 or 2 or 8 or **Millepede** or **Damping off** (see page 157)
	— tunnelled before sowing	1
	— tunnelled after sowing	2
Stems	— brown streaks outside	13 or 20
	— brown streaks inside	18
	— brown or purple spots	12 or 21
	— wilted, dying	8 or 18
	— mouldy	17
	— infested with aphids	4 or 5
	— brown or blackened at base	8
Leaves	— yellowed or yellow patches	6 or 8 or 15 or 18
	— silvery patches	10
	— spotted	12 or 13 or 20 or 21
	— notched	9
	— holed	**Slugs & Snails** (see page 157)
	— white, mauve or brown mould	6 or 7
	— infested with aphids	4 or 5
	— bronzed, speckled	**Red spider mite** (see page 56)
Flowers	— absent	11
	— present, but pods absent	14
Pods	— absent	14 or 16
	— distorted	4 or 6 or 10
	— torn	16
	— spotted, dry texture	6 or 13 or 20 or 21
	— spotted, wet texture	12
	— spotted, mouldy texture	7 or 17
	— silvery patches	10
Beans & Peas	— tunnelled, maggots present	19
	— brown spot in centre	15

3 MICE

Mice can be serious pests, as they are capable of clearing whole rows of pea seeds and seedlings overnight. Old fashioned remedies are to dip the seed in paraffin or alum, or to put spiny branches along the rows. A mouse bait, such as Racumin, can be used if the site is known to have a mouse problem.

4 BLACK BEAN APHID

A serious pest of broad beans in spring and French beans in July and August. Large blackfly colonies stunt growth, damage flowers and distort pods.

Treatment: Spray with pyrethrins or insecticidal soap at the first signs of attack. Repeat as necessary.

Prevention: Pinch out the tops of broad beans once four trusses of pods have formed.

APHIDS ON LEAVES

5 PEA APHID

Not often a serious pest, but in a hot, damp summer large colonies can severely damage peas. Growth is stunted and flowers are damaged.

Treatment: Spray with pyrethrins or insecticidal soap at the first signs of attack. Repeat as necessary.

Prevention: No practical method available.

6 | DOWNY MILDEW

Yellowish blotches on the leaves of peas, with a pale mauve or brown mould on the underside. Attacks occur in cool, wet seasons. Infected pods are spotted and distorted.

Treatment: Fungicides once used to control this disease are no longer available.

Prevention: Practise crop rotation. Burn affected plants after picking the crop.

MOULDY LEAVES

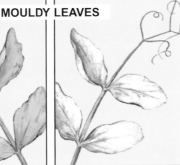

7 | POWDERY MILDEW

White powdery patches appear on both sides of the leaves of peas. Attacks occur in dry seasons and are worst in sheltered gardens. Infected pods are covered with white patches.

Treatment: Fungicides once used to control this disease are no longer available.

Prevention: Burn affected plants after picking the crop.

BLACKENED STEMS

8 | FOOT ROT & ROOT ROT

Leaves turn yellow and shrivel; roots and stem bases turn brown or black and soon start to rot.

Treatment: Lift and burn badly affected plants. Water soil with Cheshunt Compound to check the spread of the disease to other plants.

Prevention: Rotate crops.

NOTCHED LEAVES

1 cm (⅓ in.) brown beetles

9 | PEA & BEAN WEEVIL

Tell-tale signs are U-shaped notches at the edges of the young leaves. Growth is retarded but older plants generally soon recover. Seedlings, however, can be killed by a severe attack.

Treatment: Spray with pyrethrins at the first signs of attack.

Prevention: Hoe around the plants in April and May.

SILVERY PODS

10 | PEA THRIPS

Silvery patches appear on leaves and pods. The pods are distorted and the yield is reduced. Attacks are worst in hot, dry weather. Minute black or yellow insects are just visible.

Treatment: Spray with insecticidal soap or pyrethrins.

Prevention: Dig over the soil after removing an infected crop.

11 | NO FLOWERS

Peas and beans sometimes fail to produce flowers. This uncommon complaint can be due to a severe infestation of capsid bug (see page 84) or pea thrips which causes the flower buds to wither. But the most likely cause of a shortage of flowers is the presence of too much nitrogen in the soil. Always use a balanced fertilizer containing phosphates and potash for peas and beans.

12 | HALO BRIGHT

Small brown spots on leaves, each one being surrounded by a yellow 'halo'. Pods develop water-soaked spots. Plants are stunted and yields are reduced. Attacks are worst in a wet season.

Treatment: Lift and destroy diseased plants.

Prevention: Practise crop rotation. Never soak seed before sowing.

SPOTS ON LEAVES

French beans, Runner beans

Broad beans

13 | CHOCOLATE SPOT

Small brown spots on leaves; dark streaks along the stems. Pods may be affected and the seeds discoloured. In a bad attack the spots join together and the plant is killed.

Treatment: Fungicides once used to control this disease are no longer available.

Prevention: Apply some fertilizer before sowing and do not grow the plants too closely together.

BEAN & PEA TROUBLES continued

14 NO PODS

One of the major problems with runner beans is their tendency to lose their flowers without forming pods. Sparrows can be the culprits, and so can bumble bees. Cool weather at flowering time results in a lack of pollinating insects, but the failure of beans to set is always worst in a hot dry season. Keeping the roots moist by digging in compost, by mulching and watering is helpful, but recent research has shown that the practice of spraying the flowers is of little value. The best way to avoid trouble is to grow a white- or pink-flowering variety.

ROTTEN PODS

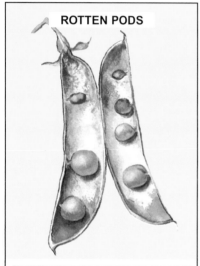

17 GREY MOULD (Botrytis)

The pods of French beans and occasionally peas may develop a grey velvety mould in wet weather. This mould may also coat the stem surface.

Treatment: Pick and burn affected pods. No systemic chemicals are available to treat this disease.

Prevention: Fungicides once used to control this disease are no longer available.

BROWN-CENTRED PEAS

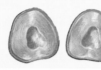

15 MARSH SPOT

Tell-tale sign is a brown-lined cavity in the centre of each pea. The cause is a shortage of manganese in the soil. The only outward sign is a slight yellowing between the leaf veins.

Treatment: None.

Prevention: Incorporate compost into the soil before sowing. Apply a sequestered compound if you can find a supplier.

BROWN-STREAKED TISSUE

18 FUSARIUM WILT

Outward signs are stunted growth, yellowing or rolled leaves and little or no crop. If you cut open the stem of an infected plant the tell-tale signs of wilt are revealed. Reddish-brown longitudinal streaks run through the stem tissue, but no external browning occurs.

Treatment: Remove and burn affected plants.

Prevention: Grow wilt-resistant varieties.

TORN PODS

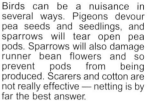

16 BIRDS

Birds can be a nuisance in several ways. Pigeons devour pea seeds and seedlings, and sparrows will tear open pea pods. Sparrows will also damage runner bean flowers and so prevent pods from being produced. Scarers and cotton are not really effective — netting is by far the best answer.

MAGGOTY PEAS

1 cm (⅓ in.) greenish maggots

19 PEA MOTH

Maggoty peas are well known to all vegetable growers, especially in S. England. Pea moth maggots burrow through the pods and into the seeds, making them unusable. Early and late sown crops often escape damage.

Treatment: None.

Prevention: Sow a quick-maturing variety early in the season.

20 ANTHRACNOSE

Brown sunken spots on pods. Stem cankers appear and leaves bear brown patches. At a later stage these brown spots and patches may turn pink. In a bad attack the plant may be killed.

Treatment: Lift and destroy diseased plants. No chemical spray is available.

Prevention: Rotate crops.

DRY SPOTS ON PODS

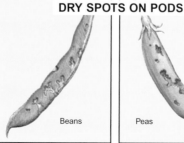

Beans   Peas

21 LEAF & POD SPOT

Brown sunken spots on pods. Peas may be discoloured. Leaves and stems bear similar brown spots and in a bad attack they may join together. Early crops suffer most, especially in a wet season.

Treatment: Lift and destroy diseased plants.

Prevention: Rotate crops.

Beet, Leaf

Many people find spinach difficult to grow. If the weather is dry it can quickly run to seed, and so it gets crossed off next year's list. But there is an answer if you like this vegetable — you can turn to the leaf beets. The varieties of leaf beet (also known as chard) are very easy to grow, succeeding in ordinary soil and not bolting when the weather turns dry. There are other benefits — you can pick a spring sowing from July to the following June if you cover the plants with cloches in winter. In addition the arching leaves make it attractive enough to earn a place in the flower border.

IN A NUTSHELL

Leaf beet 'seed' is really a fruit, each corky cluster containing several true seeds.

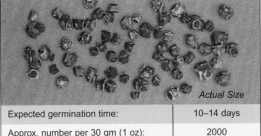

Actual Size

Expected germination time:	10–14 days
Approx. number per 30 gm (1 oz):	2000
Expected yield from a 3 m (10 ft) row:	3 kg (7 lb)
Life expectancy of stored seed:	3 years
Approximate time between sowing and picking:	12 weeks
Ease of cultivation:	Easy

SOIL FACTS

- Rich, well-manured soil is the ideal but any reasonable soil in sun or light shade will do.
- Dig the soil in autumn and incorporate a liberal amount of compost or well-rotted manure. Rake in a compound fertilizer 2 weeks before sowing.

SEED SOWING

Cover with soil

10 cm

40 cm

3 cm

CALENDAR

	JAN	FEB	MAR	APR	MAY	JUN	JUL	AUG	SEP	OCT	NOV	DEC
Sowing Time												
Picking Time												

For key to symbols — see page 7

LOOKING AFTER THE CROP

- Thin the seedlings to 30 cm (1 ft) apart when they are large enough to handle.
- Hoe regularly to keep the land weed-free. Bolting is most unlikely, but remove any flower-heads which may appear.
- Water at fortnightly intervals during dry spells. Mulching will help to conserve moisture.

HARVESTING

- Pull off outer leaves when they are large enough for kitchen use — do not wait until they have reached their maximum size. Harvest carefully (do not disturb the roots) and regularly, leaving the central foliage to develop for later pickings.
- Cover the plants with cloches or straw in late autumn to ensure winter and spring cropping.

IN THE KITCHEN

Both Swiss chard and spinach beet are used and cooked like spinach, although both of them are really members of the beet family. The flavour, however, is stronger than the refined true spinach varieties which are available these days and so you should always pick the foliage of leaf beet while it is still quite young and fresh.

STORAGE: Avoid storage if possible. If you must store it, place washed leaves in a polythene bag in the refrigerator — leaf beet will stay fresh for up to 2 days.

COOKING: See page 93 for instructions. With Swiss chard use the green foliage as a spinach substitute and cook the stalks as for asparagus (page 11), steaming the fleshy leafstalks for about 20 minutes. Alternatively you can chop them into sections and boil for 15 minutes.

VARIETIES

SWISS CHARD: Other names — silver chard, seakale beet. This attractive plant grows about 45 cm (1½ ft) high and bears distinctive foliage — the leafstalks are white and fleshy, and the white veins stand out against the crumpled, green spinach-like leaves. Varieties such as Lucullus, Fordhook Giant and White Silver 2 are occasionally listed.

RHUBARB CHARD: Other name — ruby chard. Similar in growth habit to Swiss chard, but the stalks are thinner and red. A striking plant for the border, but the flavour is inferior to the white variety. The variety Feurio is claimed to be resistant to bolting.

BRIGHT LIGHTS: The new star of the show. The stems come in a variety of colours, making it an excellent subject for the flower border. The flavour is delicate — serve raw or steamed.

SPINACH BEET: Other name — perpetual spinach. Similar to spinach in appearance and use — see page 93.

TROUBLES

All the leaf beets are virtually trouble-free, but slugs may attack young plants in spring. Sprinkle slug pellets around the plants.

Beetroot

Home-grown beetroot (fresh, stored or pickled) can be eaten all year round. It is rather slow to start but growth is rapid once the seedlings are through. The secret is to avoid any checks to growth and to pull the roots before they become large and woody. This calls for sowing short rows at monthly intervals and watering in dry weather — in this way you can gather beets in peak condition throughout the summer months. Most, but not all, are red and most, but not all, are bolt-resistant.

IN A NUTSHELL

Beetroot 'seed' is really a fruit, each corky cluster containing several true seeds. Pelleted seed is available.

Actual Size

Expected germination time:	10–14 days To hasten germination soak 'seeds' for several hours before sowing
Approx. number per 30 gm (1oz):	2000
Expected yield from a 3 m (10 ft) row:	4 kg (9 lb) Globe varieties
Life expectancy of stored seed:	3 years
Approximate time between sowing and lifting:	11 weeks (Globe varieties) 16 weeks (Long varieties)
Ease of cultivation:	Easy

SOIL FACTS

- For prize-winning long roots you will need deep, sandy soil but almost any reasonable land will produce good crops if it is adequately prepared.
- Pick a sunny spot and dig in autumn or early winter — add well-rotted compost if the humus content is low. Apply lime if the soil is known to be acid. In spring prepare the seed bed — rake in a general-purpose fertilizer 2–3 weeks before sowing.

- For a very early crop which will be ready in late May or early June, sow a bolt-resistant variety under cloches or in a frame in early March.
- Tha main sowing period begins outdoors in mid April. A second sowing of Globe varieties in mid May will provide a regular supply of tender roots.
- When growing for winter storage sow in late May or June — the roots from earlier sowings may be too coarse at lifting time in October.
- For a late autumn crop sow Detroit-Little Ball in July.

SEED SOWING

Cover with soil

2 'seeds'

10 cm

30 cm

3 cm

LOOKING AFTER THE CROP

- When the seedlings are about 3 cm (1 in.) high, thin out to leave a single plant at each station. Throw away these thinnings — do not attempt to plant them. Protection against birds may be necessary at this stage.
- The ground must be kept weed-free. Use a hoe, taking great care not to touch the roots.
- Dryness leads to woodiness and low yields — a sudden return to wet conditions can lead to splitting. To avoid these problems, water moderately at fortnightly intervals during dry spells. Mulching will conserve moisture.
- When the roots have reached golf-ball size, pull up alternate plants and use these thinnings for cooking. Leave the remainder to reach maturity.

HARVESTING

- Pull out roots of Globe varieties as required. They should not be left to grow larger than cricket balls — there should be no white rings when a root is cut in half.
- Roots grown for storage should be lifted in October. Long varieties should be carefully prised out of the soil with a fork, making sure that the prongs never touch the roots. Shake off the soil and discard all damaged specimens. Place the roots between layers of dry sand in a stout box and store in a shed. The crop will keep until March.
- After pulling for immediate use or for storage, twist off the foliage to leave a 5 cm (2 in.) crown of stalks. Cutting off the leaves with a knife will result in bleeding.

CALENDAR

	JAN	FEB	MAR	APR	MAY	JUN	JUL	AUG	SEP	OCT	NOV	DEC
Sowing Time												
Lifting Time												

IN THE KITCHEN

Beetroots are mainly used to add colour and flavour to salads. Boiled or pickled, they are sliced to accompany the lettuce, tomatoes and radishes in the typical British salad. As a hot vegetable, boiled or baked, beets are more popular in the U.S. than in England, and in Eastern Europe they provide the basis of *borsch* soup. Other uses include chutney and wine-making.

FREEZING: Use small beets which are no more than 5 cm (2 in.) across. Wash and boil as described in this section. After skinning and cooling, cut the roots into slices or cubes and freeze in a rigid container. Use within 6 months.

STORAGE: Keep in a polythene bag in the refrigerator — roots will stay fresh for up to 2 weeks.

COOKING: Beets should be washed in cold water, removing neither the leaf stalks nor the thin root at the base. On no account should you peel or damage the skin — bleeding results in loss of colour and flavour. Boil for ¾-2 hours, depending on size, in salted water. After boiling remove the skin by rubbing. Serve hot as a vegetable or allow to cool for pickling in vinegar or serving fresh in a salad. The young leaves of ordinary beetroot varieties and the more mature foliage of the yellow and white types can be cooked in the same way as spinach. Try baked beets for a change. Wash carefully and arrange in a baking dish. Bake at 165ºC (325ºF) until tender (¾–2 hours, depending on size).

VARIETIES

GLOBE varieties
Other names: Round or Ball varieties

The Globe varieties are by far the most popular group for the ordinary gardener. These beets are generally quick-maturing and are the ones chosen to provide roots for cooking in summer. There are now monogerm types available which produce a single seedling from each 'seed' — this makes thinning a much easier task — reduce space between 'seeds' to 5 cm (2 in.).

For early sowing choose a bolt-resistant type — one which will not readily run to seed in poor growing conditions. For May or June sowing you have the whole range to choose from — the Detroit group is usually chosen to provide a maincrop for late summer use or storage.

The red-rooted varieties remain the usual choice, adding colour to salads and occasionally to tablecloths. Try a white- or yellow-fleshed variety for a change. The leaves can be cooked as 'greens' and the roots have an excellent flavour.

Red

BOLTARDY: Widely available — the usual choice for early sowing. Bolt-resistant. Smooth-skinned with deep red flesh.

DETROIT 2: With the older Detroit it is a standard Globe variety for later planting. Renowned for its flavour.

MONOPOLY: Bolt-resistant like Boltardy with the added advantage of being a monogerm variety (one seedling per 'seed').

RED ACE: An F₁ hybrid which is excellent for exhibition — the flesh colour is dark red. Better than most in dry weather.

DETROIT 2-LITTLE BALL: A popular choice for late sowing. Produces baby beets which are excellent for pickling and bottling.

DETROIT 2-NEW GLOBE: A good choice for the show bench. The shape is uniform, the texture is good and the flesh is free from rings.

Yellow

BURPEE'S GOLDEN: A fine variety from the U.S. which is widely available in Britain. The skin is orange, and the yellow flesh does not bleed when cut. Many consider the flavour to be superior to red varieties — leaves can be cooked as 'greens'.

White

ALBINA VEREDUNA: A popular white variety — sometimes sold as Snowhite. Not widely available like Burpee's Golden or the popular reds, but well worth looking for. The flavour is excellent and the leaves can be cooked as 'greens', but it does not store well.

CYLINDRICAL varieties
Other names:
Tankard or Intermediate varieties

Not many types are listed in the catalogues, although these beetroots are a good choice if you are growing for winter storage. Each root provides many slices of similar size.

CYLINDRA: An oval beet with excellent keeping qualities. Deep red flesh. It is the most popular Cylindrical variety.

ALTO: Not many cylindrical varieties are available. This one is an early-maturing F₁ hybrid which is ring-free and rated highly for its flavour.

LONG varieties
Other names:
Long-rooted or Tapered varieties

The Long varieties require sandy, free-draining soil outdoors and a large pan indoors, so they are not really suitable for the average household. Their popularity has declined, but they remain favourites with the keen exhibitor.

CHELTENHAM GREEN TOP: By far the most popular and highly recommended Long variety. Stores well.

CHELTENHAM MONO: A broad-shouldered Long variety like Cheltenham Green Top, with the advantage of one plant per 'seed'.

Monopoly

Cheltenham Green Top

BEETROOT TROUBLES

Beetroot is an easy crop to grow, and is generally trouble-free. Black bean aphid and mangold fly are occasionally troublesome, but yields are not usually seriously affected. You may find that the leaves are discoloured — beetroot is one of the most sensitive indicators of trace element deficiency in the soil.

	Symptom	Likely Causes
Seedlings	— eaten	**Birds** or **Slugs** (see page 157)
	— toppled over	**Damping off** (see page 157)
	— blackened	3
Leaves	— holed	**Flea beetle** (see page 30)
	— blistered	1
	— rolled	5
	— spotted	6
	— infested with blackfly	**Black bean aphid** (see page 20)
	— mouldy patches	**Downy mildew** (see page 94)
	— mottled	5
Plants	— run to seed	4
Roots	— small and leathery	**Dry soil** or **Fertilizer shortage**
	— large and leathery	**Delayed harvesting**
	— blackened inside, cankered outside	2
	— eaten	**Mice** (see page 20) or **Squirrels** or **Swift Moth** (see page 43) or **Cutworm** or **Millepede** (see page 157)
	— covered with purple mould	**Violet root rot** (see page 43)
	— scabby patches	**Common scab** (see page 85)
	— split	**Splitting** (see page 43)
	— forked	7

BLISTERED LEAVES

1   MANGOLD FLY (Leaf Miner)

Small white grubs burrow inside the leaves, causing tunnels which later turn into blisters. Attacks occur from May onwards, and the effects are most serious on young plants. Badly damaged leaves turn brown and growth is retarded.

Treatment: Pick off and destroy affected leaves. Chemical sprays for this pest are no longer available.

Prevention: None.

3   BLACK LEG

Black leg is a serious disease of seedlings, causing them to turn black and shrivel. It occurs when seeds are sown too thickly in compacted soil which becomes waterlogged in wet weather. If an attack occurs, remove diseased plants and water remainder with Cheshunt Compound.

4   BOLTING

Plants sometimes run to seed before roots have developed. Dry soil or a shortage of organic matter is the usual cause, but it will occur if you sow too early or if you wait too long before thinning the seedlings. Grow a resistant variety such as Boltardy or Monopoly if bolting has been a problem in the past.

7   FANGING

Forked roots are usually caused by adding fresh manure shortly before sowing. Other causes are growing beetroot in stony soil or in heavy ground which has not been properly cultivated. The answer is to use land which has been manured for a previous crop or to add well-rotted compost in the autumn before sowing.

BLACKENED ROOTS

2   HEART ROT

Leaves wilt in the summer and the tops of the roots develop brown, sunken patches. A cut root reveals blackened areas within the flesh. The cause is boron deficiency, and attacks are worst on light, over-limed land in a dry season.

Treatment: Repeated spraying with a trace element spray may help.

Prevention: If soil is known to be boron deficient, apply 30 gm (1 oz) of borax per 16 sq.m (180 sq.ft).

ROLLED LEAVES

5   SPECKLED YELLOWS

Yellow patches develop between the veins, and in a severe attack the whole leaf turns yellow and then brown. The tell-tale sign is the inward rolling of the leaf edges. The cause is manganese deficiency.

Treatment: Apply a sequestered compound. Repeated spraying with a trace element spray may help.

Prevention: Do not overlime the soil.

SPOTTED LEAVES

6   LEAF SPOT

Brown spots appear on the leaves. The pale central area of each spot sometimes drops out. Leaves may be badly disfigured by these numerous small spots but the effect on the yield of roots is not serious.

Treatment: None. Pick off and destroy badly diseased leaves.

Prevention: Practise crop rotation. Apply a balanced fertilizer before sowing seed.

Brassicas

The single genus *Brassica* provides the cornerstone of the average vegetable plot. Botany books talk about *B. bullata*, *B. capitata*, *B. gemmifera* and so on, but to us they are cabbages, Brussels sprouts, etc. Not all are leafy vegetables — both turnips and swedes are brassicas and so is kohl rabi. But for the gardener the word 'brassica' is usually reserved for the varieties grown as greens — the all-important group which flourish so well in our climate and which share the same cultural likes and dislikes. Brassicas have been a staple part of our diet for thousands of years — long before newcomers like potatoes and runner beans came to our shores. But we must forget old prejudices — in recent years there has been a steady stream of new brassica varieties offering new tastes, and during the same period our ideas about the way to cook brassicas have also changed — the days of school cabbage and boarding house Brussels sprouts should now be a thing of the past!

SECRETS OF SUCCESS

- Do not grow brassicas on the same plot more often than one year in three. The main reason for this move-around is to avoid the build-up of soil pests and diseases which thrive on the cabbage family — the dreaded club root disease is the prime example.
- Dig deeply in autumn — the roots must be allowed to reach the water reserves well below the surface.
- Brassicas require firm soil — leave several months between digging and planting in order for the surface to consolidate.
- Lime if necessary — brassicas will disappoint if the soil is acid. Aim for a pH of 6.5–7.5.
- Transplant at the right stage and make sure that you plant firmly.
- Consider using protective discs (see page 28) around the base of each seedling if cabbage root fly has been a problem in the past.
- Many pests and diseases can attack brassicas — treat problems as soon as they are seen.

SOWING

Leafy brassica	Sow in a seed bed, then transplant to a permanent bed	Sow where the plants are to grow to maturity
Broccoli	All varieties	—
Brussels sprouts	All varieties	—
Cabbage	Nearly all varieties	Chinese cabbage varieties
Cauliflower	All varieties	—
Kale	Nearly all varieties	Rape kale varieties

- As shown above, nearly all leafy brassicas are planted in a seed bed and then transferred to another part of the plot where they will grow to maturity. In this way the 'permanent bed' can be utilised for another vegetable until the seedlings are ready for transplanting.
- Choose a sunny but sheltered spot for the seed bed. The soil must be fertile — if it was not manured for a previous crop then add compost when digging in autumn. Before sowing rake (do not fork) the surface and add a general-purpose fertilizer. You can incorporate a nematode-based insecticide if cabbage root fly has been a nuisance in the past. Tread to remove air pockets and to make the surface firm — rake lightly and then follow the sowing instructions.

PLANTING

- The permanent bed (the area where the plants will grow to maturity) should be deeply dug in autumn — ideally it will have grown peas or beans a few months earlier. If the soil has not been recently manured it is essential that compost is incorporated during this autumn digging.
- Do not fork over the ground in spring — simply tread down, rake lightly and remove surface debris. A firm footing for the seedlings is essential.
- The seedlings will be ready for transplanting 5–7 weeks after sowing — look up the specific brassica in this book for details. Water the row the day before the seedlings are to be lifted.
- Lift carefully, retaining as much soil as possible around the roots. Do not dig up too many at one time, and keep the roots covered so that they do not dry out. Mark out the planting row with string and make holes at the required distances with a trowel or dibber — if the soil is dry fill the holes with water and begin transplanting once they have drained.
- Look up the specific plant for details of planting depth. Make sure that the plants are properly firmed in with fingers, dibber or the back of a trowel.

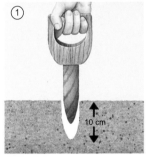
① 10 cm

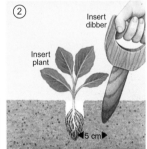
② Insert dibber / Insert plant / 5 cm

③ Press towards plant

④ Tug test: Test one plant — leaf should tear before plant is uprooted

- Water the base of each transplant as soon as planting is finished — keep the rose on the watering can to ensure that the plants will not be disturbed. If the weather is warm and dry before the transplants are established, cover them with newspaper and water the soil frequently.

BRASSICA TROUBLES

Kale is generally a trouble-free vegetable, but the other members of the brassica family are subject to a wide range of pests and diseases. The worst of these brassica enemies are cabbage root fly, cabbage caterpillars, mealy aphid, whitefly, club root, flea beetle and pigeons. But you must not assume that an insect or fungus disease is the cause every time something goes wrong. As the following pages make clear, the most likely cause of blown Brussels sprouts, heartless cabbages and button-headed cauliflowers is you — the ground was left too spongy or the seedlings were not planted firmly. You may have left acid soil unlimed or you may have planted a brassica crop in land which produced poor cabbages or cauliflowers last year. If you are new to gardening, read the appropriate page carefully before growing one of the brassicas.

	Symptom	Likely Causes
Seedlings	— eaten	11 or 13 or 16 or 27
	— toppled over	3 or **Damping off** (see page 157)
	— peppered with small holes	16
	— severed at ground level	27
Stems	— tunnelled, maggots present	28
	— blackened zone near soil level	6
Leaves	— swollen, distorted	18
	— narrow, strap-like	9
	— curled, blistered	20
	— whitened	17
	— diseased	1 or 5 or 7 or 8
	— coloured between green veins	22 or 23
	— holed	10 or 11 or 13 or 16 or 26
	— infested with greenfly	20
	— tiny white moths	21
	— caterpillars	10 or 26
Roots	— swollen	3 or 4
	— tunnelled, maggots present	2
	— eaten	24
Plants	— bluish leaves, wilting in sunshine	2 or 4
	— blind; plants not growing	9 or 18 or **Blind transplants**
	— wilting, dying	24 or 28
Brussels sprouts	— buttons open and leafy	15
Cabbage	— no hearts	2 or 12
	— split hearts	14
Cauliflower	— small heads	2 or 9 or 19 or 25
	— brown heads	25

1 | DOWNY MILDEW

Yellowing of upper surface. White furry fungus growth beneath. Usually restricted to young plants; over-crowding and moist atmosphere encourage its spread. Growth severely checked.

Treatment: Chemical sprays are no longer available for this purpose.

Prevention: Sow seeds in sterilised compost. Choose a fresh site for raising seedlings if downy mildew has been a problem in the past.

TUNNELLED ROOTS

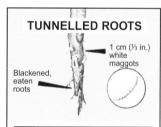

1 cm (⅓ in.) white maggots

Blackened, eaten roots

2 | CABBAGE ROOT FLY

Tell-tale signs are blue-tinged leaves which wilt in sunny weather; recent transplants are particularly susceptible. Young plants die; older ones grow slowly. Cabbages fail to heart, cauliflowers form tiny heads.

Treatment: Apply a nematode-based insecticide immediately after planting out, or put discs made out of roofing felt around the base of the stems. Alternatively place fine netting over the young plants.

3 | GALL WEEVIL

Much less serious and much less common than club root. Swellings generally form close to ground level. Growth may be checked slightly, but there is rarely any serious effect on yield.

Treatment: Not worth while. Spread can be reduced by watering around plants with pyrethrins.

Prevention: Soil-pest killers which have been used to control pests which live underground are no longer available.

SWOLLEN ROOTS

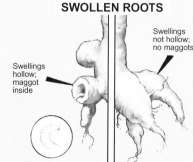

Swellings not hollow; no maggots

Swellings hollow; maggot inside

4 | CLUB ROOT (Finger & Toe)

Tell-tale signs are discoloured leaves which wilt in sunny weather. A serious disease which can be disastrous in a wet season. Plants may die or grow very slowly.

Treatment: None. Lift diseased plants and burn. In the case of a severe attack do not plant brassicas on the site for several years.

Prevention: Make sure the land is adequately limed and well drained. No chemical treatment for dipping roots is currently available.

5 | WHITE BLISTER (White Rust)

White spots appear on leaves. The fungus may spread in a mild, damp season to form a white felt over the leaves. Growth is stunted and plants may die. Sprouts are more susceptible than other brassicas.

Treatment: Cut off and burn diseased leaves. Thin out plants to reduce over-crowding.

Prevention: Do not grow brassicas on land affected in the previous season.

6 | WIRE STEM

Base of stem becomes black and shrunken. Seedlings often die; the plants which survive grow very slowly and stems break easily.

Treatment: None.

Prevention: Avoid growing seedlings in wet and cold soil or compost. Cheshunt Compound may help. Avoid over-crowding.

SHRUNKEN STEMS

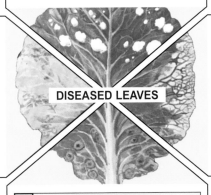

DISEASED LEAVES

7 | BLACK ROT

An uncommon but serious disease. Seedlings are killed — mature plants are severely stunted, bearing yellow leaves and characteristically black veins. Lower leaves generally fall. If the stem is cut across a dark brown ring is revealed. Worst attacks occur in a warm, wet summer.

Treatment: None. Lift diseased plants and burn.

Prevention: None. Rotate crops.

8 | LEAF SPOT (Ring Spot)

Brown rings up to 3 cm (1 in.) across appear on mature leaves. Badly infected foliage may turn yellow and fall. Most likely to occur in S.W. areas.

Treatment: Cut off and burn diseased leaves. No sprays are available.

Prevention: Do not grow brassicas on land affected by leaf spot in the previous season.

9 | WHIPTAIL

Leaves are thin and strap-like. Plant growth is poor, cauliflower heads may be very small or fail to develop. Caused by molybdenum deficiency due to acid soil.

Treatment: Repeated spraying with a trace element spray.

Prevention: Make sure soil is adequately limed before sowing or planting.

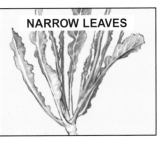

NARROW LEAVES

10 | CABBAGE CATERPILLARS

Look for cabbage caterpillars when holes begin to appear in leaves. The cabbage moth tends to burrow into the heart. The risk period is April-October, and attacks are worst during a hot dry summer and in coastal areas.

Treatment: Spray with pyrethrins as soon as the first attacks occur. Repeat as necessary.

Prevention: Inspect underside of leaves if you see white butterflies hovering over the plants. Remove and crush any eggs which have been laid.

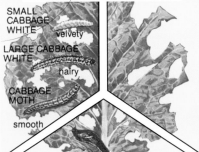

LARGE HOLES IN LEAVES

SMALL CABBAGE WHITE   velvety

LARGE CABBAGE WHITE

hairy

CABBAGE MOTH

smooth

11 | PIGEONS

Pigeons are a serious pest in many areas, stripping away the soft portions of the leaves until only the stalks and veins remain. Droppings make the produce tedious to prepare for cooking. Troublesome throughout the year, especially in winter.

Treatment: None.

Prevention: Bird scarers are of limited value. Use nylon netting, making sure that the plants are completely enclosed.

12 | HEARTLESS CABBAGES

There are several reasons why cabbage plants fail to heart. Too little organic matter in the soil and too little compaction of the ground before planting are common reasons. So is failing to plant the seedlings firmly. Drought increases the risk; so does a shady site. Proper feeding will help, but use a balanced fertilizer, or a potassium-rich soluble feed, and not straight nitrogen.

13 | SLUGS & SNAILS

Leaves and stems may be severely attacked during wet weather. The pests are generally not seen during the day, so look for the tell-tale slime trails. Young plants are particularly susceptible and may be killed.

Treatment: Scatter slug pellets around the plants at the first signs of attack or use a nematode product.

Prevention: Keep surrounding area free from rubbish.

14 | SPLIT HEARTS

There are two major reasons why cabbage heads suddenly split. In summer the usual cause is rain after a long period of dry weather. Foliar feeding at the first sign of trouble helps to harden the leaf tissue, but it is better to prevent trouble by watering regularly during drought. In winter the cause is a sudden sharp frost; consider lifting and storing mature heads if very cold weather is forecast.

page 30

BRASSICA TROUBLES continued

15 BLOWN BRUSSELS SPROUTS

Brussels sprouts sometimes produce open, leafy sprouts instead of hard, round buttons. These blown sprouts should be removed promptly. The causes are similar to the factors responsible for heartless cabbages — not enough well-rotted organic matter in the soil, too little consolidation of the ground before planting and failure to plant firmly. Make sure the plants are kept well watered during dry weather and avoid planting too closely. Choose an F₁ hybrid variety.

WHITENED LEAVES

BLIND PLANTS

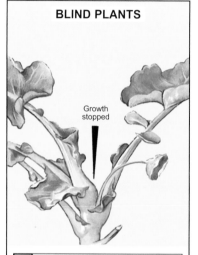

Growth stopped

17 FROST

Frost can be extremely damaging to brassicas. If the plants are not firmly anchored in the soil then frost can reach the roots and lead to the death of the plant. Frosts can also damage the leaves of non-hardy varieties. The blanched areas are quickly attacked by fungi or bacteria and extensive rotting can occur.

Treatment: Remove and burn damaged leaves.

Prevention: Always plant firmly. Frost damage is worse on soft growth so always use a properly balanced fertilizer when preparing the soil.

18 SWEDE MIDGE

Attacks are uncommon, but the results are devastating. Leaf stalks near the growing point are swollen and distorted, and the plants become blind. Look carefully for the minute white larvae on the leaf stalks. Northern and S.W. districts are most at risk.

Treatment: Lift and burn badly affected plants. Insecticides once used to control this disease are no longer available.

Prevention: No practical method available.

SMALL HOLES IN LEAVES

16 FLEA BEETLE

A serious pest, especially in April and May during warm, settled weather. Young leaves bear numerous, small round holes. Growth is slowed down and seedlings may be killed. The tiny beetles jump when disturbed.

Treatment: Spray the seedlings with pyrethrins as soon as the first signs of damage are noticed. Water damaged plants if the weather is dry.

Prevention: Treating seed with an insecticidal seed dressing before sowing will prevent early attacks.

19 BUTTON CAULIFLOWERS

Many gardeners fail to grow satisfactory cauliflowers. Buttoning often takes place, which is the production of very small heads early in the season. These button heads quickly run to seed. Unfortunately there are many causes. It may be due to an early attack by a pest such as flea beetle or the shortage of a trace element such as boron or molybdenum. Or the cause may be cultural — poor soil, insufficient consolidation of the ground before planting, loose planting, drought or failure to harden off the seedlings properly before planting.

20 MEALY APHID

Large clusters of waxy, greyish 'greenflies' occur on the underside of leaves and tips of plants from June onwards in hot, dry weather. Affected leaves curl and turn yellow. Sooty moulds develop if the attack is severe and the pests can be numerous enough to render sprouts unusable.

Treatment: Not easy to control. Spray thoroughly with pyrethrins or thiacloprid.

Prevention: Dig up and destroy old brassica stalks.

INSECTS ON LEAVES

21 CABBAGE WHITEFLY

Outbreaks have become much more widespread in the past few years. Tiny white moths and larvae feed on the underside of leaves. Affected plants are weakened and sooty moulds develop. The adults are active throughout the year and fly into the air when disturbed.

Treatment: Not easy to control. Spray with pyrethrins at 3 day intervals until the infestation has been cleared. Best results are obtained by spraying in the morning or evening.

Prevention: No practical method available.

22 MAGNESIUM DEFICIENCY

Yellowing between the leaf veins begins on the older leaves, and these yellow areas may eventually turn orange, white, red or purple. Magnesium deficiency is much more common than manganese deficiency.

Treatment: Apply a trace element spray around the plants. Repeated spraying with a foliar feed may help.

Prevention: Incorporate compost into the soil during autumn digging. Use a fertilizer containing magnesium.

MOTTLING BETWEEN VEINS

23 MANGANESE DEFICIENCY

It is not always easy to distinguish between manganese and magnesium deficiency by looking at a single leaf. Manganese deficiency symptoms, however, usually start on young as well as old leaves, and the leaf edges are often curled inwards and scorched.

Treatment: Apply a trace element spray around the plants. Repeated spraying with a foliar feed may help.

Prevention: Incorporate compost into the soil during autumn digging.

24 CHAFER GRUBS

The visual symptoms of chafer grub attack are wilting leaves and dying plants. On lifting affected specimens damaged roots are seen and fat, curved grubs may be found in the soil. These slow-moving pests can feed throughout the year. Gardens made from newly-dug grassland are the areas most likely to suffer.

Treatment: None

Prevention: Hand pick and destroy the grubs when autumn digging. Use a nematode-based insecticide.

ROOTS EATEN

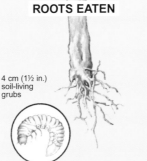

4 cm (1½ in.) soil-living grubs

BROWN CURDS

25 BORON DEFICIENCY

Cauliflowers are extremely sensitive to boron deficiency in the soil. Young leaves are distorted, and the heads are small and bitter. The main symptom is the development of brown patches on the curds.

Treatment: Repeated spraying with a foliar feed may help.

Prevention: Incorporate compost into the soil during autumn digging. If soil is definitely known to be boron deficient, apply 30 gm (1 oz) of borax per 16 sq.m (180 sq.ft).

SKIN-COVERED HOLES

2 cm (⅔ in.) green caterpillars

26 DIAMOND-BACK MOTH

These green caterpillars can be a serious summer nuisance in coastal areas. They feed on the underside of the foliage and, unlike the cabbage caterpillars, generally leave the upper skin intact. When disturbed they drop from the plant on a silken thread. In a severe attack the leaf is completely skeletonized.

Treatment: Spray with pyrethrins as soon as the first attack occurs.

Prevention: None.

SEVERED STEMS

3–5 cm (1–2 in.) soil-living caterpillars

27 CUTWORM

These large grey or brown caterpillars live just below the surface. Young plants are attacked at night and stems are severed at ground level. Leaves and roots may also be eaten. Plants are most at risk in June and July.

Treatment: Hoe the soil around the plants regularly during the danger months. Pick up and destroy caterpillars which are brought to the surface.

Prevention: Use a nematode-based insecticide.

TUNNELLED STEMS

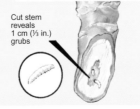

Cut stem reveals 1 cm (⅓ in.) grubs

28 CABBAGE STEM FLEA BEETLE

Infested plants wilt and die. Cut open the stem of one of the plants if you suspect cabbage stem flea beetle; the tell-tale sign is the presence of small, cream-coloured grubs. Attacks occur between August and October.

Treatment: Lift and burn infested plants.

Prevention: Do not grow brassicas on land affected by cabbage stem flea beetle in the previous season.

Broccoli

There is some confusion over the naming of broccoli types in the catalogues and textbooks. The ones which form a single large white head in winter are listed in this book with the cauliflowers. The green broccoli varieties are harvested in autumn and are classed as calabrese. The varieties which are cut-and-come-again plants producing late winter and spring spears are white and purple sprouting broccoli. The frozen spears from the super-market are really calabrese — the common garden ones are varieties of purple sprouting broccoli.

IN A NUTSHELL

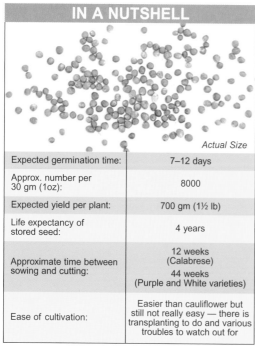

Actual Size

Expected germination time:	7–12 days
Approx. number per 30 gm (1oz):	8000
Expected yield per plant:	700 gm (1½ lb)
Life expectancy of stored seed:	4 years
Approximate time between sowing and cutting:	12 weeks (Calabrese) 44 weeks (Purple and White varieties)
Ease of cultivation:	Easier than cauliflower but still not really easy — there is transplanting to do and various troubles to watch out for

SOWING & PLANTING

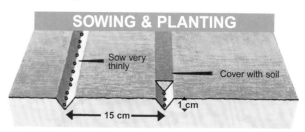

- Thin the seedlings to prevent them from becoming weak and spindly. They should be about 8 cm (3 in.) apart in the rows.
- The seedlings are ready for transplanting when they are 8 cm (3 in.) high. Water the rows the day before moving the transplants to their permanent quarters. Plant firmly, setting the seedlings about 3 cm (1 in.) deeper than they were growing in the seed bed. Leave 45 cm (1½ ft) between purple and white sprouting broccoli, 30 cm (1 ft) between green sprouting broccoli. Water after planting.

LOOKING AFTER THE CROP

- Hoe regularly and provide some means of protection for the young plants against birds.
- Summer care consists of watering in dry weather and applying a mulch to conserve moisture. Occasional feeding with a liquid fertilizer will improve the crop. Broccoli is a trouble-prone crop so watch for pests. Spray with permethrin if caterpillars appear.
- With the approach of winter draw up soil around the stems and stake the plants if the site is exposed. Always firm the stems if they are loosened by wind or frost. Pigeons can be a menace at this time of the year — netting may be necessary.

HARVESTING

- The time to cut is when the flower shoots ('spears') are well formed but before the small flower buds have opened. Once in flower the spears are woody and tasteless.
- Cut or snap off the central spear first — in a few varieties this will be a cauliflower-like head. Side shoots will be produced and these should be picked regularly, but never strip a plant completely.
- The spears are generally 10–15 cm (4–6 in.) long and cropping should continue for about 6 weeks. If you let any of them flower, however, production will stop at an earlier stage.

SOIL FACTS

- Broccoli, like other brassicas, can fail in loose and starved soil. Ideally the ground should be firm and rich in organic matter.
- Pick a reasonably sunny site for the place where the plants will grow to maturity. Dig in autumn — work in plenty of well-rotted manure or compost if the soil is poor. Lime, if necessary, in winter.
- In spring apply a compound fertilizer. Consider using protective discs (see page 28) if cabbage root fly is known to be a problem. Do not fork over the surface before planting the seedlings — tread down gently, rake lightly and remove surface rubbish.

- The date you can expect to start cutting depends on the variety and the weather. Early Purple Sprouting will be ready for its first picking in January if the winter is mild but mid spring is the peak harvesting period for the purple and white varieties.
- The calabrese varieties will be ready for cutting in autumn — choose Green Magic if you are in a hurry. Cropping will extend into winter if prolonged frosts do not occur.

CALENDAR

	JAN	FEB	MAR	APR	MAY	JUN	JUL	AUG	SEP	OCT	NOV	DEC
Sowing Time				▓	▓							
Planting Time						▓	▓	▓				
Cutting Time		EARLY vars.		LATE vars.					GREEN vars.			

For key to symbols — see page 7

IN THE KITCHEN

Broccoli may look like a small version of cauliflower but its flavour is usually closer to asparagus. Calabrese is the most asparagus-like and white sprouting broccoli is the closest in taste to cauliflower — it can be used as a substitute for making 'cauliflower' cheese. Don't judge broccoli from the flavour of shop-bought spears which are then boiled — to discover the real flavour you should steam (not boil) the spears and this should take place within hours of picking.

FREEZING: An excellent vegetable for freezing. Soak in salted water for 15 minutes, then rinse and dry. Blanch for 3–4 minutes — cool and drain. Pack carefully and freeze in rigid containers.

STORAGE: Keep in a polythene bag in the refrigerator — broccoli will stay fresh for up to 3 days.

COOKING: The standard method is to peel off the skin if it is tough, remove any large leaves and then cook in boiling salted water for 10 minutes. Drain carefully and then serve hot with white sauce or melted butter, or cold with a vinaigrette. Steaming is preferred by the food experts — stand the spears upright in 5 cm (2 in.) of gently boiling water for 15 minutes. Keep the pan covered so that the heads are steamed. On the Continent you will find broccoli cooked in many ways — *broccoli alla romana* (braised in white wine), *broccoli alla siciliana* (braised with anchovies, olives and red wine) and broccoli fritters (washed and dried heads dipped into batter and then deep fried until golden-brown).

VARIETIES

PURPLE SPROUTING varieties

This is the hardiest and the most popular broccoli for growing at home. It is extremely useful for heavy soils and cold areas where little else can overwinter. The heads turn green when cooked. There are three popular varieties — planting all three will give you broccoli spears for many months.

RED ARROW: Introduced with the claim that it gave higher yields than the popular older varieties. Now hard to find.

EARLY PURPLE SPROUTING: The most popular variety — ready for cutting in February or March. Prolific and hardy with a long cropping season — the one to choose if you plan to grow only one sort of broccoli for spring use.

LATE PURPLE SPROUTING: Like the other purples, winter-hardy and robust — plants grow about 1 m (3 ft) tall. The spears will not be ready for picking until April.

RUDOLPH: Grow this variety if you want an early start to the cropping season — large spears begin to appear in September from an early sowing.

WHITE SPROUTING varieties

This group produces small cauliflower-like spears. The varieties are less popular than the purple sprouting sorts but some people prefer the flavour and the white appearance of this crop. If you propose to grow white sprouting broccoli then the choice is very limited.

EARLY WHITE SPROUTING: The one to grow if you want to cut the crop in March and early April.

WHITE EYE: A hard-to-find alternative to Early White Sprouting — the first spears are ready for cutting in February. A heavy cropping variety.

CALABRESE varieties

Calabrese or green sprouting broccoli is a useful but much underrated vegetable. Unlike the purple and white sprouting types, it produces its crop of delicately-flavoured spears before the onset of winter. Some varieties produce a succession of spears stretching from early autumn until the first frosts — if you want plants which bear a single large head in August then choose Green Magic.

MARATHON: A calabrese variety which is highly rated for its disease resistance and its reliability in poor conditions. Sow in July and start cutting in September.

SAMSON: The tightly-packed blue-green heads will be ready for cutting in October from a June sowing. A good variety with a fine flavour.

GREEN MAGIC: An early maturing variety — sow in late March for a summer crop. The large head should be cut first, after which you can pick the smaller side-shoots as they appear.

PARTHENON: Marathon offered a number of advantages over the standard varieties of calabrese, and Parthenon takes it a step further. The heads are heavier and smoother, and the colour is deep green. Flavour is excellent.

GREEN SPROUTING: Not the usual sort of calabrese — unlike the F_1 hybrids it produces a profusion of individual spears. An April sowing will be ready for cutting from August onwards.

DE CICCO: Another cut-and-come-again variety. The main head is smaller than Green Magic, but the later side-shoots are more prolific. Quick-growing — sowing to cutting is less than 3 months.

SHOGUN: An F_1 hybrid which bears large blue-green heads with many lateral shoots below them. It is tolerant of cold conditions and a wide range of soil types. Early maturing — good for freezing.

PERENNIAL variety

Perennial broccoli is a tall-growing vegetable — leave about 1 m (3 ft) between the plants. In spring or early summer about 8 small and pale green heads are produced, each one looking like a small cauliflower. Grow the variety **NINE STAR PERENNIAL** — plant it against a fence and fork in a general-purpose fertilizer each spring. Apply a mulch in early summer, never let the flower buds open and you will obtain heads year after year.

TROUBLES

See pages 28–31

Early Purple Sprouting

Marathon

Brussels sprout

Loose, open sprouts are caused by bad gardening, not bad weather. The ground must be firm — never wait until spring to dig or fork over the soil. At sowing time merely tread down the surface, rake lightly and remove surface rubbish. You can begin picking in September and finish in March by growing both early and late varieties. The usual choice is an F_1 hybrid. New ones continue to appear and some older ones disappear — Peer Gynt, once a favourite, has gone from the catalogues. The old standard varieties have none of the uniformity of the F_1 hybrids, but some are still available.

IN A NUTSHELL

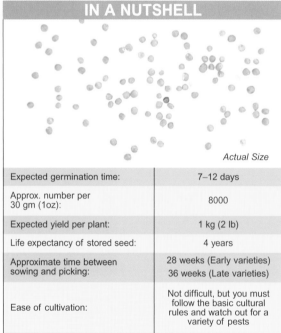

Actual Size

Expected germination time:	7–12 days
Approx. number per 30 gm (1oz):	8000
Expected yield per plant:	1 kg (2 lb)
Life expectancy of stored seed:	4 years
Approximate time between sowing and picking:	28 weeks (Early varieties) 36 weeks (Late varieties)
Ease of cultivation:	Not difficult, but you must follow the basic cultural rules and watch out for a variety of pests

SOIL FACTS

- The main cause of failure is planting in loose, infertile soil. The ground must be *firm* and adequately supplied with humus.
- Pick a reasonably sunny spot with shelter from high winds for the place where the plants will grow to maturity. Dig in autumn — work in plenty of well-rotted manure or compost if the soil is poor. The ground must not be acid — lime, if necessary, in winter.
- In spring apply a fertilizer — consider using protective discs (see page 28) if cabbage root fly is usually a problem. Do not fork over the surface before planting the seedlings — tread down gently, rake lightly and remove surface rubbish.

SOWING & PLANTING

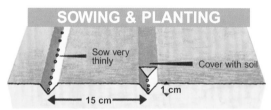

Sow very thinly — Cover with soil — 15 cm — 1 cm

- Thin the seedlings to about 8 cm (3 in.) apart in the rows to prevent them from becoming weak and spindly.
- The seedlings are ready for transplanting when they are 10–15 cm (4–6 in.) high. Water the rows the day before moving the transplants to their permanent quarters. Plant firmly, setting the seedlings with their lowest leaves just above the soil surface. Leave 75 cm (2½ ft) between the plants and water after planting.

LOOKING AFTER THE CROP

- Birds are a problem — protect the seedlings from sparrows and the mature crop from pigeons.
- Hoe regularly and water the young plants in dry weather. The mature crop rarely needs watering if the soil has been properly prepared. Brussels sprouts respond remarkably well to foliar feeding in early summer. Both caterpillars and aphids can be a menace — spray with permethrin.
- As autumn approaches earth-up around the stems and stake tall varieties before the high winds of winter arrive. The old practice of removing the tops of the plants to hasten maturity is no longer recommended.

HARVESTING

- Begin picking when the sprouts ('buttons') at the base of the stem have reached the size of a walnut and are still tightly closed. Snap them off with a sharp downward tug or cut them off with a sharp knife.
- Work steadily up the stem at each cropping session, removing yellowed leaves and any open ('blown') sprouts as you go. Remember to remove only a few sprouts at any one time from each individual stem.
- When all the sprouts have gone, cut off the stem tops and cook as cabbage. Dig up and dispose of the stems.

- Sow an early variety outdoors in mid March and plant out in mid May to provide sprouts during October and November. To obtain September sprouts, sow the seeds under cloches in early March and plant out in early May.
- For a later crop which will produce sprouts between December and March, sow a late variety in April and plant out in June.

CALENDAR

	JAN	FEB	MAR	APR	MAY	JUN	JUL	AUG	SEP	OCT	NOV	DEC
Sowing Time			↥									
Planting Time												
Picking Time												

For key to symbols — see page 7

IN THE KITCHEN

Overcooked sprouts, straw-coloured and soggy, are a much-quoted example of bad British cookery. The secret of success is to pick them whilst they still feel hard and boil briskly for the minimum time required to turn them chewy but not mushy. Even this small amount of boiling is not essential — small sprouts can be shredded and served as part of a salad. Freezing is often recommended and is indeed the only way of coping with a glut, but it is not wholly satisfactory. Boil frozen sprouts for only 2—3 minutes before serving.

FREEZING: Use only small, firm sprouts. Strip off the outer leaves if damaged and soak for 15 minutes in cold water. Blanch for 3 minutes, cool and then drain thoroughly. Dry the sprouts on a paper towel and pack into polythene bags, leaving no air space, before freezing.

STORAGE: Keep unwashed in a polythene bag in the refrigerator — Brussels sprouts will stay fresh for up to 3 days.

COOKING: Boiling is the standard method of cooking sprouts. Cut off the basal stalk and strip away the outer leaves. Cut a cross at the base with a sharp knife. Wash in cold water — if there are aphids within the sprouts soak in salted water for 15 minutes. Add 3 cm (1 in.) of water to a large pan and bring to the boil. Add the sprouts slowly so that the water does not stop boiling — cover the pan and keep the water bubbling merrily for 7–8 minutes. Drain thoroughly, add a knob of butter (optional) and serve. Christmas Dinner calls for something a little extra — boil the sprouts for 5 minutes and then braise with cooked chestnuts in butter for a further 5 minutes. Alternatively you can braise the parboiled sprouts with onions in a small amount of stock and bacon fat.

VARIETIES

F₁ HYBRID varieties

The modern F_1 hybrids are the usual choice. This popularity is due to the compact growth habit of most of them and the large number of uniform buttons which crowd the stems. The sprouts tend to mature all at the same time, which is an advantage if you intend to freeze them, but it is often quoted as a disadvantage if you wish to pick over a protracted period. This disadvantage is overrated — the F_1 hybrids generally hold their mature buttons for many weeks without 'blowing'.

BRIGITTE: A sweet nutty flavour and good disease resistance are the two outstanding features here. The tight buttons are available from mid October to mid December.

MAXIMUS: It is suggested that this variety is sown at periods between early March to late April to provide fine quality sprouts from September to February. Regarded by some experts as the replacement for Peer Gynt.

TRAFALGAR: A tall-growing variety which produces firm, medium-sized sprouts. It is claimed in some catalogues to be the sweetest Brussels sprout.

BOSWORTH: This British-bred variety has been highly praised — it holds the RHS Award of Garden Merit. It is easy to pick, has good cold-weather tolerance, and the flavour is rated highly.

MONTGOMERY: Another modern F_1 hybrid with some of the features of the Bedford varieties. The strong stems resist wind damage and you can expect a prolific late crop of dark green sprouts.

CRISPUS: You will find this one in many catalogues. It is an early to mid-season variety. It bears small, dark-green buttons. Picking starts in September — buttons will stand for several weeks if picking is delayed.

BRILLIANT: An early variety for picking in September and October which has good disease and bolt resistance. Yields are high and the flavour is said to be excellent.

HASTINGS: Not in many catalogues, but this early variety has a few features which are worth considering. The short stems make it a good choice for an exposed site, and the buttons have good keeping qualities on the stems.

RAMPART: Another late variety which holds its sprouts for a long period without blowing. Tall-growing — the sprouts are quite large and noted for their flavour.

Crispus

STANDARD varieties

The heritage varieties, sometimes called ordinary or open-pollinated varieties, have now been largely overshadowed by the F_1 hybrids. Their sprouts have none of the uniformity or high quality of the modern hybrids and they quite quickly blow off if not picked off the stem once they have matured. Though no longer recommended by some experts they still retain one or two advantages. Here you will find the largest sprouts and perhaps the best flavours.

EARLY HALF TALL: An alternative choice to the F_1 hybrid Peer Gynt if you want a compact plant which will crop between September and Christmas.

BEDFORD: The market gardeners of Bedfordshire originated this variety, noted for its large sprouts on tall stems. There are Bedford-Fillbasket if you want the heaviest yields and the largest sprouts, and Bedford-Asmer Monitor if you want a compact plant for a small garden.

NOISETTE: The gourmet's sprout — small buttons with a pronounced nutty flavour. A French favourite — they say it should be braised in white wine.

EARLY HALF TALL: A compact plant which will crop between September and Christmas. Its rival was Peer Gynt — once the favourite sprout but no longer in the catalogues.

EVESHAM SPECIAL: A few catalogues still offer this heritage sprout which produces an abundant supply of solid sprouts from September to December.

DARKMAR 21: This Bedford-style sprout is not an F_1 hybrid, but it has its supporters as the large sprouts are available from mid November to early February.

Bedford-Fillbasket

TROUBLES

See pages 28–31

Cabbage

If you have the space and inclination it is quite possible to have heads ready for cutting all year round. Nearly all of the varieties in the catalogues fall neatly into one of the three major groups — Spring, Summer or Winter cabbage. The seasonal name refers to the time of harvesting, not planting. You can cut-and-come-again with Spring and Summer cabbages, and even if you grow just one variety it is a good idea to plant just a short row every few weeks. Savoys are less popular than the other types.

TYPES

| SPRING | SUMMER | WINTER | SAVOY | RED | CHINESE |

IN A NUTSHELL

Don't sow too many at one time — just a small row every few weeks

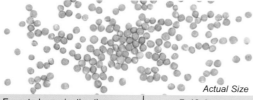

Actual Size

Expected germination time:	7–12 days
Approx. number per 30 gm (1oz):	8000
Expected yield per plant:	300 gm – 1.5 kg (½–3 lb)
Life expectancy of stored seed:	4 years
Approximate time between sowing and cutting:	35 weeks (Spring varieties) 20–35 weeks (Summer, Winter, Savoy)
Ease of cultivation:	Not difficult if you follow the cultural rules and if club root, cabbage root fly and other pests stay away

SOIL FACTS

- Cabbage requires well-consolidated soil, so leave several months between digging and planting. Some humus must be present but this must never be freshly applied.
- Pick a reasonably sunny spot for the site where the plants are to grow — you can use an area recently vacated by a non-brassica crop (see page 27). Dig in autumn — work in some compost or manure if the soil is poor. The ground must not be acid — lime, if necessary, in winter.
- About a week before planting apply a general fertilizer for all types except Spring cabbage — this group needs to be grown slowly n a sheltered spot. Consider using protective discs (see page 28) if cabbage root fly is usually a problem. Do not fork over the surface before planting — tread down gently, rake and remove surface rubbish.

SOWING & PLANTING

Sow very thinly

Cover with soil

15 cm

1 cm

- Thin the seedlings to prevent them from becoming weak and spindly. They should be about 8 cm (3 in.) apart in the rows.
- The seedlings are ready for transplanting when they have 5 or 6 leaves. Water the rows the day before moving the transplants to their permanent quarters.
- Allow 30 cm (1 ft) between the plants if the variety is compact — leave 45 cm (1½ ft) either way if the variety produces large heads. With Spring cabbage leave only 10 cm (4 in.) between plants in rows 30 cm (1 ft) apart — the thinnings provide spring greens in March.

LOOKING AFTER THE CROP

- Birds are a problem — protect the seedlings from sparrows. Hoe carefully until the crop is large enough to suppress weeds.
- Water if the weather is dry. Always apply a liquid feed as the heads begin to mature.
- In autumn earth-up the stems of Spring cabbage. During winter firm down any plants loosened by wind or frost.

HARVESTING

- In March thin out the Spring cabbage rows and use the young plants as spring greens. Leave the remaining plants to heart up for cutting in April or May.
- Cabbages are harvested by cutting with a knife close to the ground. With Spring and Summer cabbages cut a 1 cm (½ in.) deep cross into the stumps — a secondary crop of small cabbages will appear from the cut surfaces.
- In most cases cabbages are cut as required for immediate use. Both Red and Winter white cabbages can be harvested in November and then stored for winter use. Cut off roots and stem, remove outer leaves and then place in straw-lined boxes in a cool, dry place. The crop should keep until March.

IN THE KITCHEN

Boiling is just one of the many methods of using cabbages in the kitchen. First of all, there is raw cabbage — not as unappetising as it may sound. Shredded white or red cabbage is a useful salad ingredient, but white cabbage is more usually mixed with grated carrots, apples, etc. and tossed with mayonnaise to produce coleslaw. The standard method of serving Chinese cabbage is to add a vinaigrette dressing to the shredded leaves. Then there is pickled cabbage — in vinegar for red cabbage or in brine for white cabbage *(sauerkraut)*. For most of us cabbage is a vegetable for cooking and not for eating raw or pickled, but boiling should not be regarded as the only or even the best way of cooking. There is stir frying — the recommended method for Chinese cabbage and a welcome alternative for ordinary varieties. Baked cabbage stuffed with minced meat is popular in eastern Europe and cabbage leaves can be used as a substitute for vine leaves to make the Greek dish *dolmades*. Cabbage soup, cabbage casserole, braised cabbage — there are many recipes to turn to if you are tired of plain boiled cabbage.

FREEZING: Use only fresh, crisp heads. Wash and coarsely shred — blanch for 1 minute. Pack into polythene bags for freezing.

STORAGE: Keep wrapped in plastic cling film in the refrigerator — cabbage will stay fresh for up to 1 week — Chinese cabbage for several weeks.

COOKING: Boiling cabbage properly is something of an art. Wash and prepare just before cooking — shred or cut into wedges depending on your taste. Fill a large pan with 3 cm (1 in.) of lightly salted water and bring to the boil. Add the coarse leaves a handful at a time — the water should not stop boiling. Put the leaves of the young heart on top of the old leaves and replace the lid. Keep on medium heat for 5 minutes (shredded cabbage) or 10 minutes (cabbage wedges). Drain and then toss with butter and black pepper. Or put in a baking dish, cover with cream sauce and grated cheese, and then brown under the grill. Red cabbage needs different treatment — braise with butter, vinegar, sugar, onions and sliced apples — the *apfelrotkohl* of Germany.

VARIETIES

SPRING cabbages

April

These cabbages are planted in the autumn to provide tender spring greens (collards) in early spring and mature heads later in the season. They are generally conical in shape and smaller than the summer and winter varieties.

DURHAM EARLY: Dark green and conical. Popular, especially as a source of spring greens. An early-maturing type producing medium-sized heads.

OFFENHAM: A broad-leaved, dark green variety to sow in early August for cutting as 'spring greens' or leaving to form heads later in the season.

APRIL: Highly recommended — very early, compact and reliable. The shape is conical and there are few outer leaves.

WHEELER'S IMPERIAL: An old variety which still has its fans. The dark green heads are small and pointed.

PIXIE: Small and tightly packed heads make this early variety an ideal choice for close planting in beds. A replacement for the old variety Dorado.

FLOWER OF SPRING: No worries about the weather with this one — it is very hardy. The heads are solid and cone-shaped. Sow in August for April heads.

SPRING HERO: Something different — a ball-headed spring cabbage. This F₁ hybrid is both early and hardy, producing round heads which weigh up to 1 kg (2 lb) each. Sow in August, not July.

SUMMER cabbages

Derby Day

These cabbages mature in summer or autumn. They are usually ball-headed, with some conical exceptions such as the ever-popular Greyhound and the F₁ hybrid Hispi. The normal pattern is to sow outdoors in April, transplant in May and cut in August or September. For June cabbages sow an early variety under cloches in early March and transplant in April.

GREYHOUND: The compact, pointed heads mature quickly, making Greyhound an excellent variety for early sowing.

HISPI: This variety is even earlier than the old favourite Greyhound. Same shape — dark green leaves and good flavour. Stands for a long time without splitting.

PRIMO (GOLDEN ACRE): The favourite ball-headed summer cabbage — compact and very firm.

DERBY DAY: So named because it will be ready for cutting by Derby Day from a February sowing.

CANDISA: A quick maturing variety which produces compact heads which can be grown as a baby vegetable. Flavour is rated very highly.

MINICOLE: An F₁ hybrid which has become popular. The small, oval heads are produced in early autumn and will stand for up to 3 months without splitting.

WINNIGSTADT: An old favourite — the large, pointed heads are ready for cutting in September or October.

	JAN	FEB	MAR	APR	MAY	JUN	JUL	AUG	SEP	OCT	NOV	DEC
Sowing Time							▓	▓				
Planting Time									▓	▓		
Cutting Time			▓	▓	▓					▓		

	JAN	FEB	MAR	APR	MAY	JUN	JUL	AUG	SEP	OCT	NOV	DEC
Sowing Time		▓	▓		▓							
Planting Time				▓	▓							
Cutting Time						▓		▓	▓	▓		

For key to symbols — see page 7

WINTER cabbages

Celtic

These cabbages mature in winter. They are generally ball-headed or drum-headed, green or white, all suitable for immediate cooking. The white varieties are also used for coleslaw and can be stored for months — see page 36. The normal pattern is to sow in May, transplant in July and cut from November onwards.

CELTIC: Once the crown prince of winter cabbages — an F_1 hybrid of a savoy and winter white cabbage. Ball-headed, rock-hard, blue-green and capable of standing for months without splitting.

CHRISTMAS DRUMHEAD: The early one — dwarf, blue-green and ready from late October.

JANUARY KING: Drum-headed savoy type of cabbage — you can tell it by its red-tinged leaves. A December-January variety.

NOELLE: A January King type variety noted for its flavour and keeping qualities.

TUNDRA: An excellent choice — ready in November but still suitable for cutting in March. Unrivalled for winter hardiness.

	JAN	FEB	MAR	APR	MAY	JUN	JUL	AUG	SEP	OCT	NOV	DEC
Sowing Time				▓	▓							
Planting Time						▓	▓					
Cutting Time		▓	▓								▓	▓

SAVOY cabbages

Vertus

These cabbages are easily recognisable by their crisp and puckered dark green leaves. They are grown as winter cabbages but there is a wider harvesting span — there are varieties which mature in September and others which come to maturity as late as March.

BEST OF ALL: A good choice if you want a large drum-headed type which will mature in September.

VERTUS: Flattened heads of tightly-packed greyish-green leaves. This variety is late maturing and stands well over winter without splitting.

SAVOY KING: This F_1 hybrid has been named by some as the best savoy of all. The foliage is light green — unusual for a savoy, and the heads are unsurpassed for size. Sow early for a September crop.

WINTESSA: Like Vertus this variety has a good reputation for standing well after the heads mature.

	JAN	FEB	MAR	APR	MAY	JUN	JUL	AUG	SEP	OCT	NOV	DEC
Sowing Time				▓	▓							
Planting Time							▓					
Cutting Time		▓	▓							▓	▓	▓

RED cabbages

Kalibos

These cabbages are extremely popular in many parts of Europe, but Britain is an exception. We buy it pickled in jars and we see them on display in the supermarket, but we do not generally plant them on the vegetable plot. Grow it like a summer cabbage, cutting in early autumn for cooking or late autumn for storing over winter.

RED DRUMHEAD: A popular variety, producing firm hearts which are dark red in colour. A compact plant suitable for the small plot.

KALIBOS: The one to choose if you want a pointed red cabbage. Sweeter than most — use it raw in salads. Colour fades when boiled.

RUBY PERFECTION: Round firm heads — its compact growth makes it a good choice where space is limited.

	JAN	FEB	MAR	APR	MAY	JUN	JUL	AUG	SEP	OCT	NOV	DEC
Sowing Time			▓	▓	▓							
Planting Time				▓	▓	▓						
Cutting Time									▓	▓	▓	

CHINESE cabbages

Jade Pagoda

These cabbages are the 'chinese leaves' sold by supermarkets. Tall and cylindrical, they look more like a cos lettuce than a cabbage. Cultivation is also uncabbage-like — sow at about 10 cm (4 in.) spacings in drills 30 cm (1 ft) apart, then thin to leave 30 cm (1 ft) between the plants. Bolting is the problem — do not transplant and remember to water regularly in dry weather. Loosely tie the heads with raffia in August.

YUKI: A variety for spring sowing — it is a quick-growing plant which produces short cylindrical heads.

KASUMI: A reliable barrel type with good bolt resistance, but the heads are not tightly packed.

WONG BOK: One recommendation is to broadcast seeds over a small area, and then cut the crisp leaves as they mature.

	JAN	FEB	MAR	APR	MAY	JUN	JUL	AUG	SEP	OCT	NOV	DEC
Sowing Time						▓	▓	▓				
Cutting Time									▓	▓	▓	

TROUBLES

See pages 28–31

Capsicum

On this page we deal with the sweet pepper group — the large, mild-flavoured varieties which are available in all the supermarkets and in the seed catalogues. Their small and fiery relatives, the chilli peppers, are less popular — see page 126 for details. Capsicum is a relative of the tomato and requires similar conditions — it is really a greenhouse plant but can be grown outdoors in southern counties if you are lucky. The plants grow about 1 m (3 ft) tall under glass or 60 cm (2 ft) outdoors, and they are ripe when plump and green. Leaving them will not improve the flavour.

IN A NUTSHELL

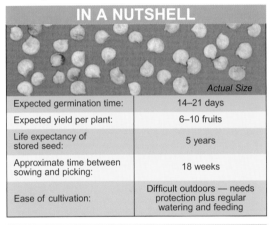

Actual Size

Expected germination time:	14–21 days
Expected yield per plant:	6–10 fruits
Life expectancy of stored seed:	5 years
Approximate time between sowing and picking:	18 weeks
Ease of cultivation:	Difficult outdoors — needs protection plus regular watering and feeding

SOIL FACTS

- For outdoor cultivation, well-drained fertile soil in a sunny, sheltered location is necessary. Add a general-purpose fertilizer before planting.
- In the greenhouse grow in pots filled with compost or plant in growing bags — 3 per bag.

SOWING & PLANTING

- Raise seedlings under glass at 15°–21°C (60°–70°F). Sow 2 seeds in a compost-filled fibre pot — remove weaker seedling. Harden off before planting outdoors.

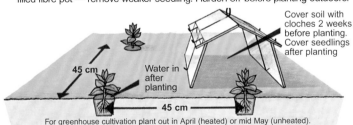

45 cm

Water in after planting

45 cm

Cover soil with cloches 2 weeks before planting. Cover seedlings after planting

For greenhouse cultivation plant out in April (heated) or mid May (unheated).

CALENDAR

	JAN	FEB	MAR	APR	MAY	JUN	JUL	AUG	SEP	OCT	NOV	DEC
Sowing & Planting (Outdoor crop)			▣			▣						
Sowing & Planting (Greenhouse crop)			▣▣	▼▼								
Picking Time												

For key to symbols — see page 7

LOOKING AFTER THE CROP

- It is necessary to repot in several stages until the plants are ready to be moved to their permanent site.
- Mist plants regularly to keep down red spider mite and encourage fruit set. Some form of support is necessary — attach stems to stakes or horizontal wires. Pinching out the growing tip is not recommended.
- Water regularly but do not keep the compost in bags or pots sodden. Add a potassium-rich feed with each watering once the fruits have begun to swell.

HARVESTING

- Pick the first fruits when they are green, swollen and glossy. Cut as required — a mature green pepper will turn red in about 3 weeks under glass.

IN THE KITCHEN

Sweet peppers have many uses in the kitchen. Narrow rings provide a crunchy ingredient for summer salads or they can be served as a hot vegetable after frying. Chunks can be grilled as part of a *kebab* or added to casseroles or stews — green and red peppers are essential ingredients for *ratatouille* (French vegetable stew). Or the whole fruit may be used — fill it with minced meat, diced chicken, etc. and then bake.

STORAGE: Keep in a sealed rigid container in the refrigerator — capsicums will stay fresh for up to 2 weeks.

COOKING: Wash and dry the peppers, then slice off the stalk and small 'lid'. Remove the seeds with a spoon and the inner pith with a small knife. Slice, cube or leave whole depending on the recipe. If it is to be cooked, blanch in boiling water for 5 minutes before stuffing or adding to a casserole.

VARIETIES

REDSKIN: A dwarf variety for growing in pots, bags or beds in a sheltered spot. The pointed fruit turn bright red when mature.

CORNO DI TORO ROSSO: Red Bulls Horn in English — a reference to the long, tapered shape of this red, fleshy pepper.

GYPSY: An F₁ hybrid which is regarded as an improvement on the older variety Canape. 'Early maturing' and 'very heavy crops' according to the catalogues.

CALIFORNIA WONDER: The block-shaped red and green fruits have a mild flavour — a reliable open-pollinated variety.

TROUBLES

RED SPIDER MITE

Sweet peppers are susceptible to red spider mite — keep careful watch for pale mottling and bronzing of the leaves. Tiny mites can be found on the underside. Spray thoroughly with pyrethrins.

APHID

Greenfly can be a nuisance on both the outdoor and greenhouse crop. The answer is to spray with insecticidal soap.

WHITEFLY

Brown patches appear at the bottom of the fruit — a frequent problem where growing bags are used. Incorrect watering is the usual cause.

Carrot

If you want to impress the family or win a prize at the local show, the secret of growing exceptionally long and straight carrots is to make a deep hole shaped like a giant ice-cream cone, using a crowbar. Fill the hole with potting compost and sow three seeds of St Valery at the top. Thin the seedlings to leave the strongest. Of course this is no way to grow carrots for the kitchen — these days we want shorter ones which are easier and quicker to grow. Short varieties, golf-ball round or finger long, are the first to be sown and mature quickly. Intermediate-rooted varieties are the best all-rounders — some are pulled for immediate use and the rest are left for winter storage.

IN A NUTSHELL

Mix seed with sand to prevent sowing too thickly. Better still, sow pelleted seeds 3 cm (1 in.) apart.

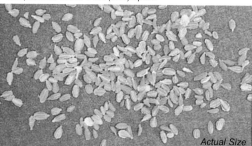

Actual Size

Expected germination time:	17 days
Approx. number per 30 gm (1oz):	20,000
Expected yield from a 3 m (10 ft) row:	4–5 kg (9–11 lb)
Life expectancy of stored seed:	4 years
Approximate time between sowing and lifting:	12 weeks (Early) 16 weeks (Maincrop)
Ease of cultivation:	Not difficult if soil is good and carrot fly keeps away

SOIL FACTS

- Carrots are hard to please. The soil must be deep, fertile and rather sandy if you want to produce fine long specimens. If your soil is rather heavy or stony, grow short-rooted varieties. Where land has been manured during the past year, don't grow carrots at all.

- Pick a sunny spot — dig in autumn in the usual way, but do not add manure nor compost. Prepare the seed bed 1–2 weeks before sowing — rake a general-purpose fertilizer into the surface.

- For a very early crop which will be ready in June, sow a short-rooted variety under cloches or in a cold frame in early March.

- For an early crop which will be ready in July, sow a short-rooted variety in a sheltered spot in late March or April.

- For maincrop carrots sow intermediate- or long-rooted varieties between mid April and early June for lifting in September and October.

- For a tender crop in November and December, sow a short-rooted variety in August and cover with cloches from October.

SEED SOWING

Sow very thinly

Cover with soil

15 cm

1 cm

LOOKING AFTER THE CROP

- Thin out the seedlings when they are large enough to handle. The plants should be about 5–8 cm (2–3 in.), apart. Take care when thinning or the root-ruining carrot fly will be attracted to your garden by the smell of the bruised foliage. Water if the soil is dry and thin in the evening. Firm the soil around the remaining plants and burn or bury the thinnings.

- Pull out or hand hoe any weeds between the seedlings, but once well-established the use of a hoe is not recommended. The dense foliage cover provided by the closely-packed plants should keep down annual weeds — others should be removed by hand.

- Water during periods of drought in order to keep the ground damp — a downpour on dry soil may cause root splitting

HARVESTING

- Pull up small carrots as required from June onwards. Ease out with a fork if the soil is hard.

- October is the time to lift maincrop carrots for storage. Use a fork to lift the roots and then remove the surface dirt. Damaged roots should be used in the kitchen or thrown away — only sound carrots should be stored. Cut off the leaves to about 1 cm (½ in.) above the crowns and place the roots between layers of sand in a stout box. Do not let the carrots touch — store in a dry shed and inspect occasionally so that any rotten roots can be disposed of before infecting their neighbours. The crop will keep until March.

CALENDAR

	JAN	FEB	MAR	APR	MAY	JUN	JUL	AUG	SEP	OCT	NOV	DEC
Sowing Time												
Lifting Time												

For key to symbols — see page 7

IN THE KITCHEN

Some of the vegetables in this book may be new to you, but everybody knows the carrot. Few vegetables can match its versatility — cut into sticks as snacks, shredded for salads, sliced for stews and casseroles or boiled whole as a hot vegetable. Even so, there are uses which are not commonplace — pickling, stir-frying, jam-making, wine-making and even as the basic ingredient of carrot cake — a delicious U.S. dessert. For eating raw, remember to lift carrots when they are still quite small — this is the time of maximum sweetness.

FREEZING: Lift carrots for freezing when they are finger-sized. Trim the ends and wash, then blanch for 5 minutes. Cool and rub off skins if necessary. Freeze in polythene bags.

STORAGE: Keep as cool as possible. Store them in a polythene bag in the refrigerator — carrots will stay fresh for up to 2 weeks.

COOKING: Top and tail the carrots with a knife and remove any damaged or diseased parts. Don't peel unless the carrots are old — small roots should merely be scrubbed with a brush. Cook young carrots whole — larger ones should be sliced diagonally. Boiling is the usual method of cooking, and the common fault is to drown them. Use just enough lightly salted water to cover the carrots and then boil for 10-20 minutes, depending on size and age. Drain and serve with a knob of butter and chopped parsley. Steaming takes longer (½-1 hour), but retains more of the flavour. Stir-frying is perhaps the tastiest method — lightly fry thin slices with chopped onions. Growing carrots at home means you can have supplies fresh from the garden or taken out of store for 9 months of the year, but there is the annoying problem of some of the roots being riddled with maggot holes. If not too badly damaged, use for grating as a salad ingredient or for boiling and then mashing as a hot vegetable.

VARIETIES

SHORT-ROOTED varieties

Golf ball round or finger long, these short-rooted carrots mature quickly. They are the first to be sown, and the early crop is either used immediately or frozen. The favourites are Amsterdam Forcing and Early Nantes, but there are now many others. Small, perhaps, but top of the league for flavour. Sow every 2–3 weeks between early spring and July to provide a steady supply of succulent roots.

AMSTERDAM FORCING: Reputed to be the earliest of all for growing in the open or under cloches — cylindrical with a blunt (stump) end. There is little core and it is an excellent carrot for freezing.

EARLY NANTES: The roots are longer and more tapered than Amsterdam Forcing, but it is similar in many ways — early, tender and good for freezing.

CARACAS: A short carrot which is broad at the top and pointed at the base. It received an RHS Award of Garden Merit. Caracas is recommended for close planting in containers and for growing in vegetable plots where space is short.

EARLY SCARLET HORN: A good carrot of the Nantes type which is recommended for sowing under cloches in early March.

PARIS MARKET: The best of the baby carrots — just about 3 cm (1 in.) across with a sweet flavour. Matures quickly — a good choice for containers.

PARMEX: Once the most popular round variety, but now shares the crown with Paris Market. Carrots are 3–5 cm (1–2 in.) smooth globes.

Flyaway

INTERMEDIATE-ROOTED varieties

These medium-sized carrots are the best all-rounders for the average garden. They are generally sown later than the short varieties, the young roots being pulled for immediate use and the remainder left to mature as maincrop carrots for winter storage.

CHANTENAY RED CORED: The popular choice, which seems to appear on everybody's list of recommended varieties of medium-sized carrots. Thick and stump-rooted, the flesh is deep orange and the skin very smooth. There are many good selections, such as Royal Chantenay.

BERLICUM BERJO: An improvement on the old variety Berlicum — the cylindrical roots are stump-ended and it has a good reputation for keeping well, high yields and attractive colour.

AUTUMN KING: The roots are unusually large for carrots in this group, but they are distinctly stump-rooted with none of the finely-pointed taper of the long-rooted varieties. Autumn King has several virtues — it is extremely hardy and will stay in the soil over winter, and carrot fly find it less attractive than some other varieties.

JAMES SCARLET INTERMEDIATE: An old favourite with a good reputation for all-round performance. It is half-long, broad and tapered.

FLYAWAY: If your plot has been plagued by carrot fly choose a variety which has a high degree of resistance — Flyaway is the most popular one. The smooth roots are stump-ended.

MOKUM: An F_1 hybrid which produces cylindrical roots up to 20 cm (8 in.) long. It matures very rapidly, and can be sown from March until July.

SUPERSNAX: An early variety which is bolt resistant. Its main claim to fame is that it is unmatched for sweetness — an excellent choice for salads.

LONG-ROOTED varieties

These are the long, tapered giants of the show bench. They are usually grown in specially prepared soil and are not really suitable for general garden use unless your ground is deep, rich and light.

NEW RED INTERMEDIATE: Despite its name, one of the longest of all carrots. It has good keeping qualities.

ST VALERY: This is the one which the exhibitors so often choose. The roots are long, uniform and finely tapered.

New Red Intermediate

CARROT and PARSNIP TROUBLES

Carrots are not considered easy to grow successfully — if your soil is heavy and sticky then long, straight roots are virtually an impossibility. The answer is to choose a short-rooted variety in such a situation, but this won't help you against carrot fly. In some areas pest attacks reach such proportions that the growing of this vegetable is hardly worthwhile. No variety is resistant, and no single control method can be relied upon to be completely successful. The answer is to use a combination of control measures — see the section below. Parsnips are less susceptible to pests — canker is the major disease and growing a resistant variety is the answer.

	Symptom	Likely Causes
Seedlings	— failed to appear	Sowing too deeply
	— toppled over	Damping off (see page 157)
Leaves	— mottled yellow, later red	9
	— reddish, later yellow	1
	— badly distorted	10
	— collapsed, leaf stalks black	7
	— tunnelled, blistered	Celery fly (see page 49)
	— covered with blackfly	Black bean aphid (see page 20)
Plants	— toppled over, brown affected area	Basal stem rot (see page 56)
Roots in the garden	— split	12
	— forked	8
	— hollowed out	13
	— green-topped	2
	— small	5
	— covered with purple mould	6
	— covered with white mould	7
	— scurfy black patches	4
	— black patches, decay inside	11
	— tunnelled	1 or Wireworm (no cure)
	— eaten	Cutworm (see page 157) or Millepede (see page 157) or Slugs & Snails (see page 157)
Roots in store	— covered with purple mould	6
	— covered with white mould	7
	— sunken black areas	3
	— soft, evil-smelling	Soft rot (see page 85)

TUNNELLED ROOTS

1 cm (⅓ in.) creamy maggots

1 | CARROT FLY

Tell-tale signs are reddish leaves which wilt in sunny weather. At a later stage the leaves turn yellow. This pest is the major disorder of carrots and also attacks parsnips. Seedlings are killed; mature roots are riddled and liable to rot. Attacks are worst in dry soils.

Treatment: None.

Prevention: Grow carrots well away from tall plants. Sow thinly and destroy all thinnings — no chemical treatment for the soil before sowing is available. Cover the seedlings with fine netting in spring. If carrot fly is known to be a problem in your area, lift early varieties no later than August and delay the sowing of Maincrop carrots until June — lift Maincrops as soon as they are large enough.

2 | GREEN TOP

The tops of carrot roots are sometimes found to be green when the crop is harvested. Unlike potatoes green carrots are not harmful but they are unsightly. Green top is caused by sunlight on the exposed crowns, and it is easily prevented by earthing-up to cover the tops of the roots during the growing season.

3 | BLACK ROT

A storage disease of carrots, which renders the root useless. The large black lesions are easily seen in store, but there are no symptoms on the growing crop.

Treatment: Burn diseased roots immediately.

Prevention: Store roots properly. Do not use the land for carrots next year.

BLACKENED CARROT ROOTS

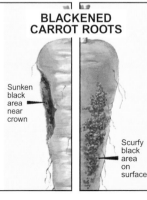

Sunken black area near crown

Scurfy black area on surface

4 | CLAYBURN

This carrot disorder is neither common nor serious, and is always associated with pockets of clay in a loamy soil. Harmful salts contained in the clay cause the damage, but the culinary value is not affected.

Treatment: None.

Prevention: Dig out clay from soil used for growing carrots if you are growing for exhibition.

5 | SMALL ROOTS

Aphids and virus will stunt growth and reduce yield, but even in the absence of pests and diseases many gardeners produce disappointingly small carrots. Poor soil conditions are usually to blame — you must dig the soil deeply and break up clays by adding well-rotted compost or manure at least one or two seasons before growing carrots. If the plants are slow growing, spray with a foliar feed at regular intervals or water with a liquid feed. Carrots respond well to this in-season feeding.

MOULDY ROOTS

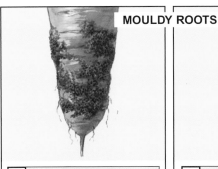

6 | VIOLET ROOT ROT

An occasional disease of carrots and parsnips. The only above-ground symptom is a slight yellowing of the foliage, but harvested roots show a felt-like mass of purplish threads covering the lower parts.

Treatment: None. Destroy all diseased roots.

Prevention: Never store any roots which are affected by violet root rot or the whole crop will be lost. Do not grow root crops or asparagus on land affected in the previous season.

7 | SCLEROTINIA ROT

The major disease of carrots in store. White woolly mould covers and soon destroys the roots. Occasionally it attacks the growing crop — lower leaf stalks and crown turn black.

Treatment: None. If attacks are seen in the garden, water healthy plants with Cheshunt Compound after removing diseased plants. Remove rotten roots immediately.

Prevention: Keep weeds under control. Store only sound roots in a dry, airy place. Do not grow carrots, parsnips or celery on land affected by sclerotinia rot in the past 2 seasons.

FORKED ROOTS

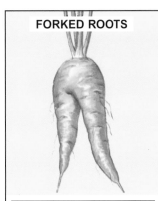

8 | FANGING

Fanging is usually caused by adding manure or compost to the soil shortly before seed sowing. Other causes are growing carrots in stony soil or in heavy ground which has not been properly dug.

Treatment: None.

Prevention: Use land which has been manured for a previous crop. Don't make the bed too firm.

DISCOLOURED LEAVES

9 | MOTLEY DWARF VIRUS

Central leaves show a distinct yellow mottling, outer leaves have a reddish tinge. This virus is spread by the carrot-willow aphid. Growth is greatly reduced and the yield is small if the plants are attacked at the seedling stage.

Treatment: None.

Prevention: Keep young carrots free from aphids by spraying with pyrethrins or insecticidal soap.

DISTORTED LEAVES

10 | CARROT-WILLOW APHID

Greenfly attacks can be serious in a warm, dry summer. The leaves are distorted, discoloured and stunted. Plants are weakened, but even more serious is the transmission of motley dwarf virus by this pest.

Treatment: Spray at the first sign of attack with pyrethrins or insecticidal soap.

Prevention: No practical method available.

BLACKENED PARSNIP ROOTS

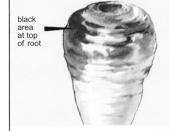

black area at top of root

11 | PARSNIP CANKER

A serious disease of parsnips, which can be caused by several factors — soil acidity, presence of fresh organic matter in the soil, root damage and irregular rainfall. The blackened areas on the roots crack and the parsnips rot.

Treatment: None.

Prevention: Lime soil. Don't sow too early. Do not grow a susceptible variety on the same site next year — choose a resistant variety such as Gladiator or Countess.

12 | SPLITTING

Much more serious than the fanging of carrots, because these roots will not store. The cause is heavy rain or copious watering after a prolonged dry spell.

Treatment: None. Use split roots immediately.

Prevention: Water regularly in times of drought. Apply a mulch of compost around the crop in dry weather.

SPLIT ROOTS

HOLLOWED-OUT ROOTS

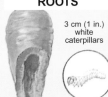

3 cm (1 in.) white caterpillars

13 | SWIFT MOTH

These soil-living caterpillars, which move backwards when disturbed, hollow out the roots of carrots and parsnips.

Treatment: None. Burn affected roots. Destroy caterpillars.

Prevention: Cultivate thoroughly before planting and hoe regularly. Eradicate nearby weeds.

Cauliflower

Cauliflower is more difficult to grow than cabbage. It needs rich and deep soil, and during the growing season there must not be any check on growth. Failure to provide these requirements will often result in the production of tiny 'button heads'. This means that proper soil preparation, careful planting and regular watering are essential, and so is the choice of suitable varieties. Types are available which will produce heads at almost any time of the year. There are compact summer varieties, large-headed autumn ones, and the winter cauliflowers which are really heading broccoli and not true cauliflowers.

IN A NUTSHELL

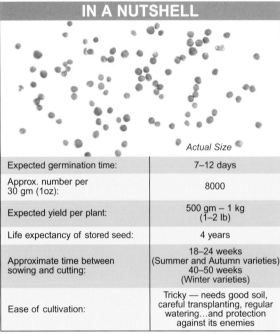

Actual Size

Expected germination time:	7–12 days
Approx. number per 30 gm (1oz):	8000
Expected yield per plant:	500 gm – 1 kg (1–2 lb)
Life expectancy of stored seed:	4 years
Approximate time between sowing and cutting:	18–24 weeks (Summer and Autumn varieties) 40–50 weeks (Winter varieties)
Ease of cultivation:	Tricky — needs good soil, careful transplanting, regular watering…and protection against its enemies

SOIL FACTS

- Cauliflower needs well-consolidated soil, so the basic requirement is to leave several months between digging and planting.
- Pick a reasonably sunny site for the place where the plants will grow to maturity. Avoid a frost pocket for winter varieties. Dig in autumn — work in plenty of well-rotted manure or compost. Lime, if necessary, in winter.
- In spring apply a fertilizer — consider using protective discs (see page 28) if cabbage root fly is known to be a problem. Do not fork over the surface before planting the seedlings — tread down gently, rake lightly and remove surface rubbish.

- **Summer varieties:** In late March or early April transplant seedlings which have been raised under glass from a January sowing to provide a June–July crop. Or sow outdoors in early April and transplant in June for cropping in August–September.
- **Autumn varieties:** Sow outdoors between mid April and mid May and transplant in late June.
- **Winter varieties:** Sow outdoors in May and transplant in late July.

SOWING & PLANTING

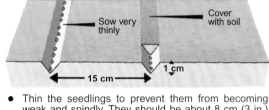

Sow very thinly

Cover with soil

1 cm

15 cm

- Thin the seedlings to prevent them from becoming weak and spindly. They should be about 8 cm (3 in.) apart in the rows.
- The seedlings are ready for transplanting when they have 5 or 6 leaves. Water the rows the day before moving and lift the seedlings carefully with as much soil as possible around the roots. Plant firmly, setting the seedlings at the same level as in the seed bed. Leave 60 cm (2 ft) between summer and autumn varieties, 75 cm (2½ ft) between winter varieties.

LOOKING AFTER THE CROP

- Hoe regularly and provide some means of protection for the young plants against birds.
- Cauliflowers must never be kept short of water, especially in the early stages, or very small heads will quickly form. Feed occasionally as this crop is a hungry one.
- With summer varieties bend a few leaves over the developing curd to protect it from the sun.
- Protect the winter crop from frost and snow by breaking a few leaves over the curd.

HARVESTING

- Begin cutting some of the cauliflowers while they are still fairly small rather than waiting for them all to mature and produce a glut. You have waited too long once the florets start to separate.
- Cut in the morning when the heads still have dew on them, but in frosty weather wait until midday. If you wish to keep the heads for up to 3 weeks before use, lift the plants, shake the earth off the roots and hang upside down in a cool shed. Mist the curds occasionally.

CALENDAR

	JAN	FEB	MAR	APR	MAY	JUN	JUL	AUG	SEP	OCT	NOV	DEC
Sowing Time												
Planting Time												
Cutting Time			WINTER vars.				SUMMER vars.			AUTUMN vars.		

For key to symbols — see page 7

IN THE KITCHEN

There are two popular ways of serving cauliflower. It is either boiled and served with or without a white sauce or it is covered with a cheese sauce after boiling and baked in the oven to provide the old stand-by — cauliflower cheese. It is a pity not to be more adventurous with this fine vegetable — serve the sprigs raw with mayonnaise as the French do or dip them in batter and fry until golden-brown. In this way you can have your cauliflower cold as *crudités* or hot as cauliflower fritters, and you can also find recipes for soups, soufflés and pickles.

FREEZING: Divide into sprigs — only use firm, tight heads. Blanch for 3 minutes in water to which lemon juice has been added. Cool and drain — pack carefully and freeze in polythene bags.

STORAGE: Keep wrapped in plastic cling film in the refrigerator — cauliflower will stay fresh for up to 1 week.

COOKING: Compact heads can be boiled whole but it is more usual to divide them up into sprigs. Leave the small basal leaves attached — cut a cross with a sharp knife at the bottom of each stalk. Most cauliflower is overcooked — it should be slightly crisp, not soggy. Correct cooking calls for adding a little lemon juice to 3 cm (1 in.) of water in a pan and then bringing it to the boil. Remove from the heat and add the sprigs carefully so that the stalks and not the florets are in the water. Replace the lid and boil for about 10 minutes. Drain thoroughly before serving with a white or parsley sauce. Alternatively dress with melted butter and black pepper.

VARIETIES

SUMMER varieties

These cauliflowers mature during the summer months from seed sown in a cold frame in September, in a greenhouse or on the windowsill in January or outdoors in April. They are compact plants — you can choose an early variety, such as Snowball, which will produce heads in June or July, or you can grow a later-maturing type like All the Year Round which will be ready for cutting in August from an outdoor sowing.

ALL THE YEAR ROUND: An old favourite. The curds are large and you can crop all summer and early autumn by sowing early under glass and then outdoors in April or May.

SNOWBALL: The usual choice if you want an early variety. The tight heads are not large — for well-rounded 1 kg (2 lb) cauliflowers of the Snowball type choose a F_1 hybrid Snow Crown.

DOK-ELGON: All the Year Round has had its day, according to many experts. This is the one to grow for kitchen or exhibition if you want a late summer cauliflower.

CANDID CHARM: Not easy to find but worth looking for. The time between sowing and harvest is unusually short, and the large heads are well protected by the leaf cover.

IGLOO: This is the one to choose if you want to produce baby caulis. Set close together at planting time in spring — leave some plants to mature as a midsummer crop.

MAYFLOWER: Reputed to be one of the earliest cauliflowers. Sow in January under glass and plant out in March for a June crop of large pure white heads.

Snowball

AUTUMN varieties

These cauliflowers mature during the autumn months and are of two quite different types. There are the large and vigorous varieties such as Autumn Giant and Flora Blanca, and there are the more compact Australian varieties such as Barrier Reef and Canberra.

AUTUMN GIANT: Once Autumn Giant and its various strains dominated this group — now the newer types have taken over. Still worth choosing if you want large heads in early winter — Veitch's Self Protecting is the usual selection but there are others.

CLAPTON: A good variety to choose if club root has been a problem. It is noted for its upright growth habit so plant closer than the standard recommendation on page 44. Sow in May for an October crop.

WALLABY: An Australian cauliflower which is grown for its unusually large heads. The usual cutting time is September-October. Good for freezing.

TREVI: Colour is the outstanding feature. The curd is pale green — something different for the crudité plate. Sow in May for a September crop. Good flavour.

Clapton

WINTER varieties

'Winter cauliflower' is the technically incorrect name for the group of varieties listed below. The standard types mature in spring, not winter, and they are really heading broccoli. Although less delicately-flavoured than true cauliflowers the popular varieties of winter cauliflower are easier to grow.

ENGLISH WINTER: This was once the basic hardy variety, producing large heads between March and June. The numerous strains include St George (April), Leamington (April) and Late June (June).

JEROME: An overwintering type which stands up really well to frost and snow as the curd is protected by the dense foliage. The heads are ready for cutting in February-March. Winner of an RHS Award of Garden Merit.

GALLEON: Another overwintering type — the large heads are harvested in April or May. As with Jerome the leaves provide excellent protection against frost and snow. The flavour has been highly praised.

AALSMEER: The outstanding characteristics claimed for this overwintering variety are the vigour of its growth and the deepness of the curds within the head.

VILNA: Once in many catalogues but now difficult to find. It is fully hardy and the rather loose heads are ready for cutting in May.

Aalsmeer

TROUBLES

See pages 28–31

Celeriac

You will find Monarch and perhaps one or two other varieties in the catalogues, but you will find this Continental vegetable in very few gardens and allotments. It is a knobbly, swollen stem-base measuring about 10–15 cm (4–6 in.) across which has a distinct celery flavour. It has advantages over its ever-popular rival — no earthing-up, no pest problems, good storage etc, but it is not for everyone. You have to raise your own seed-lings and provide rich, moisture-retentive soil, plus plenty of water in dry weather.

IN A NUTSHELL

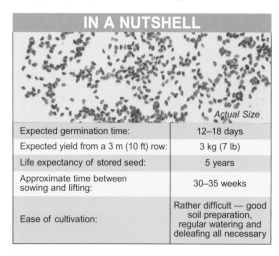

Actual Size

Expected germination time:	12–18 days
Expected yield from a 3 m (10 ft) row:	3 kg (7 lb)
Life expectancy of stored seed:	5 years
Approximate time between sowing and lifting:	30–35 weeks
Ease of cultivation:	Rather difficult — good soil preparation, regular watering and deleafing all necessary

SOIL FACTS

- Fertile, moisture-retentive soil is essential. Pick a reasonably sunny spot and dig in autumn. Incorporate as much manure or compost as you can.
- About a week before planting apply a general-purpose fertilizer.

SOWING & PLANTING

- Raise seedlings under glass in early spring. Plant 2 seeds in a compost-filled fibre pot — remove weaker seedling. Harden off before planting outdoors.

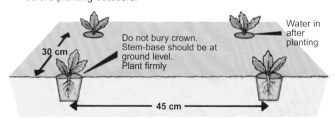

30 cm

Do not bury crown. Stem-base should be at ground level. Plant firmly

Water in after planting

45 cm

CALENDAR

	JAN	FEB	MAR	APR	MAY	JUN	JUL	AUG	SEP	OCT	NOV	DEC
Sowing Time			■ ■									
Planting Time					❦ ❦							
Lifting Time												

For key to symbols — see page 7

LOOKING AFTER THE CROP

- Hoe regularly and feed occasionally — a mulch in early summer will help to conserve moisture.
- Remove side shoots — from midsummer onwards remove the lower leaves so as to expose the crown.
- In late September draw soil around the swollen stem-bases.

HARVESTING

- Aim for maximum size — neither flavour nor texture deteriorate with age. Lifting begins in October — in most areas you can cover the roots with straw and then lift as required until early spring.
- If your soil is heavy and the site exposed, it is better to lift the crop in November. Twist off the tops, cut off the roots and store in boxes filled with damp sand. Keep in a cool shed.

IN THE KITCHEN

If you are fond of celery then you will certainly like celeriac. Grate it coarsely or cut it into strips to add zest to a winter salad — the French mix it with mustard mayonnaise to produce *céleri-rave à la rémoulade*. Use the leaves to garnish salads or add flavour to soups or serve the 'root' hot as a winter vegetable. A versatile vegetable indeed!

FREEZING: Cut into cubes and blanch for 3 minutes. Dry and open freeze — then store in polythene bags.

COOKING: Celeriac is a difficult vegetable to clean — scrub thoroughly. Slice thickly and peel like a turnip, then cube. Boil for ½ hour in lightly salted water to which lemon juice has been added. Drain and serve with melted butter or a white sauce.

VARIETIES

ASTERIX: An early, heavy cropping F_1 hybrid. Claimed to be more disease and bolt resistant than Monarch.

MONARCH: This is the variety you are most likely to find in the catalogues.

GIANT PRAGUE: The roots are larger and the flavour is stronger than the average celeriac. Harvest in October — stores well.

PRINZ: The early roots are large and it is both disease and bolt resistant.

BRILLIANT: Keeps its place in a few catalogues because of its flavour and excellent storage properties.

SNOW WHITE: A 'nutty' flavour, according to the suppliers. Large and white when cooked.

TROUBLES

SLUGS

These pests find young plants attractive — use slug pellets if necessary.

CARROT FLY

Not often a serious pest, but if carrot fly has plagued your garden in previous seasons then see control measures on page 42.

CELERY FLY

Attacks are much less frequent than on celery, and all that is usually necessary is to pick off the occasional blistered leaflet. If the problem is more serious, see control measures on page 49.

Celery

Growing celery in the traditional way involves a lot of effort. Trenches must be prepared and the stems must be earthed-up at intervals until only the green leafy tips are showing. The main purpose of earthing-up (blanching) is to lengthen and reduce the stringiness of the stalks.
There are self-blanching varieties and so both trenching and earthing-up are not necessary. These varieties are less crisp and less flavoursome, and cannot be left in the ground once the frosts arrive, but they do make celery growing easier. Easier, but not easy.

IN A NUTSHELL

Actual Size

Expected germination time:	12–18 days
Approx. number per 30 gm (1oz):	70,000
Expected yield from a 3 m (10 ft) row:	5 kg (11 lb)
Life expectancy of stored seed:	5 years
Approximate time between sowing and lifting (Trench varieties):	40 weeks
Approximate time between sowing and lifting (Self-blanching varieties):	25 weeks
Ease of cultivation:	Difficult — especially the Trench varieties

SOIL FACTS

- All varieties require a sunny site and well-prepared soil. For self-blanching types dig a bed in April — incorporate a generous dressing of manure or compost.
- For trench varieties prepare a 'celery trench' in April as shown — allow to settle until planting time.
- Just before planting rake a general-purpose fertilizer into the surface inch of the bed or trench.

- Buy celery seedlings for planting in late May–mid June. Or raise your own by sowing seed under heated glass between mid March and early April — make sure that the seedlings do not receive any check to growth and ensure that the plants are properly hardened off before planting.
- Self-blanching varieties will be ready for lifting between August and October. The trench varieties are grown for winter use from October onwards.

SOWING & PLANTING

- Sow seeds under glass and harden off the seedlings before planting outdoors. Seedlings are ready for transplanting when there are 5 or 6 leaves.

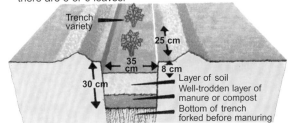

- Fill the trench with water after planting. Self-blanching varieties are planted 25 cm (10 in.) apart in a square block (not in rows) so that the crowded plants will shade each other.

LOOKING AFTER THE CROP

- Celery is a thirsty and hungry crop — water copiously in dry weather and liquid feed during the summer months.
- Blanch trench varieties in early August when they are about 30 cm (1 ft) high. Remove any side shoots, surround the stalks with newspaper or corrugated cardboard and tie loosely, after which the trench should be filled in with soil. In late August mound moist soil against the stems and in mid September complete earthing-up to give a steep-sided mound with only the foliage tops showing. Do not let soil fall into the celery hearts. In frosty weather cover the tops with straw.
- With self-blanching celery tuck straw between the plants forming the outside line of the bed.

HARVESTING

- Lift self-blanching varieties as required — finish harvesting before the frosts arrive. Remove the outer plant first, using a trowel so that neighbouring plants will not be damaged.
- Lift trenching varieties according to type — white types up to Christmas and the coloured ones in January. There is no need to wait for a sharp frost — there is little scientific evidence that frost improves quality. Start at one end of the earthed-up row — replace soil to protect remaining plants.

CALENDAR

	JAN	FEB	MAR	APR	MAY	JUN	JUL	AUG	SEP	OCT	NOV	DEC
Sowing Time			▪	▪								
Planting Time					🌱	🌱						
Lifting Time												

For key to symbols — see page 7

IN THE KITCHEN

For most people celery is a vegetable to be eaten raw rather than cooked. Sticks served whole for eating with cheese or chopped for inclusion in green salads, or diced and mixed with apple, shrimps and mayonnaise as an *hors d'oeuvre*. Celery sticks filled with cream cheese or paté are a party favourite. The proper preparation of celery for eating raw shows the versatility of this vegetable — cut off the roots and remove the outer stalks for cooking. Trim off the leaves and use for flavouring soup or as a garnish. Now separate the sticks and scrub thoroughly — do not leave them standing upright for hours in water before eating or they will lose their crispness. For celery curls, immerse thin strips in ice-cold water for 2 hours.

FREEZING: Cut scrubbed sticks into 3 cm (1 in.) lengths and blanch for 3 minutes — cool and drain. Pack into polythene bags and freeze. Frozen celery is no use in salads as the crispness is lost, but it is perfectly satisfactory for cooked dishes.

STORAGE: Keep in a polythene bag in the refrigerator — celery will stay fresh for up to 3 days.

COOKING: There are many ways of cooking celery, but boiling is not one of them. Outer stalks should be cut into sections or slices and used in stews, soups or stir-fried. The leaves can be chopped and added to meat dishes as a substitute for parsley or you can deep fry them as a crisp accompaniment for fish. The best way to cook celery hearts is to braise them in the Continental way. Simmer in boiling water for 10 minutes and then braise for about 45 minutes over low heat, the drained celery hearts being arranged over a bed of carrots and onions in meat or chicken stock in an ovenproof dish. Thicken the liquid and continue to braise for a few more minutes.

VARIETIES

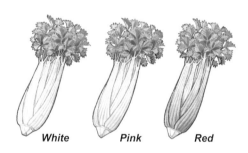

White   *Pink*   *Red*

TRENCH varieties

These varieties are not easy to grow, as trenching and subsequent earthing-up are time-consuming jobs. Choose from this group if you are an exhibitor or if you have rich, deep soil and like a challenge. Otherwise grow self-blanching celery. The white trench varieties have the best flavour but are the least hardy. Grow a pink or red celery if you want a New Year crop.

Giant White

GIANT WHITE: The traditional white-stalked celery — tall, crisp and full of flavour. Once in all the catalogues, now hard to find. Various strains are sold by a few suppliers — you may find Prize White, Prizetaker and Hopkins Fenlander in the catalogues.

GIANT PINK: Once popular, but now you will have to look for it in the specialist catalogues.

GIANT PASCAL: The sticks of this strong-growing celery are excellent for soups and salads, but it really comes into its own on the show bench.

GIANT RED: This old favourite has stood the test of time, and is the variety you are most likely to find in the catalogues. It is strong growing and very hardy, with sticks which are greenish-purple before turning purple after blanching.

DWARF WHITE: A short-growing variety which needs less careful blanching than Giant White. Has joined the hard-to-find group of Trench celeries.

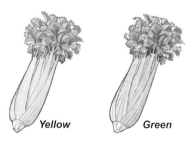

Yellow   *Green*

SELF-BLANCHING varieties

These varieties have taken some of the hard work out of celery growing. They require neither trenching nor earthing-up, and they mature before the end of summer. They are milder-flavoured and less stringy than trench varieties, and they are not winter hardy.

Utah Green

GOLDEN SELF-BLANCHING: The basic yellow variety — low-growing and early maturing with a fair but not outstanding flavour. Ready for cropping, like the other yellows, from August.

VICTORIA: Highly regarded by the experts. An RHS Award of Garden Merit winner and the star performer in various trials. An early variety which is quick-growing and full of flavour. It is able to flourish in soils not recommended for celery.

LORETTA: The variety you are most likely to find in the catalogues. Growth is vigorous and upright, and it is rated very highly for crispness and flavour.

UTAH GREEN: A strain of American Green, the basic green variety. Solid hearts, crisp and stringless. A good choice, but gardeners generally prefer to grow a yellow variety.

CELERY TROUBLES

Celery is not an easy crop to grow successfully, and its culture is made even more difficult by four serious problems which can plague this crop. Three of these problems are easily noticed whenever they occur — celery fly, celery leaf spot and slugs. The fourth problem is shortage of water, and here the effects are less obvious but no less devastating. Prolonged dryness at the roots will invariably lead to the production of plants with inedible hearts.

	Symptom	Likely Causes
Seedlings	— toppled over	**Damping off** (see page 157) or **Basal stem rot** (see page 56)
Leaves	— tunnelled, blistered	[1]
	— covered with brown spots	[2]
	— yellow, withered	**Boron deficiency** (see page 158)
	— yellow, not withered	**Cucumber mosaic virus** (see page 54)
Stalks	— tough, bitter	[1]
	— pithy, not crisp	**Dry soil**
	— split vertically	[5]
	— split horizontally	**Boron deficiency** (see page 158)
	— mouldy at base	**Sclerotinia rot** (see page 43)
	— eaten above ground level	[6]
	— eaten at ground level	**Cutworm** (see page 157)
Hearts	— missing, flower stalk only	[3]
	— rotten	[4]
Roots	— eaten	**Carrot fly** (see page 42)

BLISTERED LEAVES

1   CELERY FLY (Leaf Miner)

White 5 mm (¼ in.) maggots tunnel within the leaves causing blisters to develop. Attacks occur from May onwards, and the effects are most serious on young plants. Whole leaves may shrivel and die, and the stalks are stunted and bitter.

Treatment: Pinch out and destroy affected leaflets. Spraying with a contact insecticide has little effect.

Prevention: Never plant seedlings with blistered leaves.

3   BOLTING

Bolting is a serious problem, which unfortunately is common in dry seasons. At lifting time the heart is found to contain just one inedible flower stalk instead of the expected cluster of edible stalks. There are several possible causes, the most likely being dry soil conditions around the roots. Never let plants go thirsty during drought. Bolting can also be caused by planting out seedlings which have grown too large or have been checked by cold or dryness.

6   SLUGS & SNAILS

Slugs will feed on many types of vegetables in the garden when the conditions are damp, but celery seems to have a special attraction. The stalks may be attacked at any stage of growth — slugs are often most troublesome after earthing-up. Reduce the danger by scattering slug pellets thinly around the plants and by removing weeds and surface rubbish.

2   CELERY LEAF SPOT (Blight)

Brown spots appear first on the outer leaflets and then spread to all of the foliage. In a wet season the whole plant may be destroyed if the disease is not checked.

Treatment: Fungicides are no longer available for tackling this disease.

Prevention: Treated seed is sometimes recommended but is very hard to find. Never plant seedlings with spotted leaves.

SPOTTED LEAVES

ROTTEN HEARTS

4   CELERY HEART ROT

This disorder is noticed at lifting time. On cutting the plant open, the heart is found to be a slimy brown mass. The bacteria which cause the rot enter the stalks through wounds caused by slugs, frost or careless cultivation.

Treatment: None. Destroy diseased plants.

Prevention: Grow celery on well-drained land. Keep slugs under control and take care when earthing-up. Bacteria build up in the soil after an attack so do not grow celery on land affected in the previous season.

SPLIT STALKS

5   SPLITTING

Celery stalks are sometimes spoilt by vertical splitting. This disorder is usually caused by dry soil around the roots, but it can be due to an excess of nitrogen in the soil.

Treatment: None.

Prevention: Water thoroughly in dry weather, especially during the early stages of growth. Feed the plants regularly with a liquid fertilizer which contains more potash than nitrogen.

Chicory

Chicory leaves add colour and crispness to an autumn or winter salad, but it is not for everyone. Some people find it tart and refreshing — others find it bitter. There are two types. The forcing chicories produce plump, leafy heads ('chicons') from roots kept in the dark during the winter months — white is the usual colour. The other chicories are the non-forcing ones which are not blanched. The Italian group of red varieties known as *radicchio* have become popular in supermarkets — see page 122.

IN A NUTSHELL

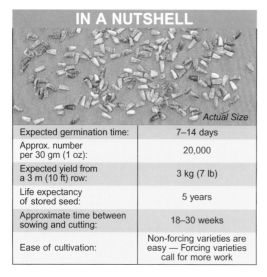

Actual Size

Expected germination time:	7–14 days
Approx. number per 30 gm (1 oz):	20,000
Expected yield from a 3 m (10 ft) row:	3 kg (7 lb)
Life expectancy of stored seed:	5 years
Approximate time between sowing and cutting:	18–30 weeks
Ease of cultivation:	Non-forcing varieties are easy — Forcing varieties call for more work

SOIL FACTS

- Chicory is not fussy about soil type, but it does need a sunny site.
- Dig the soil in autumn or winter and incorporate compost if the soil is short of humus. Prepare the seed bed a few days before sowing — rake a general-purpose fertilizer into the surface.

SEED SOWING

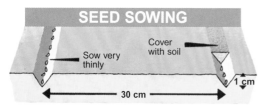

Sow very thinly

Cover with soil

30 cm

1 cm

LOOKING AFTER THE CROP

- Hoe to keep down weeds — water when the weather is dry. Thin the seedlings to 15 cm / 6 in. (forcing varieties) or 30 cm / 12 in. (non-forcing varieties) apart.
- Forcing varieties: Lift parsnip-like roots in November. Discard ones which are fanged or less than 3 cm (1 in.) across at the crown. Cut back leaves to 3 cm (1 in.) above the crown — cut back roots to a length of 15 cm (6 in.). Pack them horizontally in a box of sand in a cool shed — keep until required. Force a few at a time between November and March. Plant 5 in a pot — surround each root with moist compost, leaving the crown exposed. Cover the pot with an empty larger one — block up drainage holes to prevent the entry of light. Keep at 10°–16°C (50°–60°F) to promote chicon formation.

HARVESTING

- Forcing varieties: The chicons are ready when they are about 15 cm (6 in.) high — this will take 3–4 weeks from the start of forcing. Cut just above the level of the crown. Water the compost and replace the cover — smaller, secondary chicons will then be produced.
- Non-forcing varieties: Cut heads in late autumn — use immediately or store in a cool shed for later use. Provide some frost protection over plants if they are not to be cut until the winter.

IN THE KITCHEN

Crisp and raw — that's the best way to serve chicory. Shop-bought chicons are bitter because they have been exposed to daylight — home-grown ones kept in the dark until preparation time are much less bitter. A few tips — discard outer layer of leaves, do not leave chicory soaking in water and add tomatoes or a sweet dressing to the salad if you are not a chicory fan.

STORAGE: Keep in a black polythene bag in the refrigerator. Non-forcing chicory will stay fresh for up to 1 month, but chicons should not be stored for longer than necessary.

COOKING: Add chicons to boiling, salted water — allow to simmer for 10–15 minutes. Drain and serve with cheese sauce or braise for 20 minutes in butter, nutmeg, pepper and lemon juice.

VARIETIES

WITLOOF: Belgian chicory — the traditional forcing variety. Good and reliable, but needs forcing under a 20 cm (8 in.) layer of soil to keep chicons tightly folded.

ZOOM: An F_1 hybrid forcing variety which produces compact chicons. Easier to grow than Witloof.

SUGAR LOAF: The traditional non-forcing variety. Matures in October — looks rather like a cos lettuce. Pain de sucre in some catalogues.

PALLA ROSSA: Treat as a forcing or non-forcing chicory. Red-leaved, not hardy.

ROSSA DE VERONA: A red variety which has a round cluster of leaves. Cabbage-like in appearance.

CALENDAR

		JAN	FEB	MAR	APR	MAY	JUN	JUL	AUG	SEP	OCT	NOV	DEC
Sowing Time	FORCING vars.					▓	▓						
	NON-FORCING vars.					▓	▓	▓					
Cutting Time	FORCING vars.	▓	▓									▓	▓
	NON-FORCING vars.										▓	▓	

TROUBLES

SOIL PESTS

Cutworms and swift moth caterpillars can be troublesome, so consider using a nematode-based insecticide before sowing seed if soil pests have been a problem in the past. Slugs will ruin leaves in mild, damp weather — apply slug pellets if damage is seen.

Cucumber, Greenhouse

A straight, cylindrical and long cucumber may be a thing of beauty on the show bench, but it is a difficult thing to grow. Cucumbers under glass need warmth, watering and feeding, tying and stopping, protecting and so on. Ideally the humidity should be higher than that provided for tomatoes, but many people grow the two together quite successfully. The temptation these days is to grow cucumbers outdoors, but you must grow under glass if you want fruits in May or June.

IN A NUTSHELL

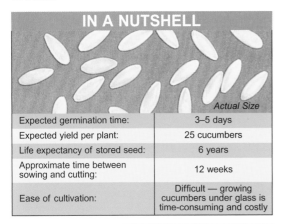

Actual Size

Expected germination time:	3–5 days
Expected yield per plant:	25 cucumbers
Life expectancy of stored seed:	6 years
Approximate time between sowing and cutting:	12 weeks
Ease of cultivation:	Difficult — growing cucumbers under glass is time-consuming and costly

SOIL FACTS

- Usually only a few plants are grown — do not plant in border soil. Use potting compost in large pots or buy growing bags.

SOWING & PLANTING

- Raise seedlings under glass — warmth 21°–26°C (70°–80°F) is essential. Place a single seed edgeways 1 cm (½ in.) deep in seed compost in a fibre pot. Sowing should take place in late February or early March for planting in a heated greenhouse or late April for an unheated greenhouse or frame. Keep compost moist — feed if necessary.

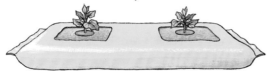

- Plant out in late March (heated greenhouse) or late May (unheated greenhouse) — 1 per pot, 2 per growing bag. Water in after planting.

LOOKING AFTER THE CROP

- The temperature after germination must be maintained at a minimum of 10°C (60°F) (Ordinary varieties) or 16°C (70°F) (All-Female varieties).
- Keep the compost thoroughly moist but never waterlogged — little and often is the rule. Keep the air as moist and well ventilated as the other plants in the house will allow. Spray the floor (not the plants) to maintain high humidity.
- Train the stem up a vertical wire or cane. Pinch out the growing point when this leader reaches the roof. The tip of each side shoot is pinched out at 2 leaves beyond a female flower. Female flowers have a miniature cucumber behind them — male flowers have just a thin stalk. Pinch out tips of flowerless side shoots when 60 cm (2 ft) long.
- Remove all male flowers from Ordinary varieties — fertilized fruit is bitter.
- Feed every 2 weeks with a tomato fertilizer once the first fruits have started to swell.

HARVESTING

- Cut (do not pull) when the fruit has reached a reasonable size and the sides are parallel. Cropping will cease if you allow cucumbers to mature and turn yellow on the plant.

VARIETIES

ORDINARY varieties

These are the cucumbers for the exhibitor. They are the traditional cucumbers of the summer salad — long, straight, smooth and dark green.

TELEGRAPH: An old variety, named when the telegraph was a new invention. Despite its age, Telegraph is still popular.

TELEPATHY: An F₁ hybrid which is an improvement on Telegraph — the fruits are longer and appear earlier. Unfortunately it is hard to find.

CONQUEROR: A good choice for a cold greenhouse or frame if you can find it. The fruits are long and smooth.

ALL-FEMALE varieties

These modern F₁ hybrids have several advantages. As they bear only female flowers the tiresome job of removing male flowers is unnecessary. They are also much more resistant to disease and rather more prolific. There are two drawbacks — the fruits tend to be shorter than the Ordinary varieties and a higher temperature is required. If your house is unheated, choose an Ordinary variety.

PEPINEX: The first of the females, formerly known as Femina. A good example of the group — high yields, lack of bitterness and no gummosis.

PASSANDRA: A mini-cue variety. Its key features are early cropping and high yields, with good resistance to both mildews and virus.

CUCINO: Another mini-cue variety which is promoted as a 'mini-munch' variety for the lunch box. It is a heavy cropper and can be grown outdoors in a sheltered sunny spot.

GALILEO: A high-yielding variety which matures early and is resistant to powdery mildew. Fruits are long and dark green.

EUPHYA: A variety noted for its high resistance to powdery mildew. Another one is Tyria.

FEMSPOT: Early with good disease resistance, but it needs a minimum temperature of 10°C (60°F).

TROUBLES

See pages 54–56

CALENDAR

	JAN	FEB	MAR	APR	MAY	JUN	JUL	AUG	SEP	OCT	NOV	DEC
Sowing Time												
Cutting Time												

For key to symbols — see page 7

Cucumber, Outdoor

Things have changed over the past 40 years. Outdoor types of cucumber were all short and dumpy with bumps and warts. They were grown on raised beds or ridges — hence the name 'ridge cucumbers'. Now there are smooth-skinned varieties which grow to 30 cm (1 ft) and are left to scramble on the ground or are supported by netting or poles. Modern outdoor varieties have one or more benefits — seed-free, good disease resistance and the flavour and juiciness associated with their greenhouse relatives. Standard ridge cucumbers, however, are still available and so are gherkins for pickling.

IN A NUTSHELL

Soak seeds overnight before sowing.

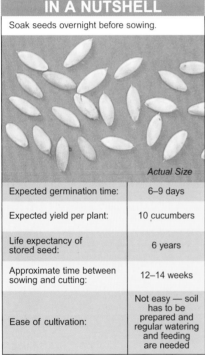

Actual Size

Expected germination time:	6–9 days
Expected yield per plant:	10 cucumbers
Life expectancy of stored seed:	6 years
Approximate time between sowing and cutting:	12–14 weeks
Ease of cultivation:	Not easy — soil has to be prepared and regular watering and feeding are needed

SOIL FACTS

- A sunny spot protected from strong winds is essential — outdoor cucumbers are neither hardy nor long-suffering.

- The soil must be well drained and rich in humus. Most households will need only a few plants, so prepare planting pockets as shown above about 2 weeks before seed sowing or planting.

- Sow outdoors in late May or early June. In the Midlands and northern areas cover the seedlings with cloches if you can for a few weeks. Cropping should start in early August.

- For an earlier crop sow seeds under glass in late April. Plant out the seedlings in early June when the danger of frost has passed.

SOWING & PLANTING

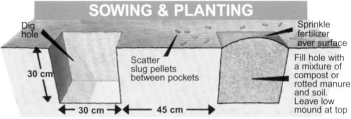

Dig hole · Scatter slug pellets between pockets · Sprinkle fertilizer over surface · Fill hole with a mixture of compost or rotted manure and soil. Leave low mound at top · 30 cm · 30 cm · 45 cm

- Sow 3 seeds 3 cm (1 in.) deep and 5 cm (2 in.) apart at the centre of each pocket. Cover with a large jar or cloche to hasten germination. When the first true leaves have appeared thin out to leave the strongest seedling.

- Alternatively you can raise the seedlings indoors, but this method is less satisfactory. Place a single seed edgeways 1 cm (½ in.) deep in seed compost in a 8 cm (3 in.) pot. Keep at 20°–25°C (68°–78°F) until germinated — gradually harden off seedlings before planting in pockets outdoors. Disturb the roots as little as possible when planting out — water in thoroughly.

LOOKING AFTER THE CROP

- Pinch out the growing tip when the plants have developed 6 or 7 leaves. Side shoots will then develop, and these can be left to trail over the ground or be trained up stout netting. Any shoots not bearing flowers should be pinched out at the 7th leaf.

- Keep the soil moist. Water *around* the plants, not over them. Mist lightly in dry weather.

- Place black polythene over the soil in summer before fruit formation. This will raise soil temperature, conserve moisture, keep down weeds and protect the fruit from rot.

- Once the first fruits have started to swell, feed with liquid tomato fertilizer.

- Fertilization is essential — never remove the male flowers.

HARVESTING

- Cut the fruits before they reach maximum size, as this will encourage further fruiting. Most types will be 15–20 cm (6–8 in.) long — harvest gherkins when they are 10 cm (4 in.) long.

- Use a sharp knife — don't tug the fruits from the stem. The harvesting period is quite short, as the plants are killed by the first frosts. Despite this, good soil, proper care and continuous picking will result in the production of many fruit until the end of September.

CALENDAR

	JAN	FEB	MAR	APR	MAY	JUN	JUL	AUG	SEP	OCT	NOV	DEC
Sowing Time (outdoors)					▌							
Sowing Time (indoors)				▼	🌱							
Cutting Time												

For key to symbols — see page 7

IN THE KITCHEN

Cucumber is generally served raw so that its crisp, refreshing flavour can be enjoyed to the full. Thin slices (there is no need to peel them) are a basic ingredient of the green and mixed salad, and every Greek restaurant offers the cucumber-enriched yoghurt dish known as *tzatziki*. Cucumber sandwiches evoke memories of pre-war summers — the expression 'cool as a cucumber' was in everyday use more than a century ago. Hollowed-out cucumber chunks filled with cream cheese can be served as a party snack and carrot juice, lemon juice and cucumber mixed in a blender makes an excellent summer drink.

FREEZING: Not a good idea for cucumbers as the crispness is lost.

STORAGE: Keep wrapped in plastic cling film in the refrigerator — cucumbers will stay fresh for up to 1 week.

COOKING: Cucumber is not just a salad vegetable — cut firm fruits into slices, dip in egg and breadcrumbs and fry like courgettes. Or you can treat them like miniature marrows and stuff them — boil hollowed-out halves for 5 minutes and then fill with chopped meat, onions, breadcrumbs, etc. Bake until brown.

PICKLING: Pickled gherkins are a delicious accompaniment to meat dishes, from the lordly roast to the humble hamburger. Wash the fruits and rub with a cloth to dry and remove any prickles. Place in a dish and cover with salt for 24 hours. Rinse thoroughly and pack into glass jars. Cover the gherkins with warm malt vinegar and add ½ teaspoonful of dill seed. Cover each jar with an air-tight lid — the pickles will be ready in about 2 months.

VARIETIES

SLICING varieties

Seed catalogues used to offer a wide range of standard (ridge) varieties for growing outdoors. These cucumbers were medium-sized, thick and covered with a rough, knobbly surface. King of the Ridge, Bedfordshire Prize etc were vigorous and heavy croppers but very few of these types are now available. Their place has been taken by the F₁ hybrids, which offered a better shape, improved hardiness, less disease and increased length. The final improvement came with the Japanese varieties which are represented in nearly all the catalogues by Burpless Tasty Green. These are the longest and smoothest of all the outdoor cucumbers. They require training up a pole or a stout netted frame.

BURPLESS TASTY GREEN: A popular variety. It is in nearly all the catalogues and according to most experts it is the one to choose. The fruits are not giants like most Japanese varieties — cut them when they are about 25 cm (10 in.) long, and enjoy the crisp, juicy flesh from which both bitterness and indigestibility have been removed.

LA DIVA: This variety bears 15 cm (6 in.) long smooth-skinned cucumbers which are seedless and free from bitterness.

MARKETMORE: Nearly all gardeners who grow cucumbers outdoors choose either Burpless Tasty Green or this one. Marketmore's distinctive feature is its resistance to mildews and its reliability.

EMERALD: A seedless variety which is claimed to be an improvement on Marketmore. Good disease resistance.

SWING: An all-female variety which produces heavy crops of 20 cm (8 in.) seedless fruits which have small spines.

CHINESE SLANGEN: An example of the long-fruiting Japanese types — cucumbers measuring 50 cm (20 in.) have been produced. Unfortunately it is hard to find many Japanese rivals to greenhouse cucumbers in the catalogues these days.

MASTERPIECE: The straight 20 cm (8 in.) fruits are slightly spiny. Provide some form of support.

BANGKOK: A seedless variety which crops heavily. The 15 cm (6 in.) cucumbers are slightly ribbed.

BEDFORDSHIRE PRIZE: This old favourite is still available, but is not easy to find. The pale green ridged fruit should be picked while still small to avoid bitterness.

PASKA: A variety which seems to tick all the boxes but is now listed by very few suppliers. It is an all-female type which produces seedless 20 cm (8 in.) long fruits which are bitter-free. It also shows good resistance to virus and the mildews.

La Diva

PICKLING varieties

A group of a few outdoor cucumber varieties which bear small and warty fruits which are designed for pickling.

GHERKIN: A fast-growing variety which produces an abundant crop of small fruits. 'Gherkin' is often used as a general name for all pickling varieties.

PARTNER: An F₁ hybrid with good disease resistance which is recommended as both a pickling and slicing variety.

VENLO PICKLING: The most popular and widely recommended variety, but it does have a few hard-to-find rivals such as Partner and Cornichon de Paris.

CORNICHON DE PARIS: An old French variety which produces 3 cm (1 in.) long fruits which are ideal for pickling.

Burpless Tasty Green

CUCURBIT TROUBLES
CUCUMBER • MARROW • COURGETTE • SQUASH • PUMPKIN

Greenhouse cucumbers are a delicate crop, and a host of bacterial and fungal infections can attack them. Most of these troubles arise through incorrect soil preparation or careless management of the growing plants, so study page 51 if you are a beginner. Outdoor cucumbers and marrows are much simpler to grow and are generally trouble-free, although slugs, grey mould, powdery mildew and cucumber mosaic virus can cause serious losses.

	Symptom	Likely Causes
Seedlings	— eaten	9 or **Woodlice** (see page 157) or **Flea beetle** (see page 30)
	— toppled over	**Damping off** (see page 157)
Stems	— gnawed at base	**Millepede** (see page 157)
	— brown shrivelled patches	18
	— mouldy patches	6 or 16 or 22
	— soft brown rot at base	19
Leaves	— holed	10 or **Woodlice** (see page 157)
	— wilted	1 or 4 or 5 or 18 or 19 or 20
	— yellow, moving up plant	20
	— mottled yellow and green	1
	— covered with silky webbing	21
	— covered with spots	16 or 17
	— covered with mould	6 or 22
	— infested with greenfly	**Aphid** (see page 157)
	— tiny moths, sticky surface	**Greenhouse whitefly** (see page 103)
	— papery patches	23
	— brown patches, yellow halo	18
Roots	— blackened, rotten	5
	— covered with galls	4
Fruit	— no flowers	**Lack of humidity**
	— no fruit	2
	— covered with mould	6 or 12
	— sunken spots	7 or 9
	— tip rotten, oozing gum	13
	— eaten	10 or 11
	— young fruits withered	14
	— bitter	15
	— poor yield	3
	— misshapen, warty	8

MOTTLED LEAVES

1 | CUCUMBER MOSAIC VIRUS

Cucumber mosaic virus is a common and extremely serious disease. Marrows are even more susceptible than cucumbers. The leaves are mottled with yellow and dark green patches. The leaf surface becomes puckered and distorted. Plants are severely stunted and may collapse in a bad attack.

Treatment: None. Destroy all infected plant material; wash hands and tools thoroughly before touching other plants.

Prevention: This disease is spread by greenfly, so spray immediately with pyrethrins if these pests are seen.

2 | NO FRUIT

A common complaint of marrows and courgettes is the failure of fruit to set. The usual cause is poor pollination and it is wise to give nature a helping hand. This calls for fertilizing 2 or 3 female flowers (tiny marrow behind petals) by dusting a male flower (thin stalk behind petals) into the mouth of each one. This job should be done in the morning, preferably on a dry day. Make sure the soil is kept moist.

3 | POOR YIELD

Greenhouse cucumbers sometimes lose their vigour shortly after the first fruits have been picked. To keep the plants cropping it is necessary to follow a few simple rules. Remove the first fruits when they are quite small. Encourage root activity by adding a mulch around the stems. Feed every 2 weeks with a tomato fertilizer. Cut the fruits when they have reached a reasonable size; if the fruits mature then flower production will cease.

4 | EELWORM

Both indoor and outdoor crops may be attacked by root knot eelworm. Gall-like growths develop on the roots. Leaves are discoloured.

Treatment: None. Lift and destroy badly wilted plants.

Prevention: Do not grow cucumbers in infested soil for at least 6 years.

ROOT TROUBLES

5 | ROOT ROT

Several fungal diseases can affect the root system; black root rot is the worst. The tap root turns black and the plant wilts.

Treatment: None. Lift and destroy collapsed plants.

Prevention: Grow plants in compost. Avoid cold growing conditions under glass and do not overwater.

FRUIT TROUBLES

6 | GREY MOULD (Botrytis)

A grey furry mould appears on rotting fruit. Botrytis can cause serious losses outdoors in a wet season and under glass if the humidity is high. Stems are frequently infected, the point of entry being a damaged or dead area.

Treatment: Remove and burn infected fruit and leaves. No fungicides are available for spraying against this disease.

Prevention: Avoid overwatering. Always remove decaying leaves, fruit etc to prevent infection spreading if grey mould is a regular problem.

7 | GUMMOSIS

A serious disease of greenhouse cucumbers grown under wet and cool conditions. Infected fruits develop sunken spots through which oozes an amber-like gum. A dark mould develops on the surface of this gum.

Treatment: Destroy all diseased fruit. Raise the temperature and reduce the humidity.

Prevention: Keep the greenhouse or frame warm and ensure adequate ventilation.

8 | CUCUMBER MOSAIC VIRUS

Misshapen small fruits bearing distinctive dark green warts. The surface is either white or yellow with patches or spots of green. The severity of the symptoms increases with the temperature of the greenhouse.

Treatment: None. Healthy plants should not be handled after infected fruit have been cut. However, there is no health risk if virus-affected cucumbers or marrows are eaten.

Prevention: See page 54.

9 | ANTHRACNOSE

Pale green sunken spots and patches appear near the blossom end of the fruits. The affected areas turn pink as mould develops over the surface, and eventually they become black and powdery. As the disease spreads the affected fruits turn yellow and die.

Treatment: None. Destroy infected fruit. No fungicides are available.

Prevention: Grow cucumbers in sterilised soil or compost. Make sure that the greenhouse is adequately ventilated.

10 | SLUGS & SNAILS

As marrows increase in size they become susceptible to attack by slugs and snails. The outer layers are scraped away and the soft flesh is then eaten.

Treatment: Scatter slug pellets around the plants at the first signs of attack.

Prevention: Keep area free from rubbish. Place polythene or a tile beneath each growing fruit.

11 | MICE

Mice occasionally gnaw the flesh of ripening pumpkins, marrows and squashes, but they are a more serious pest at a much earlier stage — they find the seeds irresistible.

Treatment: None.

Prevention: There is no point in taking precautionary measures unless you have had damage in the past. Cover the sown area with spiny twigs or put down a bait such as a mouse killer product.

12 | SCLEROTINIA ROT

Dark rotten areas on greenhouse cucumbers develop white cottony mould. In this mould large black cyst-like bodies are formed.

Treatment: None. Pick and destroy infected fruit immediately.

Prevention: Avoid splashing the fruit during watering and prevent them from coming into contact with soil.

13 | BLACK ROT

Rotting of the ends of cucumbers, and the oozing of gum in the shrivelled diseased area, indicate attack by the fungus which causes stem rot (page 56).

Treatment: None. Pick and destroy infected fruit immediately. Stop spraying the floor temporarily.

Prevention: Grow cucumbers in sterilised soil or compost.

14 | WITHERING OF YOUNG FRUIT

Cucumbers and marrows stop growing when they are only a few inches long and withering spreads back from the tip. Unfortunately there are many possible causes, such as draughts, heavy pruning and the use of fresh farmyard manure. The most likely reason is faulty root action due to poor drainage, overwatering or poor soil preparation. The secret is to maintain steady growth by careful watering. If withering of young fruit does take place, remove the damaged fruit and spray with a foliar feed. For the next week withhold water and ventilate the greenhouse, but keep the floor damp as usual.

15 | BITTERNESS

If the fruit is normal in appearance then one of the growing conditions is at fault. A sudden drop in temperature or soil moisture and a sudden increase in sunshine or pruning are all common causes. The second type of bitterness is associated with misshapen club-like fruits grown under glass. Here the cause is pollination; remember that male flowers must be removed. This tedious job can be avoided by growing an All-Female variety such as Pepinex. Bitter cucumbers are generally unusable, but you can try the old practice of cutting the fruit a couple of inches from the blossom end and rubbing the cut surfaces together.

CUCURBIT TROUBLES continued

SPOTS ON LEAVES

16 | ANTHRACNOSE (Leaf Spot)

Small pale spots rapidly enlarge and turn brown. Each spot has a yellowish margin. In a bad attack the spots fuse and the leaf withers. Large areas of pink mould develop on the stems and leaf stalks — these areas later turn black.

Treatment: Remove and burn spotted leaves. Lift and burn badly diseased plants.

Prevention: Grow cucumbers in sterilised soil or compost. Make sure the greenhouse is adequately ventilated.

17 | BLOTCH

Less common than anthracnose, and the spots are usually smaller and paler. Leaves decay rapidly in a severe attack. Unlike anthracnose, the disease does not affect the stems, and pink mould does not develop.

Treatment: Remove and burn spotted leaves. No fungicides are available. Lift and burn badly diseased plants.

Prevention: Grow cucumbers in sterilised soil or compost — choose an All-Female variety.

SHRIVELLED BLOTCHES

18 | STEM ROT

Leaf blotches have a distinct yellow halo. Affected area turns brown and shrivelled. Stems are attacked (gummy stem blight) and may be killed. Fruit are also affected (black rot, see page 55).

Treatment: Remove and burn all diseased plant material. Stop damping down temporarily.

Prevention: Grow cucumbers in sterilised soil or compost.

COLLAPSED STEMS

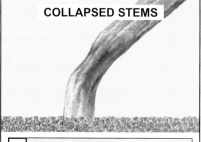

19 | BASAL STEM ROT

This bacterial disease has several common names, including soft rot, cucumber foot rot and canker. The brown slimy rot attacks the base of the stems of greenhouse crops. The leaves wilt and the plant may collapse.

Treatment: Fungicides once used to control this disease are no longer available. Apply a moist mulch around the stem to cover the diseased zone. Lift and destroy affected plants if attack is severe.

Prevention: Avoid overwatering and keep water away from the base of the stem.

YELLOWING LEAVES

20 | VERTICILLIUM WILT

Lower leaves turn yellow and the discoloration moves upwards. Finally all leaves become dry and wilted. Tell-tale signs are brown streaks inside the stem tissue (see page 103). Young plants in cold, wet conditions, are most susceptible.

Treatment: Keep air moist and warm. Shade the greenhouse and do not overwater.

Prevention: Grow cucumbers in sterilised soil or compost.

SILKY WEBBING

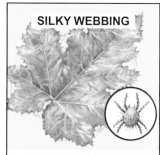

21 | RED SPIDER MITE

Fine silky webbing occurs over the leaves and stems. The foliage appears speckled and bleached, and the tiny mites can be found on the underside. Growth is retarded and the shoots are thin and weak. The mites are green in summer and red in winter.

Treatment: Spray with pyrethrins at the first sign of attack and every 7 days.

Prevention: Maintain a damp atmosphere in the greenhouse.

22 | POWDERY MILDEW

Leaves and stems are covered with white powdery patches. This disease occurs outdoors in a warm dry summer and under glass. It is encouraged by dry soil combined with a moist atmosphere.

Treatment: Fungicides are no longer available.

Prevention: Keep the soil moist at all times and ventilate adequately under glass.

WHITE POWDERY MOULD

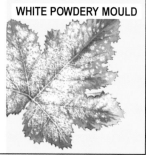

PAPERY PATCHES

23 | SUN SCALD

Pale brown, papery patches sometimes occur on the margins of the leaves and shrinkage of the dry areas takes place. Exposure to bright sunlight is the cause.

Treatment: None.

Prevention: Paint glass with Coolglass. Damp down adequately, but not at midday as water droplets can act as magnifying lenses.

Endive

Endive is a basic feature of salads on the Continent, but not so in Britain despite the fact that it has a more distinctive taste than lettuce. It is an odd fact of language that the French call this vegetable *chicorée frisée*, and have the word *endive* for our plump chicory (page 50)! By sowing at monthly intervals in spring and summer you can have heads for six months or more. The Curly-leaved varieties are grown for summer and autumn use — the Broad-leaved varieties with their lettuce-like leaves are hardier and will survive the winter if covered with cloches. Final note — blanching is necessary to remove the bitterness.

IN A NUTSHELL

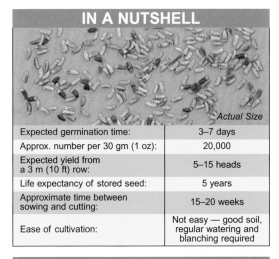

Actual Size

Expected germination time:	3–7 days
Approx. number per 30 gm (1 oz):	20,000
Expected yield from a 3 m (10 ft) row:	5–15 heads
Life expectancy of stored seed:	5 years
Approximate time between sowing and cutting:	15–20 weeks
Ease of cultivation:	Not easy — good soil, regular watering and blanching required

SOIL FACTS

- Good soil is needed — endive is not happy in sticky clay. Pick a sunny spot for summer- and autumn-sown crops — a semi-shady site is suitable for spring-sown endive.
- Dig in autumn — incorporate manure or compost if the soil is short of humus. About a week before planting apply a general-purpose fertilizer.

SEED SOWING

Sow seed thinly

Cover with fine soil. Firm down surface after sowing

30 cm

2 cm

- Sow Curly-leaved varieties in March–August or Broad-leaved varieties in July–September for late autumn and winter use.

CALENDAR

	JAN	FEB	MAR	APR	MAY	JUN	JUL	AUG	SEP	OCT	NOV	DEC
Sowing Time												
Cutting Time												

For key to symbols — see page 7

LOOKING AFTER THE CROP

- Thin the seedlings as soon as the first true leaves appear. Continue thinning at intervals until the plants are 20 cm / 8 in. (Curly-leaved varieties) or 30 cm (1 ft) apart (Broad-leaved varieties).
- Hoe regularly and feed occasionally with a liquid fertilizer. It is essential to water thoroughly in dry weather — plants will run to seed if you fail to do so.
- Begin the blanching operation about 12 weeks after sowing. Choose a few plants, as required, and make sure the leaves are dry. Loosely tie up the leaves with raffia and cover with a plastic flower pot. Block the drainage holes to exclude light. The heads will be ready in 3 weeks (summer) or 5 weeks (winter).

HARVESTING

- Sever the head with a sharp knife when the leaves have turned creamy white.

IN THE KITCHEN

Both Curly-leaved and Broad-leaved endive make an excellent addition to a mixed salad, providing both crispness and a touch of bitterness. Prepare by removing any damaged or green leaves and wash thoroughly. Dry the blanched leaves before serving — toss with a vinegar-based dressing.

FREEZING: Not suitable.

STORAGE: Endive should be used immediately. If this is not possible, store in a black polythene bag in the refrigerator for up to 3 days.

COOKING: Endive can be cooked like spinach but it is much better to prepare braised endive. Wash the head thoroughly, shake off excess water and dry. Fry a chopped onion in a little butter and add to a casserole. Place endive on top and add enough stock to prevent sticking. Replace lid and bake in a moderate oven for 20 minutes.

VARIETIES

BROAD-LEAVED varieties

EN CORNET DE BORDEAUX: A long-established French variety which will provide leaves all winter if cloches are used.

BATAVIAN GREEN: Once the most popular of the Broad-leaved endives, but it is no longer in the popular catalogues.

CURLY-LEAVED varieties

PANCALIERI: Broad heads of very frizzy foliage — dark green outer leaves surrounding near-white hearts.

NATACHA: A vigorous green variety with cream-coloured hearts. Good bolt resistance. Sow in March for June leaves.

TROUBLES

SLUGS

These pests can be a problem at blanching time. Use slug pellets if necessary.

APHID

Greenflies find endive less attractive than lettuce but are sometimes troublesome. Spray with insecticidal soap if they are numerous.

BOLTING

Endive sown in spring for early summer occasionally runs to seed in hot and dry weather. Avoid trouble by keeping the soil moist.

Kale (Borecole)

From the gardener's point of view kale is a winner. Its hardiness is unmatched by any other vegetable, and no other brassica can equal its tolerance of poor soil, pigeons, club root and cabbage root fly. Despite these virtues it is not a popular choice. The problem is in the kitchen — mature leaves of older varieties are bitter, especially when overcooked. The answer is to use a variety noted for its flavour — Red Russian is a good example. There are several types from which to make your choice, including decorative ones and a variety grown for both its leaves and broccoli-like spears. Cook it properly (see the next page) and you will lose your prejudice against this underrated vegetable.

IN A NUTSHELL

Actual Size

Expected germination time:	7–12 days
Approx. number per 30 gm (1oz):	8000
Expected yield per plant:	1 kg (2¼ lb)
Life expectancy of stored seed:	4 years
Approximate time between sowing and cutting:	30–35 weeks
Ease of cultivation:	Easy — but there is the chore of transplanting

SOIL FACTS

- Kale is much more accommodating than the other brassicas, such as cabbage, cauliflower and Brussels sprouts. It will grow in nearly all soils provided that the drainage is satisfactory.
- Pick a reasonably sunny spot for the site where the plants are to grow. As the seedlings are not transplanted until June or July, it is usual to use land which has recently been vacated by peas, early potatoes or other early summer crops. Do not dig — merely consolidate the ground, remove any weeds and rake in a little fertilizer. Lime if the land is acid. The ground should not be loose nor spongy at planting time — that is the only rule.

- If you want greens before Christmas, sow a variety of Curly-leaved kale in April. For later cropping sow Leaf & Spear or Plain-leaved kale in May. The correct time for transplanting is governed by the height of the seedlings rather than the date.
- Thin in stages to leave 45 cm (1½ ft) between the plants.
- Rape kale is sown in late June. For later management of the crop see Sowing & Planting above.

SOWING & PLANTING

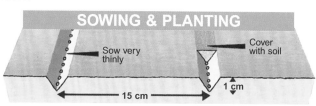

Sow very thinly — 15 cm — Cover with soil — 1 cm

- Thin the seedlings to prevent them from becoming weak and spindly. They should be about 8 cm (3 in.) apart in the rows.
- The seedlings are ready for transplanting when they are 10–15 cm (4–6 in.) high. Water the rows the day before moving the transplants to their permanent quarters. Plant firmly, setting the seedlings with their lowest leaves just above the soil surface. Leave 45 cm (1½ ft) between them — water after planting.
- Rape kale varieties are sown where they will grow to maturity. Make the seed drills 45 cm (1½ ft) apart and thin in stages to leave 45 cm (1½ ft) between the plants.

LOOKING AFTER THE CROP

- Hoe regularly and tread firmly around the stems to prevent them from rocking in the wind. Water the young plants in dry weather.
- Pick off yellowing leaves. As autumn approaches earth up around the stems to protect the roots from frost and wind rock. Stake tall varieties if growing on an exposed site.
- In winter the plants may look a sorry sight — don't worry, in early spring there will be a crop of fresh side shoots. Feed with a liquid fertilizer in March to encourage their development.

HARVESTING

- There is more skill involved in harvesting kale than growing it. With curly kale start at the crown of the plant from November onwards, removing a few young leaves each time you pick. Use a sharp knife or a sharp downward tug. Do not gather mature or yellowing leaves for kitchen use.
- This stripping of the crown will stimulate the development of succulent side shoots. These are gathered between February and May from all varieties, breaking them off or using a sharp knife for their removal. They should be 10–15 cm (4–6 in.) long and young — mature shoots are bitter when cooked.

CALENDAR

	JAN	FEB	MAR	APR	MAY	JUN	JUL	AUG	SEP	OCT	NOV	DEC
Sowing Time				■	■							
Planting Time						■	■					
Cutting Time	■	■	■								■	■

IN THE KITCHEN

The taste of mature kale leaves which have been overcooked can discourage you from ever trying this vegetable again. However, it need not be bitter — the secret is to gather only young greenstuff after it has been subjected to frost and then to cook it quickly in a small amount of water, as described below. Young shoots are even more acceptable, but kale can never be turned into a delicately-flavoured vegetable. But it is rich in iron and Vitamin C, and the strong flavour can be turned to advantage. Chop the leaves and toss in a vinegar dressing to give zest to a winter salad, or boil and serve with melted butter or white sauce.

FREEZING: Use tender shoots. Blanch for 1 minute — cool and drain thoroughly. Chop and then pack into polythene bags for freezing.

STORAGE: Keep in a polythene bag in the refrigerator — squeeze out as much air as possible before sealing. Kale will stay fresh for up to 3 days.

COOKING: Boiling is the usual method of preparation. Discard old, yellowed and damaged leaves and remove the midribs from the remainder with a sharp knife. Wash thoroughly and then add to 3 cm (1 in.) of boiling water — cover and keep on medium heat for about 8 minutes. The favourite accompaniments are poached eggs, bacon, pork and fatty meat. Kale can be used in other ways — in soups, stews or as a creamed vegetable. Perhaps the best way to serve the leaves and shoots is to boil or braise them with onions, parsley, spices and bacon or a ham bone — the dish known as Southern kale in the U.S.

VARIETIES

CURLY-LEAVED varieties

These 'Scotch' kales appear in a wide range of catalogues and are much more popular than the other types. Each leaf, has an extremely frilled and curled edge, giving a parsley-like appearance.

DWARF GREEN CURLED: The usual choice for the small plot — the 45–60 cm (1½-2 ft) plants do not require staking and the leaf flavour is as good as any.

SCARLET: The greenish-violet leaves change their colour to a reddish-violet shade once the first frosts arrive. Tall plants, reaching more than 1 m (3 ft). A medium to late variety — can be used in salads.

RED RUSSIAN: Green leaves with purple veins — the 'oak-leaf' shape is distinctive. Noted for its tenderness.

NERO DI TOSCANA: An easy-to grow variety with deeply curled strap-like leaves. Has a peppery flavour.

REDBOR: The most popular Curly-leaved variety which you will find in many catalogues. Its attractive purplish-red leaves make it a candidate for the flower border. Use the young leaves to add colour to salads.

DARKIBOR: An F_1 hybrid bearing tightly-curled, dark green leaves. Good cold resistance.

PLAIN-LEAVED varieties

These tall kales tend to be coarser than the Curly-leaved varieties, but they are extremely hardy and prolific, and they are easier to keep pest-free. Eat the young shoots in early spring — not the autumn leaves.

THOUSAND-HEADED KALE: The few catalogues which list this variety sing the praises of the side shoots for picking and cooking from February onwards. You would do better with Pentland Brig.

COTTAGERS: The plants are quite tall — 1 m (3 ft) high with leaves which turn bright purple in winter. It is hard to find, as with other Plain-leaved varieties.

Dwarf Green Curled

RAPE KALE varieties

These kales provide young tender shoots between March and May, and are not grown like other varieties. They are sown where they will mature, as they detest transplanting.

HUNGRY GAP: A late cropper, like all Rape kales. Robust and reliable, producing shoots which are suitable for freezing. Hard to find.

ASPARAGUS KALE: The Rape kale variety to grow where space is limited. You will find this variety in the textbooks, but you will have to search to find a supplier.

LEAF & SPEAR variety

There is just one variety — a cross between a Curly-leaved kale and a Plain-leaved one. Its arrival was heralded as a new era for the lowly kale, but it never became popular and is now in only a few specialist catalogues.

PENTLAND BRIG: Plants grow about 60 cm (2 ft) tall, and their kitchen use differs from other kales. Pick young leaves from the crown beginning in November — they are fringed but less so than a Curly-leaved kale. In early spring harvest the leafy side shoots and later gather the immature flower-heads ('spears') which should be cooked like broccoli. A versatile vegetable, indeed!

TROUBLES

Brassica troubles are described on pages 28–31. Kale is remarkably resistant to most major problems such as cabbage root fly and club root, but mealy aphid, whitefly and cabbage caterpillar can be a nuisance. Spray with an insecticide at the first sign of attack.

Redbor

Kohl rabi

This vegetable is more popular on the Continent than in Britain. The edible swollen part of kohl rabi is not really a root at all — it is the stem base ('globe') and so is able to succeed in shallow soils where turnips and swedes would fail. It reaches about 30 cm (1 ft) high and matures quickly, progressing from sowing to harvesting in a couple of months. Textbooks try to describe the taste of the globe but the phrases used are not much use — 'a cross between a turnip and a cabbage' for the boiled vegetable, and 'nutty with a slight taste of celery' for the grated raw globe. It can be a tasty vegetable if harvested before the globes are mature.

IN A NUTSHELL

Actual Size

Expected germination time:	10 days
Approx. number per 30 gm (1 oz):	8000
Expected yield from a 3 m (10 ft) row:	20 globes
Life expectancy of stored seed:	4 years
Approximate time between sowing and lifting:	8–12 weeks
Ease of cultivation:	Easy

SOIL FACTS

- The ideal situation is a sunny spot on light land. Dig in autumn — work in compost if the soil is poor. Lime, if necessary, in winter.
- In spring apply a fertilizer — consider using protective discs (page 28) if cabbage root fly is known to be a problem. Prepare the bed about a week later, treading down and raking the surface.

SEED SOWING

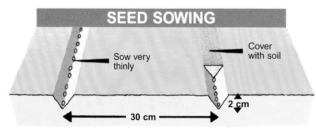

Sow very thinly

Cover with soil

2 cm

30 cm

- Sow green varieties between March and June. For a late autumn or winter crop sow a purple variety in July or August.

CALENDAR

	JAN	FEB	MAR	APR	MAY	JUN	JUL	AUG	SEP	OCT	NOV	DEC
Sowing Time												
Lifting Time												

For key to symbols — see page 7

LOOKING AFTER THE CROP

- Thin the seedlings as soon as the first true leaves appear. Continue thinning at intervals until the plants are 15 cm (6 in.) apart. Provide protection against birds.
- Hoe regularly and feed occasionally if growth is slow. Soak the ground during periods of drought.

HARVESTING

- Pull the swollen stem bases ('globes') when they are midway in size between a golf ball and a tennis ball. Do not lift and store — they deteriorate once out of the ground. Leave the plants growing in the garden and pull as required until December.

IN THE KITCHEN

Kohl rabi is a versatile vegetable which few British cooks have discovered. The young globes can be grated to provide a nutty-flavoured ingredient for summer and winter salads, but it is more usual to cook before serving. Young leaves are boiled like spinach, the globes are boiled, braised or used as an ingredient for soups or stews.

FREEZING: Trim, scrub, cut in strips and blanch for 2 minutes before freezing.

STORAGE: Keep in a polythene bag in the refrigerator — kohl rabi will stay fresh for up to 2 weeks.

COOKING: The young globes should be trimmed and scrubbed — do not peel. Boil whole or sliced for 20–30 minutes — drain and peel, then serve with melted butter or white sauce. Alternatively, the boiled globes can be mashed with butter or sour cream.

VARIETIES

KOLIBRI: This is the variety you are most likely to find in the catalogues. An F₁ hybrid with purple skin which covers the pure white flesh. It has good resistance to woodiness.

LANRO: Pale-skinned, white-fleshed — an F₁ hybrid which is noted for the quality of its texture and flavour.

SUPERSCMELZ: A pale green kohl rabi which produces 5 kg (11 lb) globes. These giants are slow to develop woodiness.

ROWEL: An F₁ hybrid which claims to be definitely superior to the old Viennas. The flesh is sweeter and it does not become woody if allowed to grow larger than a tennis ball.

TROUBLES

Brassica troubles are described on pages 28–31. Many of these problems are occasionally seen, but they are not likely to be serious. The crop matures quickly and so it is not affected by diseases which develop slowly nor pests which are at their peak when kohl rabi is absent from the garden. Birds and aphids can be troublesome.

Leek

Leeks are one of the darlings of the horticultural show bench — monsters weighing a couple of kilos or more raised with loving care and the use of magical potions. The grow-your-own gardener has a different aim. Here the goal is to produce plants for the kitchen — smaller but tastier than the show bench ones. It is interesting that they are also darlings at the other end of the scale from the giants — they are popular members of the baby vegetable group (see page 109). Leeks are the easiest member of the onion family to grow and are generally trouble-free, but they do need transplanting, earthing-up, and occupy the ground for a long time.

IN A NUTSHELL

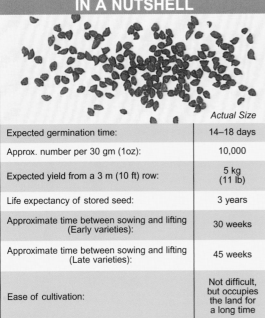

Actual Size

Expected germination time:	14–18 days
Approx. number per 30 gm (1oz):	10,000
Expected yield from a 3 m (10 ft) row:	5 kg (11 lb)
Life expectancy of stored seed:	3 years
Approximate time between sowing and lifting (Early varieties):	30 weeks
Approximate time between sowing and lifting (Late varieties):	45 weeks
Ease of cultivation:	Not difficult, but occupies the land for a long time

SOIL FACTS

- Leeks are less demanding than onions and will grow in any reasonable soil provided it is neither highly compacted nor badly drained.
- The crop will be disappointing if the land is starved of nutrients and humus. Thorough digging in winter is required — add compost or well-rotted manure if this was not done for the previous crop.
- Choose a sunny spot for where the plants will grow. Leave the soil rough after winter digging and level the surface in the spring by raking and treading. Incorporate a general fertilizer into the surface about 1 week before planting.

- For exhibiting in the autumn sow seed under glass in late January or February and plant outdoors during April.
- For ordinary kitchen use sow seed outdoors in spring when the soil is workable and warm enough to permit germination — for all but warm and sheltered areas this means mid March or later. Transplant the seedlings in June.
- For an April crop you can sow seed of a Late variety in June and transplant in July.

SOWING & PLANTING

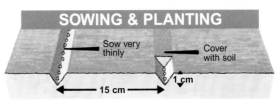

Sow very thinly — 15 cm — Cover with soil — 1 cm

- Thin the seedlings so that they are 5 cm (2 in.) apart in the rows.
- The young leeks are ready for transplanting when they are about 20 cm (8 in.) high and as thick as a pencil. Water the bed the day before lifting if the weather is dry. Trim off the root ends and leaf tips, then set out in rows 30 cm (1 ft) apart, leaving 15 cm (6 in.) between the transplants.
- Make a 15 cm (6 in.) deep hole with a dibber, drop in the leek transplant and then gently fill the hole with water to settle the roots. Do not fill the hole with soil.

LOOKING AFTER THE CROP

- Hoe carefully to keep down weeds and make sure that the plants are not short of water during dry weather. Do not deliberately fill the holes with soil.
- Blanch to increase the length of white stem. Gently draw *dry* soil around the stems when the plants are well developed. Do this in stages, increasing the height a little at a time. On no account allow soil to fall between the leaves or grittiness will be the unpleasant result at dinnertime. Finish earthing-up in late October.
- Feeding will increase the thickness of the stems. Late feeding, however, should be avoided for plants which will overwinter in the garden — late August is the time to stop.

HARVESTING

- For culinary purposes do not aim to produce giants — there is a reduction in flavour as size increases.
- Begin lifting when the leeks are still quite small — in this way you will ensure a long harvesting period. Never try to wrench the plant out of the soil — lift it gently with a fork.
- Leeks can remain in the ground during the winter months until they are required for use.

CALENDAR

	JAN	FEB	MAR	APR	MAY	JUN	JUL	AUG	SEP	OCT	NOV	DEC
Sowing Time												
Planting Time												
Sowing Time (under glass)	🪴	🪴		🌱								
Lifting Time												

IN THE KITCHEN

Leeks are a favourite ingredient for the traditional soups of many countries — England's leek & potato soup, Scotland's cock-a-leekie (leek and chicken broth) and cold vichyssoise, a French import from the U.S. In the southern counties of England the use of leeks is often restricted to soups and stews — many families have rejected this vegetable after suffering sliminess and grittiness, the twin distasteful features of badly prepared boiled leeks. Both can easily be avoided, and there are many other ways of using them apart from boiling. There is no need to cook at all — slice young leeks and mix with shredded cabbage and a dressing for a winter salad.

FREEZING: Remove green tops. Wash stems thoroughly, cut into small chunks and blanch for 3 minutes. Cool, drain and dry the pieces on a paper towel, then pack into polythene bags before freezing.

STORAGE: Keep in a polythene bag in the refrigerator — leeks will stay fresh for up to 5 days.

COOKING: Grittiness is the first problem to avoid. The best way to remove dirt is to cut off the top of the leaves and some of the coarse outer foliage — do not remove all the green tissue. Slit part way down the stem with a knife and stand in a bowl of water, green end down, for about an hour. Finally wash under a cold tap, prising leaves apart if necessary. Sliminess is the next problem — avoid it by boiling in a small amount of water for no more than 10 minutes and then draining thoroughly. Now return the leeks to the pan and heat gently for about 5 minutes to drive off the excess water. Serve with a white sauce or melted butter. There are better ways of using leeks — braise with carrots and celery in beef stock or cut into rings and stir-fry in a little butter. Leek dumplings and leek flan are age-old methods of using this versatile vegetable.

VARIETIES

EARLY varieties

These varieties are popular with exhibitors as they can be sown under glass at the beginning of the year and they will reach their maximum size in time for the autumn show. Alternatively they can be sown outdoors to provide long-stemmed leeks for the kitchen before the end of the year.

LYON 2-PRIZETAKER: A great favourite for the show bench over the years — long, thick stems with dark green leaves to catch the judge's eye. Good for the kitchen — mild flavoured.

CARLTON: Highly rated for its long straight stems. High yields can be expected from September onwards. Good resistance to bulbing at the base.

JOLANT: An RHS Award of Garden Merit winner. This mild-flavoured variety is grown to provide baby leeks or left to produce mature shanks in late summer and autumn. Growth is vigorous and the flavour is good.

ZERMATT: A long-shanked variety which is lifted between August and November. It can be grown to maturity in the usual way or it can be harvested earlier to provide baby leeks.

MID-SEASON varieties

These varieties mature during the winter months and one of them has long been the number one choice for the home gardener. They are of course all winter hardy, but vary considerably in length of stem.

MUSSELBURGH: This Scottish variety remains Britain's favourite home-grown leek — it is very hardy, reliable and fine flavoured. The stems are thick but not tall.

AUTUMN MAMMOTH: Similar to Mussel-burgh in general appearance — some-times listed as Snowstar. Popular as an exhibition variety.

NEPTUNE: This variety is rated highly for its outstanding flavour. The dark green leaves have good resistance against rust. The harvest period is between late November and January. Stands up to winter frosts.

OARSMAN: A dark-leaved variety which shows good resistance to bolting and rust. An RHS Award of Garden Merit reflects its reliability and high quality.

LATE varieties

These varieties are perhaps the most useful of all for kitchen use, maturing between late January and early April when other vegetables are scarce.

GIANT WINTER: Giant Winter and a number of its strains have been popular Late leeks for many years. The thick stems can be left in the ground throughout winter and early spring.

APOLLO: A vigorous variety which carries the recommendation that close planting is acceptable. Cropping can start in late December and continues through the winter months.

WINTER CROP: This variety has the reputation for being the hardiest of all — it is the one to try on an exposed northern plot.

BELOW ZERO: An F_1 hybrid which the suppliers claim will stand up to the harshest of winters without bolting or bulbing at the base.

Prizetaker

Musselburgh

TROUBLES

Generally trouble-free — see pages 74–75

Lettuce

In the average garden the cultivation of lettuce is a simple matter. A row or two are sown in spring and again in early summer — the seedlings are thinned when they are overcrowded and they are cut when the heads are mature. Unfortunately pests and diseases take their toll and the survivors mature at the same time. A better plan is to buy a packet of mixed varieties which mature at different times, or sow in short rows at fortnightly intervals. Grow from seed rather than transplants to avoid bolting, and ensure adequate humus and moisture in the soil to make sure the plants grow quickly.

TYPES

COS   **CABBAGE: BUTTERHEAD**   **CABBAGE: CRISPHEAD**   **LOOSE-LEAF**

IN A NUTSHELL

Germination is erratic in hot weather.

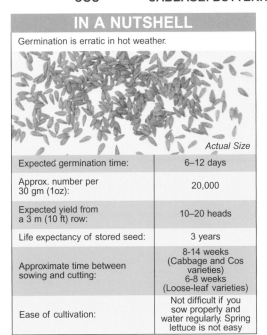

Actual Size

Expected germination time:	6–12 days
Approx. number per 30 gm (1oz):	20,000
Expected yield from a 3 m (10 ft) row:	10–20 heads
Life expectancy of stored seed:	3 years
Approximate time between sowing and cutting:	8-14 weeks (Cabbage and Cos varieties) 6-8 weeks (Loose-leaf varieties)
Ease of cultivation:	Not difficult if you sow properly and water regularly. Spring lettuce is not easy

SOIL FACTS

- Three basic needs have to be satisfied to obtain good lettuces. The soil must contain adequate organic matter, it must not be acid and it must be kept moist throughout the life of the crop.
- For summer lettuce choose a sunny or lightly shaded site. Dig the soil and incorporate compost in autumn or early winter. Shortly before sowing time rake the surface to produce a fine tilth and apply a general fertilizer. Pesticides which were once used for soil pests are no longer available.
- Spring lettuce can be grown in a sunny spot outdoors in mild areas without glass protection, but it will not succeed in poorly drained or exposed sites.

SEED SOWING

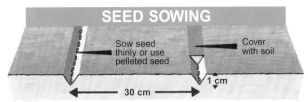

Sow seed thinly or use pelleted seed

Cover with soil

30 cm

1 cm

- To grow lettuce for transplanting, sow 2 seeds in a small fibre pot. Remove weaker seedling after germination — harden off before transplanting.

LOOKING AFTER THE CROP

- Thin the seedlings as soon as the first true leaves appear — avoid overcrowding at all costs. Water the day before thinning. Continue thinning at intervals until the plants are 30 cm (1 ft) apart — 20 cm (8 in.) for dwarf varieties.
- You can try transplanting thinnings in spring or you can plant shop-bought seedlings — do not bury the lower leaves. Lettuces hate to be moved — sow seed whenever you can where the crop is to grow and mature.
- Put down slug pellets and protect seedlings from birds. Hoe regularly. Keep unprotected plants watered, but the soil under glass should be kept on the dry side. Ventilate glass-grown lettuce whenever possible.
- Always water in the morning or midday — watering in the evening will increase the chance of disease.
- Greenfly can render the crop unusable — spray with an insecticide which is recommended for vegetables.

HARVESTING

- Lettuce is ready for cutting as soon as a firm heart has formed. Test by pressing the top of the plant gently with the back of the hand — squeezing the heart will damage the tissues.
- If left after this stage the heart will begin to grow upwards, a sign that it is getting ready to bolt. You must then cut immediately for kitchen use or throw it away.
- It is traditional to cut in the morning when the heads have dew on them. Pull up the whole plant and cut off the root and lower leaves. Put the unwanted material on the compost heap.

IN THE KITCHEN

Preparing lettuce for a salad is, of course, a straightforward job but there are still a few rules to follow. Wash both sides of each leaf to remove grit and insects — every cook knows that, but thorough drying is sometimes neglected. Shake vigorously in a salad basket or pat the leaves gently with a dry cloth — failure to do so will result in poor adhesion by the salad dressing. Keep the small leaves whole — tear the larger ones into pieces. The inner heart should be left unwashed if it is free from insects, dirt and slug holes — cut into wedges or in half rather than separating each tiny leaf. Before making the salad place the washed and dried lettuce leaves in the refrigerator for 30 minutes to crisp and chill them. Now you can arrange your usual mixture of cucumber, radishes, tomatoes, etc. or you can coat a wedge of a crisphead lettuce with the dressing of your choice and enjoy lettuce the American way.

FREEZING: Not suitable.

STORAGE: Keep unwashed in a polythene bag in the refrigerator — lettuce will stay fresh for up to 3 days (Butterhead) or 5 days (Cos or Crisphead).

COOKING: Lettuce is rarely regarded as a vegetable for cooking, but there are many ways of using the almost invariable glut in summer or the leaves of heads which have started to run to seed. *Pois à la française* which you enjoy in France is a combination of peas, lettuce and small onions braised in stock and a little butter. Stir-fried lettuce which is served in Oriental restaurants is prepared by cooking the leaves in hot vegetable oil for about 2 minutes. Braised lettuce, stuffed lettuce, lettuce soup … you will find many ideas in recipe books which are well worth trying.

CALENDAR

		JAN	FEB	MAR	APR	MAY	JUN	JUL	AUG	SEP	OCT	NOV	DEC
For a Summer/Autumn Crop: Sow outdoors in late March-late July for cutting in June-October. For an earlier crop (mid May-early June) sow under glass in early February and plant out in early March under cloches.	Sowing Time		▣	╫	▓	▓	▓	▓					
	Cutting Time						▓	▓	▓	▓	▓		
For an Early Winter Crop: Sow a mildew-resistant variety such as Robinson or Match outdoors in early August. Cover with cloches in late September — close ends with panes of glass. The crop will be ready for cutting in November or December.	Sowing Time								▓				
	Cutting Time											▓	▓
For a Midwinter Crop: Heated glass (minimum 7°C/45°F in winter) is necessary. Sow seed under glass in September or October — plant out as soon as the seedlings are large enough to handle. The lettuce will be ready for cutting in January-early March. Grow a forcing variety such as Kwiek.	Sowing Time									▣ ▣	🌱 🌱		
	Cutting Time	▓	▓	▓									
For a Spring Crop: If you live in a mild part of the country, sow a winter-hardy variety such as Winter Density outdoors in late August-early September. Thin to 8 cm (3 in.) apart in October — complete thinning to 30 cm (12 in.) spacing in early spring. The crop will be ready in May. For less favoured areas sow in mid October under cloches — harvest in April. Use a winter-hardy or a forcing variety.	Sowing Time									▓	╫		
	Cutting Time				▓	▓							

For key to symbols — see page 7

VARIETIES

COS varieties

The Cos or Romaine lettuce is easy to recognise by its upright growth habit and oblong head. The leaves are crisp and the flavour is good. They are generally a little more difficult to grow than the cabbage types and take longer to mature.

LOBJOIT'S GREEN: One of the old favourites — a large, self-folding variety. Deep green and very crisp.

AMAZE: A Cos lettuce to choose if you want to add colour to the salad plate. Red outer leaves, yellow ones inside.

LITTLE GEM: A quick-maturing Cos lettuce which is somewhat cabbage-like in appearance. Sow early for a May or June crop — tie the heads loosely with wool. Many experts consider it to be the sweetest lettuce. The heads are small and compact.

WINTER GEM: A winter version of the old favourite Little Gem. Sow between September and October in a greenhouse or cold frame for a spring crop.

WINTER DENSITY: This variety challenges Little Gem for the sweetest lettuce title, but its growing season is different. Sow in August or September for an April crop.

THE LEAF LETTUCE TECHNIQUE

This technique provides the maximum crop in the shortest time — try it if space is limited. Use a Cos variety and sow seeds at 3 cm (1 in.) intervals in rows 10 cm (4 in.) apart. Begin in April and make fortnightly sowings until the end of May. Do not thin — this technique produces a block of tightly packed lettuces. Make the first cut 4–6 weeks after sowing — leave the stumps to produce a second crop about 6 weeks later.

Winter Density

BUTTERHEAD varieties

All The Year Round

The Butterheads are still the most popular lettuce group. They are quick-maturing and will generally tolerate poorer conditions than the other types. The leaves are soft and smooth-edged — most are summer varieties but a few are hardy lettuces which are used to produce a spring crop and several others are forcing varieties for growing under glass.

ALL THE YEAR ROUND: Very popular because it is suitable for spring, summer and autumn sowing. Medium-sized, pale green and slow to bolt in dry weather.

TOM THUMB: The favourite for small plots, producing heads which are tennis ball size. Quick-maturing, fine-flavoured — grow it as a summer crop.

MARVEL OF FOUR SEASONS: The leaves of this medium-sized variety are green edged with red. Over 100 years old and still in a few catalogues — its name indicates its value for successional sowings.

HUMIL: A year-round hardy lettuce for successional sowings between March and September.

MAY QUEEN: The hearts of this old variety are yellow tinged with pink, but at first sight similar to Marvel of Four Seasons — red-tinged outer leaves and cabbage-like growth.

BUTTERCRUNCH: The central heart of creamy leaves is hard and compact — crunchy enough to make some books list it with the Crispheads. An American variety — try it for a different flavour.

EDOX: Described on the packet as something different — a red-tinged green Butterhead lettuce with a crisp heart.

SUZAN: Another variety which can be sown under glass in February or outdoors in spring to produce a summer crop. Hearts are large and pale green.

VALDOR: Highly recommended as an autumn crop — it stands up to poor weather conditions better than the average lettuce. Large heads are produced.

DIANA: This is the Butterhead lettuce which the packet recommends for the show bench. The large heads are dark green.

ARCTIC KING: Winter-hardy — the one to choose if you want a more compact spring lettuce than Imperial Winter.

KWIEK: A popular forcing lettuce for growing under glass to produce an early winter crop.

MAY QUEEN: Another under glass lettuce, recommended for early sowing under cloches. The leaves are red-tinged. May be listed as May King.

CLARION: A pale green, open-hearted variety. There is a choice of sowing times. You can sow under cloches or in a cold frame in February for a May crop, or sow outdoors in spring or summer for a later harvest. It has good disease resistance.

UNRIVALLED: Another long-season lettuce. Sow under glass in winter or outdoors in spring and summer.

CRISPHEAD varieties

Webb's Wonderful

The Crispheads produce large hearts of curled and crisp leaves. In general they are more resistant to bolting than the Butterheads, and their popularity is increasing in Britain. They have always been the popular group in the U.S. where the Iceberg type dominates the scene — Crispheads with a solid heart and few outer leaves.

WEBB'S WONDERFUL: The No.1 Crisphead lettuce in Britain — all the catalogues list this large-hearted frilly lettuce which succeeds even in hot summers.

ROBINSON: The claim to fame for this crisp-leaved lettuce is its tough constitution. It has a vigorous root system plus good disease resistance which means it can thrive in conditions where other lettuce varieties might fail.

SALADIN: A good-looking lettuce — the large heads are made up of shiny leaves. It seems that the Iceberg lettuce in the supermarket may be Saladin.

GREAT LAKES: A large, spreading Crisphead. It's the original summer Crisphead lettuce which came to us from America.

ICEBERG: You can buy the seed of this super-crisp white-hearted lettuce which has become so popular on the supermarket shelves. Sow in spring or early summer.

LAKELAND: An Iceberg-type of Crisphead which has been bred to be more reliable in Britain than the original Iceberg variety.

MATCH: This Iceberg-like lettuce has a number of plus points, including good resistance against mildew and bolting. Does better than most in hot weather. Noted for sweet flavour.

LOOSE-LEAF varieties

Salad Bowl

These varieties do not produce a heart. The leaves are curled and are picked like spinach — a few at a time without cutting the whole plant. Sow seed in April or May.

SALAD BOWL: The basic variety — an endive-like plant which produces intricately cut and curled leaves. Pick the leaves regularly and the plant will stay productive for many weeks. A reddish-brown variety (Red Salad Bowl) is available.

LOLLO ROSSA: The crisp leaves of this non-hearting lettuce are intricately frilled. These curled edges are tinged with red — a decorative as well as a tasty variety.

LETTUCE TROUBLES

Outdoor lettuce is an easy crop to grow, but it is not easy to grow well. You must guard against soil pests, slugs and birds; in cool, damp weather the twin major diseases (downy mildew and grey mould) can be destructive. Above all you must try to prevent any check to growth. Crops grown under glass are vulnerable to an even wider range of plant troubles, but few of them are serious in a well-grown crop.

	Symptom	Likely Causes
Seedlings	— poor or slow germination	**Seeds kept too warm**
	— eaten	5 or 10 or **Birds** (see page 157) or **Mice** (see page 20) or **Millepede** or **Leatherjacket** (see page 157)
	— toppled over	9 or **Damping off** (see page 157)
	— severed	10
Leaves	— holed	4 or 5
	— mouldy or powdery patches	1 or 9
	— brown-edged	1 or 9 or 13
	— large yellowish patches	1
	— brown spots	4
	— mottled	12
	— infested with greenfly	8
Plants	— run to seed	2
	— no hearts	3
	— wilted	6 or 7 or 9 or 10 or 11
	— rotten at base	9
	— base covered with grey mould	9
	— base covered with fluffy white mould	**Sclerotinia rot** (see page 43)
Roots	— eaten	9 or **Millepede** or **Leatherjacket** (see page 157)
	— tunnelled	11
	— infested with greenfly	6
	— covered with white patches	6
	— covered with gall-like swellings	7

WHITE MOULDY LEAVES

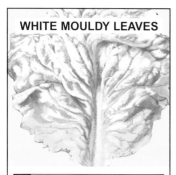

1 DOWNY MILDEW

Large yellowish patches appear between the veins of older leaves. Whitish mouldy areas develop on the underside. Later, diseased patches turn brown and die. This serious disease is worst in cool, wet conditions.

Treatment: Remove affected leaves as soon as they are seen. Chemical sprays are no longer available.

Prevention: Practise crop rotation. Avoid overcrowding. Under glass make sure that the plants are adequately ventilated and not overwatered.

2 BOLTING

Lettuces produce thick flowering stems if left in the soil after hearts have formed. Sometimes the plants run to seed before they are ready for harvesting — this condition is known as 'bolting'. The cause is a check to growth at some stage of the plant's life. Careless or delayed transplanting is perhaps the commonest cause, but both overcrowding and dryness at the root are frequently responsible. Lift and place on the compost heap; cover with soil so as not to attract aphids.

3 NO HEARTS

A wide variety of factors can prevent lettuces from forming hearts. The most likely reason is shortage of organic matter — you must enrich the land with compost or manure if you want to be sure of a well-hearted crop. Other possible causes are growing the plants in a shady site, aphid attack, overcrowding and drought.

4 RING SPOT

Not common, but occasionally damaging to winter varieties. Small brown spots appear on the outer leaves, giving a rusty appearance. The centres of the spots may fall out. Rusty streaks appear on the midribs.

Treatment: Destroy badly infected plants. Spray remaining plants with a copper fungicide.

Prevention: Practise crop rotation outdoors. Ensure good ventilation under glass.

HOLED LEAVES

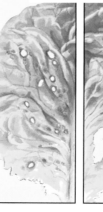

5 SLUGS & SNAILS

Both slugs and snails are a menace to lettuces at all stages of growth. Seedlings are particularly susceptible and may be killed. Leaves and stems are severely attacked in wet weather. The pests are generally not seen during the day, so look for tell-tale slime trails.

Treatment: Scatter slug pellets or use a nematode product around the plants at the first signs of attack.

Prevention: Keep surrounding area free from rubbish.

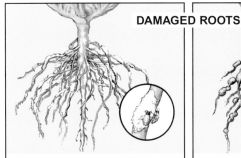

DAMAGED ROOTS

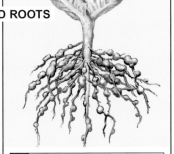

| 6 | ROOT APHID |

Greyish-coloured 'greenfly' attack the roots, which become covered with white powdery patches. Growth is stunted, and the leaves may turn yellow and wilt. Attacks are worst in late summer.

Treatment: Pull up and destroy decaying plants. Chemical treatments for this pest are not available.

Prevention: Keep plants watered in dry weather. Grow resistant varieties such as Salad Bowl if attacks recur.

| 7 | EELWORM |

Root knot eelworm occasionally attacks lettuce plants, causing stunted growth and pale-coloured leaves. Plants wilt and die if the attack is severe. Look for the tell-tale signs on lifted plants — gall-like swellings on the roots.

Treatment: None. Dig up and destroy infested plants.

Prevention: Do not grow lettuce in affected soil for at least 6 years.

GREENFLY ON LEAVES

| 8 | APHID |

Greenflies can be serious pests in two ways. They spread mosaic, a virus disease, and they also cover the plants in sticky honeydew which can make them unusable. Attacks are worst in a dry spring, when leaves may be badly puckered and distorted.

Treatment: Spray at the first signs of attack. Use thiacloprid, insecticidal soap or pyrethrins.

Prevention: None.

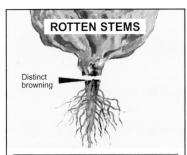

ROTTEN STEMS

Distinct browning

| 9 | GREY MOULD (Botrytis) |

Plants are infected through dead or damaged areas, and the fungus produces a reddish-brown rot when it reaches the stem. Plants wilt and may break off at soil level. Infected tissue produces abundant masses of grey mould. This disease is encouraged by low temperature and high humidity.

Treatment: Destroy diseased plants immediately. No fungicidal sprays are available.

Prevention: Handle seedlings carefully. Plant so that the leaf bases are not buried.

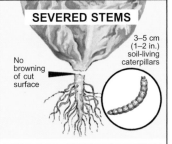

SEVERED STEMS

No browning of cut surface

3–5 cm (1–2 in.) soil-living caterpillars

| 10 | CUTWORM |

These large green, grey or brown caterpillars are a major threat to young lettuces. The plants are attacked at night and stems may be completely severed at ground level. With older plants the roots are gnawed which causes the lettuces to wilt. June and July are the main danger months.

Treatment: Hoe the soil around the plants. Destroy caterpillars which are brought to the surface.

Prevention: Use a nematode-based insecticide before planting.

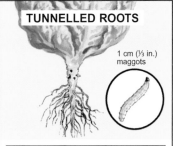

TUNNELLED ROOTS

1 cm (⅓ in.) maggots

| 11 | LETTUCE ROOT MAGGOT |

An occasional pest of lettuce grown under glass. They tunnel into the roots and eat the central tissue. Above ground the leaves wilt and growth is stunted. The main host of this pest is the chrysanthemum, where it is known as chrysanthemum stool miner.

Treatment: Dig out and destroy affected plants. No soil-acting insecticides are available for use on vegetables.

Prevention: Do not plant lettuce on land used for chrysanthemums in the previous season.

| 12 | MOSAIC VIRUS |

Yellow or pale green mottling appears on the leaves and growth is stunted. The veins appear almost transparent. It is spread by aphids.

Treatment: None. Lift and burn infected plants.

Prevention: Spray young plants with thiacloprid or insecticidal soap.

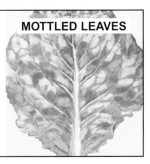

MOTTLED LEAVES

BROWN-EDGED LEAVES

| 13 | TIPBURN |

Tipburn (or 'greasiness') is a common cause of the scorching of leaf edges. It is usually due to sudden water loss by the leaves. This can happen in a warm spell in early spring or at the start of a summer heat wave.

Treatment: None.

Prevention: None.

Marrow, Courgette, Squash, Pumpkin

There are no exact dividing lines between these members of the cucumber family. Once the vegetable marrow dominated the scene — large, oblong and striped, with an insipid flavour when boiled. It is still, however, used as a casing for minced beef or other stuffing. Courgettes have now taken over with their firmer flesh and superior taste — they are nothing more than marrows cut at an immature stage. Summer squashes are non-standard shaped marrows which have become more popular in recent years, and finally the pumpkins — the giants grown for show rather than eating.

IN A NUTSHELL

Soak seed overnight before sowing.

Actual Size

Expected germination time:	5–8 days
Expected yield per plant (Marrows):	4 marrows
Expected yield per plant (Courgettes):	16 courgettes
Life expectancy of stored seed:	6 years
Approximate time between sowing and cutting:	10–14 weeks
Ease of cultivation:	Not difficult if you remember to prepare the soil properly and water regularly

SOWING & PLANTING

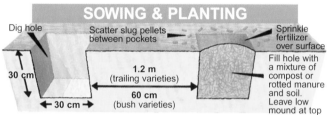

Dig hole — Scatter slug pellets between pockets — Sprinkle fertilizer over surface

30 cm — 30 cm — 1.2 m (trailing varieties) — 60 cm (bush varieties)

Fill hole with a mixture of compost or rotted manure and soil. Leave low mound at top

- Sow 3 seeds 3 cm (1 in.) deep and 6 cm (2 in.) apart at the centre of each pocket. Cover with a large jar or cloche to hasten germination. When the first true leaves have appeared thin out to leave the strongest seedling.
- Alternatively you can raise the seedlings indoors, but this method is often less satisfactory. Place a single seed edgeways 1 cm (½ in.) deep in seed compost in a 8 cm (3 in.) fibre pot. Keep at a minimum of 18°C (65°F) until germinated — harden off seedlings before planting outdoors.

LOOKING AFTER THE CROP

- Pinch out the tips of the main shoots of trailing varieties when they reach 60 cm (2 ft) long. Renew slug pellets at the first signs of damage.
- Keep the soil moist — water copiously *around* the plants, not over them. Syringe lightly in dry weather.
- Place black polythene or a mulch around the plants in summer before fruit formation.
- If the weather is cold or it is early in the season, fertilize female flowers (tiny marrow behind petals) with a male flower (thin stalk behind petals). Remove a mature male flower on a dry day, fold back petals and push gently into a female flower.
- Once the fruits start to swell feed every 14 days with a tomato fertilizer. Limit pumpkins to 2 fruits per plant. Keep marrows on a piece of tile or glass to prevent rotting and slug attack.

SOIL FACTS

- A sunny spot protected from strong winds is essential — marrows, squashes, etc. are neither hardy nor long suffering.
- The soil must be well drained and rich in humus. Most households will need only a few plants, so prepare a few planting pockets as shown on the right rather than sowing long rows.

HARVESTING

- Remove for immediate use when still quite small — courgettes 10 cm (4 in.), marrows 20–25 cm (8–10 in.) long. Push your thumbnail into the surface near the stalk — if it goes in quite easily then the marrow is at the right stage for summer picking. Continual cropping is essential to prolong fruiting. Take care — cut marrows where they lie, then lift them away.
- For pumpkins, winter squashes and marrows for winter storage, allow the fruits to mature on the plants and remove before frosts. Store in a cool room indoors — they should keep until Christmas.

- Sow outdoors in late May or early June. In the Midlands and northern areas cover the seedlings with cloches if you can for a few weeks. The first courgettes will be ready in July.
- For an earlier crop sow seeds under glass in late April. Plant out the seedlings in early June when the danger of frost has passed.

CALENDAR

	JAN	FEB	MAR	APR	MAY	JUN	JUL	AUG	SEP	OCT	NOV	DEC
Sowing Time (outdoors)					▓							
Sowing Time (indoors)				▓		▓						
Cutting Time							▓	▓	▓	▓		

For key to symbols — see page 7

IN THE KITCHEN

Courgettes are now the most popular of the edible gourds — crisp and tasty, plentiful in the shops and bountiful in the garden from just a few plants. They need neither peeling nor seeding — merely wash and trim for serving raw or cooked. For serving in salads, blanch the whole fruits for about 2 minutes in boiling water to remove bitterness — dry, slice and serve. Mature marrows require peeling before boiling and then coring by cutting the fruit lengthways and scooping out the seeds and tough fibres. Boiling produces a watery, tasteless dish — baking or braising is better. The summer squashes are also bland but the winter squashes are different — the firm, orange fibrous flesh is still one of our undiscovered tastes.

FREEZING: Courgettes (not marrows) are suitable for freezing. Cut into 1 cm (⅓ in.) slices, blanch for 2 minutes, cool, drain and pat dry. Pack into polythene bags.

STORAGE: Keep courgettes in a polythene bag in the refrigerator — the fruits will stay fresh for up to 1 week.

COOKING: Boil courgettes (5–8 minutes in very little water) if you are anti-frying, but they taste better if sliced and lightly fried. Best of all are courgette fritters — rub slices with salt to draw out water, dab dry, dip in flour or batter and then fry until golden brown. Mature marrows are excellent for wine or jam making or pickle and chutney production but boiling (10 minutes in very little water) produces an insipid vegetable. Baked stuffed marrow is better — so is braising with tomatoes and herbs. Winter squash is prepared by cutting in half through the hard rind, brushing the flesh with melted butter and then baking for 45 minutes.

VARIETIES

MARROW varieties

These varieties include all the traditional vegetable marrow shapes which are used for summer cooking and winter storage.

LONG GREEN TRAILING: Large and cylindrical with pale stripes. This is the one to grow to impress the neighbours or win prizes at the show.

TIGER CROSS: Popular bush-type marrow — dark green with prominent pale green stripes. Virus resistant. Stores well.

GREEN BUSH: Perhaps the best all-rounder — you can cut the small fruits as courgettes and let a few mature in late summer to produce striped green marrows.

BUSH BABY: For many people the average marrow is just too big for a meal. For them this marrow could be the answer. Its mature size is only three quarters of that of the average marrow.

COURGETTE varieties

These varieties are compact bush marrows which are grown exclusively for their immature fruits. They produce many small fruits over a long period … provided you keep cutting them.

ZUCCHINI: The most popular courgette variety — dark green fruits are produced in profusion. Serve raw in salad or cooked as a hot vegetable.

BAMBINO: Dark green fruits appear on the compact plants. The baby courgettes (8 cm/3 in.) are produced over a long period.

MIDNIGHT: A good choice for growing in containers. Crops heavily, producing spineless dark green courgettes.

DEFENDER: Rated very highly. Early, prolific, large fruits, virus-resistant.

Green Bush

SQUASH varieties

 Summer squash
 Winter squash

The summer squashes are non-standard shaped marrows with soft skins and pale, soft flesh. The winter squashes have a hard rind and fibrous, orange flesh.

CUSTARD SQUASH (Summer): This is the Patty Pan Squash of America — scalloped-edged, flat fruits which should be fried or boiled like courgettes. Both white and yellow varieties are available.

HUNTER (Winter): The star of the Winter squashes — bred specially for the British market. Matures a month earlier than standard varieties.

VEGETABLE SPAGHETTI (Winter): An excellent novelty — boil for 25 minutes and cut in half. Remove seeds and then scrape out spaghetti-like strands with a fork. Home-grown spaghetti!

SWEET DUMPLING (Winter): The Winter squashes are not popular, but you will find several if you search through the catalogues — Table Ace, Hubbards Squash, Butternut, Honey Bear etc. The problem is that our season is a little too short and often too cool for success. Still well worth the effort in southern counties.

Defender

PUMPKIN varieties

These varieties include the pumpkin-shaped edible gourds — thick-skinned, very large and grown to maturity on the plant.

HUNDREDWEIGHT: This was once the top variety grown to produce enormous fruits which lived up to the promise of the name. This pumpkin is sometimes listed as Mammoth.

ATLANTIC GIANT: This world-beater arrived from America to make Hundredweight seem like a lightweight. You cannot hope to match the 225 kg (500 lb) record set over there.

TROUBLES

See pages 54-56

Vegetable Spaghetti

Mushrooms

It is exciting to see the first flush of mushrooms on the compost surface. There are two reasons — it takes just a week or two for white pinheads to turn into button mushrooms, and we know that mushrooms are notoriously unpredictable. An outdoor planting is indeed a gamble. Using homemade compost and planting spawn into it reduces risk, but only the use of ready-spawned containers provides anything like the predictability associated with other vegetables.

MUSHROOMS OUTDOORS

- You may or may not be successful in raising mushrooms in a corner of your lawn. It will certainly have to be in a shady spot and the ground below will have to be enriched with well-rotted manure. Even if you are successful, there are the drawbacks of being unable to cut the grass when cropping starts and weeds cannot be treated by chemical means.

- If the above points act as a challenge rather than a deterrent, pick a damp day in spring or autumn and use golf-ball sized blocks of spawn, setting them about 5 cm (2 in.) below the surface at 30 cm (12 in.) spacings.

MUSHROOMS INDOORS

Anywhere indoors will do provided that the container or bed is shaded from direct sunlight and the temperature is in the 13º–19ºC (55º–65ºF) range. Large fluctuations in temperature will slow down production — both cold and hot conditions will stop it. You will need specially-prepared compost which is hard to make at home, although you may be lucky enough to find a local supplier. This will have to be planted with mushroom spawn and properly tended to ensure success — a much easier course is to buy a ready-spawned container of compost from a garden centre or mail order nursery.

START FROM SCRATCH METHOD

- Start with stable manure or straw plus an activator. You will need a large heap, about 1.5 x 1.5 x 1.5 m (5 x 5 x 5 ft), to be reasonably sure of success and it must be well watered at the start. Leave covered until the temperature reaches at least 60°C (140°F) — then turn every week until the heap is dark brown, crumbly and sweet-smelling.

- Fill boxes or buckets 20–30 cm (8–12 in.) deep — firm down with your fingers. When the temperature has fallen to 24°C (75°F) the surface is ready for spawning.

- Two types of spawn are available — fungus-impregnated manure (block spawn) or impregnated rye (grain spawn). Block spawn is the easier one to use — push golf-ball sized pieces about 3 cm (1 in.) below the surface at 30 cm (12 in.) spacings.

- After a couple of weeks the spawn will have started to 'run' — white threads will be seen on the surface. At this stage add a 5 cm (2 in.) layer of moist casing mixture (2 parts peat, 1 part chalk).

EASY METHOD

- Buy a bucket or bag of ready-spawned compost. Avoid any pack which has obviously been in store for a long time and make sure that you start the pack into growth within 3 weeks of purchase.

LOOKING AFTER THE CROP

- A temperature of 13º–19ºC (55º–65ºF) is necessary to promote the active development of the white fungal threads (mycelium) below the surface and the appearance of the edible fruiting bodies above. The casing should be kept moist but not wet by careful syringing with water.

HARVESTING

- The first flush will be ready for picking as button mushrooms 4–6 weeks after casing — these buttons will open into flats in about 7 days. Once the first flush has been harvested there will be a pause of about 2 weeks before the next flush appears. Cropping normally continues for about 8 weeks.

- Do not harvest mushrooms by cutting the stalks. Twist the mushroom upwards, disturbing the compost as little as possible. Cut away broken stalks and fill holes with casing mixture.

- After the final flush has been picked, use the spent manure in the garden — do not try to re-spawn for a second crop.

IN THE KITCHEN

Growing mushrooms at home is always fun because you can never really be sure what the result will be, but there is also a practical benefit — the flavour is so much better when they are eaten within hours of picking. Harvesting often takes place at the button stage when the membrane below the gills is unbroken. At this stage they are ideal for eating raw — plain or more usually in an oil and vinegar dressing. Open ('flat') mushrooms with their gills exposed are larger and have a much better flavour, but they can add a blackish colour to some dishes. Now for the golden rules. Never wash mushrooms — water will spoil the flavour. If the surface is soiled, wipe with a damp cloth. Never peel unless it is really necessary.

STORAGE: There is no really satisfactory method — the flavour declines rapidly after picking. If you have to store them, keep in a paper bag in the refrigerator for up to 3 days.

COOKING: The tastiest methods of preparation are frying (in an uncovered pan with butter and a little lemon juice for 3–5 minutes) and grilling (brushed with oil and seasoned before placing under the grill for 2–3 minutes on each side). Poach for 3–5 minutes if you are on a low-fat diet. Apart from their role as essential partners in mixed grills, hearty breakfasts and savoury omelettes, mushrooms are a basic ingredient of many classical recipes from Lancashire hotpot and *coq au vin* to *sole bonne femme* and *gebackener schwammerl*.

TROUBLES

PESTS

Several pests can cause serious problems for commercial growers, but only mushroom fly is likely to trouble the amateur. The maggots of this insect bore into the caps — spray with pyrethrins if small flies are seen.

DISEASES

Your small box or bucket is unlikely to be troubled.

Onions & Shallots from sets

Onion sets are immature bulbs which have been specially grown for planting. There are several advantages in using sets rather than seed. They mature quickly, and they are not attacked by onion fly nor mildew. Less skill and less soil fertility are required, but against these advantages are the extra cost and the extra risk of bolting. Shallot sets are full-sized — they grow into clusters of 8–12 similar sized bulbs.

IN A NUTSHELL

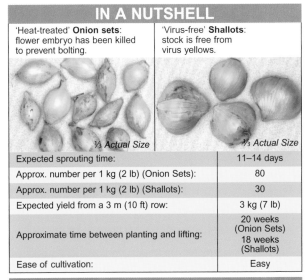

'Heat-treated' **Onion sets**: flower embryo has been killed to prevent bolting.	'Virus-free' **Shallots**: stock is free from virus yellows.
⅓ *Actual Size*	⅓ *Actual Size*
Expected sprouting time:	11–14 days
Approx. number per 1 kg (2 lb) (Onion Sets):	80
Approx. number per 1 kg (2 lb) (Shallots):	30
Expected yield from a 3 m (10 ft) row:	3 kg (7 lb)
Approximate time between planting and lifting:	20 weeks (Onion Sets) 18 weeks (Shallots)
Ease of cultivation:	Easy

SOIL FACTS

- All onions require good soil and free drainage, but sets need neither the fine texture nor the high organic content demanded by seed-sown onions.
- Dig in early winter and incorporate compost if available. Lime if necessary. Firm the surface before planting and rake in a general fertilizer such as Growmore.

PLANTING

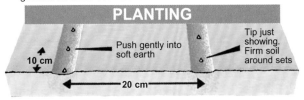

Push gently into soft earth

Tip just showing. Firm soil around sets

10 cm

20 cm

- If planting is delayed, open package and spread out sets in a cool well-lit place to prevent premature sprouting.
- Plant onion sets 10 cm (4 in.) apart in mid March–mid April. Shallots require wider (15 cm/6 in. apart) and earlier (mid February–mid March) planting.

CALENDAR

	JAN	FEB	MAR	APR	MAY	JUN	JUL	AUG	SEP	OCT	NOV	DEC
Planting Time												
Lifting Time												

For key to symbols — see page 7

LOOKING AFTER THE CROP

- Protect from birds with black thread or netting if they are a nuisance in your area.
- Keep weed-free by hoeing and hand pulling. Push back any sets which have been lifted by frost or birds. Once the sets are established and shoots have appeared then treat as for seed-sown onions (see page 72).

HARVESTING

- **Shallots:** In July the leaves will turn yellow. Lift the bulb clusters and separate them, allowing each shallot to dry thoroughly. Remove dirt and brittle stems, and store in net bags or nylon tights in a cool, dry place. They will keep for about 8 months.
- **Onions:** See page 72

IN THE KITCHEN

See page 73

VARIETIES

ONION varieties

STUTTGARTER GIANT: Once this was the leading variety, but not any more. The bulbs are flattened, not round, and the flavour is mild. It has good keeping qualities and is slow to bolt.

STURON: Sturon has established itself as a reliable globe-shaped onion which stores well. The straw-coloured bulbs are round and extremely large. Bolt resistance is excellent.

AILSA CRAIG: An old favourite — round, large and straw-coloured with white, mild-flavoured flesh.

RUMBA: A British-bred onion which flourishes under our conditions. The bulbs are large with a flavour that makes them ideal for serving raw in salads. Good bolt resistance, and the thick skin makes them a good choice for storing.

SHALLOT varieties

These small bulbs are milder in flavour than onions and are harvested in July or August. Use for cooking, garnishing or pickling — keep a few in a cool, well-lit place for planting next spring.

GOLDEN GOURMET: A good choice — a winner in independent trials and holder of an RHS Award of Garden Merit. The brown-skinned bulbs have excellent keeping qualities. Flavour has few rivals.

HATIVE DE NIORT: The usual choice by exhibitors — the bulbs are perfectly shaped with deep brown skins.

TROUBLES

See pages 74–75

Onion from seed

You can have onions fresh from the garden or out of store almost all year round from just a couple of carefully-timed sowings. Most standard varieties are sown in spring — the Japanese varieties make late summer sowing a more reliable routine for an early summer crop, but the bulbs cannot be stored. Apart from these large bulb onions there are the salad (spring onion) varieties and also the pickling varieties — small silverskin onions which are sown in April and lifted in July.

IN A NUTSHELL

Fungicide-treated and pelleted seeds are available. Germination and seedling growth are slow in spring and also erratic in hot weather.

Actual Size

Expected germination time:	21 days
Approx. number per 30 gm (1oz):	8000
Expected yield from a 3 m (10 ft) row:	4 kg (9 lb)
Life expectancy of stored seed:	1–2 years
Approximate time between sowing and lifting:	46 weeks (August-sown varieties) 22 weeks (Spring-sown varieties)
Ease of cultivation:	Easy — if a suitable seed bed is prepared

SOIL FACTS

- Many exhibitors grow their show onions in a permanent bed in order to build up fertility, but in the kitchen plot it is a much better idea to change the site annually.
- Choose an open, sunny site with good drainage. Dig thoroughly in autumn, incorporating a liberal quantity of manure or compost. Liming will be necessary if the soil is acid.
- Before sowing or planting it is necessary to prepare a traditional 'onion bed'. Apply a general fertilizer and rake the surface when the soil is reasonably dry. Tread over the area and then rake again to produce a fine, even tilth.

- For an August or September crop sow as soon as the land is workable in the spring (late February-early April depending on the location of your garden).
- Sow in mid August for an earlier crop — Japanese varieties mature in late June — standard varieties are less hardy, less reliable and later cropping (late July onwards), but they can be stored.
- In cold areas and for exhibition bulbs sow under glass in January, harden off in March and transplant outdoors in April.
- Salad onions should be sown in March-July for a June-October crop. Sow in August for onions in March-May.

SOWING & PLANTING

Water gently if soil is dry. Sow very thinly | Cover with soil | 25 cm | 1 cm

- Thin the spring-sown crop in 2 stages — first to 3–5 cm (1–2 in.) when the seedlings have straightened up and then to 10 cm (4 in.) apart. Lift the seedlings carefully — all thinnings should be removed to deter onion fly.
- Seedlings raised under glass should be transplanted 10 cm (4 in.) apart, leaving 25 cm (10 in.) between the rows. The roots must fall vertically in the planting hole and the bulb base should be about 1 cm (½ in.) below the surface. Plant firmly.
- Salad onions should be planted in rows which are only 10 cm (4 in.) apart — thin the seedlings, if necessary, to 3 cm (1 in.) spacings.
- Seeds of Japanese varieties should be sown at 3 cm (1 in.) intervals in rows spaced 25 cm (10 in.) apart. Thin seedlings to 10 cm (4 in.) intervals in spring.

LOOKING AFTER THE CROP

- Hoe carefully or weed by hand — dense weed growth will seriously affect yield. Water if the weather is dry (not otherwise) and feed occasionally. Feed an autumn-sown crop with a liquid fertilizer in March.
- Break off any flower stems which appear. Mulching is useful for cutting down the need for water and for suppressing weeds. Stop watering once the onions have swollen and pull back the covering earth or mulch to expose the bulb surface to the sun.

HARVESTING

- The salad varieties should be pulled when the bulbs are 1–3 cm (½–1 in.) across. The harvesting season is March-October.
- When the bulb is mature the foliage turns yellow and topples over. Leave them for about 2 weeks and then carefully lift with a fork on a dry day.
- The onions which are not for immediate use must be dried. Spread out the bulbs on sacking or in trays — outdoors if the weather is warm and sunny or indoors if the weather is rainy.
- Drying will take 7-21 days, depending on the size of the bulbs and the air temperature. Inspect the bulbs carefully — all soft, spotted and thick-necked onions should be set aside for kitchen use or freezing. The rest can be stored — the exceptions are the Japanese varieties which are not suitable for storage.
- Store in trays, net bags, tights or tie to a length of cord as onion ropes. Choose a cool and well-lit place; they will keep until late spring.

CALENDAR

	JAN	FEB	MAR	APR	MAY	JUN	JUL	AUG	SEP	OCT	NOV	DEC
Sowing Time (outdoors)		▓	▓					▓				
Sowing Time (indoors)	▣			✿								
Lifting Time							▓	▓	▓			

For key to symbols — see page 7

IN THE KITCHEN

The culinary uses are so varied and the basic ways of employing onions are so well known that there would be no point in trying to list them. The Ploughman's Lunch of bread, cheese, onions and ale has sustained British workers for countless generations. At the other end of the scale French classic dishes served *à la bonne femme* or with *Bercy* sauce have relied on shallots for their subtle flavour. The onion is thought to be our oldest vegetable, but there are still some basic facts which are not universally known. First of all, the proper way to chop an onion. Cut in half lengthways and place the cut side downwards on a board. Make about five cuts, first downwards and then horizontally towards but not through the base. Finally chop downwards across the length of the onion and throw away the tough basal section — you will be left with a neat pile of cubes. If watery eyes are a problem keep hands and onions under water … or buy an autochopper if all else fails. Onion rings are a popular ingredient for salads, but home-grown ones are often a great deal hotter than the mild-flavoured Spanish onions bought in shops. To increase mildness simply pour boiling water over the rings, dab dry with a paper towel and serve.

FREEZING: Cut into slices and blanch for 1 minute — leave button onions whole. Cool, drain and dry. Pack into polythene bags and freeze — use within 12 months.

STORAGE: Salad onions can be kept in the refrigerator for up to 1 week. Do not store bulbs in this way — keep in a cool place until required.

COOKING: Onions outrank even tomatoes as the great accompanists in the kitchen. For soups, stews, flans, casseroles, sauces and so on, braised chopped onions are often a basic ingredient. Remember to fry *slowly* — the onions should simmer in order to soften before browning takes place. As a hot vegetable serve boiled, baked, stir-fried, or glazed. Best of all, perhaps, are fried onion rings — dip in milk and then flour before frying until golden brown.

VARIETIES

BULB varieties

The standard varieties are grown for their large bulbs which can be stored throughout the winter months. Some have a flattened shape, others are globular. Skin colours vary from almost pure white to bright red and flavours range from mild to strong. Most of them are only suitable for spring sowing but some can be sown in August for a late July crop. The Japanese varieties make late summer sowing a much more reliable routine but their midsummer crop cannot be stored.

AILSA CRAIG: Look no further, according to some experts. A great favourite — very large, globe-shaped, excellent for exhibiting but its keeping qualities are not good.

BEDFORDSHIRE CHAMPION: Very popular — scores over Ailsa Craig by being a good keeper. Large and globular, but very susceptible to downy mildew.

RIJNSBURGER: The catalogues list many strains — Balstora, Wijbo, Bola, etc. Large, globular, white-fleshed — earliness and keeping qualities depend on the strain you choose.

LANCASTRIAN: A large globe variety with golden skin — a good choice for show bench and kitchen.

HIBALL: A hardy variety which is sown in August and lifted in the following summer.

SANTERO: The shape is oval and its two selling points are resistance to both bolting and mildew.

KEEPWELL: A Japanese variety with pale brown skin — noted for its excellent keeping quality. Consider this one if you plan to sow in August.

RED BARON: An early red-skinned onion with flattish bulbs which store well.

MARCO: A globular onion with a golden brown skin. Claimed to have three advantages — high yields, early maturing and long storage life.

LONG RED FLORENCE: This red-skinned onion is spindle-shaped — a spring sowing can be pulled early as spring onions or left to mature for August lifting. See page 121.

KAIZUKA EXTRA EARLY: A yellow-skinned Japanese variety which has replaced Express Yellow. Matures later but the yields are higher.

IMAI YELLOW: A Japanese variety which is globe-shaped and early.

SENSHYU: Rather similar to Imai Yellow, but a little flatter and later cropping.

Ailsa Craig

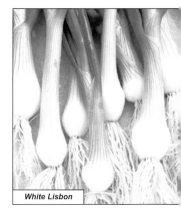
White Lisbon

SALAD varieties

Thinnings of the bulb varieties can be used as salad or 'spring' onions, but there are several varieties which are grown specifically for salad use. These Salad varieties, also known as scallions or bunching onions, are white-skinned and mild-flavoured.

WHITE LISBON: By far the most popular of the Salad varieties. Quick-growing and silvery-skinned, a small patch of ground can provide salad onions for six months of the year.

ISHIKURA: Something new in Salad onions. The long, straight stems do not form bulbs — simply pull out a few at a time and let the rest of the pencil-like plants grow on for harvesting later.

PICKLING varieties

Several onion varieties are grown for their small silverskin bulbs (button onions) which are lifted in July or August and pickled for use as cocktail onions. These varieties should be sown in April in sandy soil — do not feed. The seedlings should not be thinned.

PARIS SILVER SKIN: The favourite Pickling onion; lift when the bulb is the size of a marble.

BARLETTA: A difficult-to-find variety for making cocktail onions — no particular advantage or disadvantage compared with Paris Silver Skin.

Paris Silver Skin

ONION & LEEK TROUBLES

Although many plant disorders can attack onions, only four are likely to seriously trouble the gardener. They are onion fly, stem and bulb eelworm, neck rot and white rot. Plants grown from seed are more susceptible to onion fly, so raise onions from sets if you have been disappointed in the past. Leeks are much less prone to attack than onions.

	Symptom	Likely Causes
Seedlings	— eaten	**Cutworm** (see page 157)
	— killed	4
	— toppled over	**Damping off** (see page 157)
Sets	— lifted out of ground	**Frost** or **Birds**
	— two or more plants produced	6
Leaves	— tunnelled	12
	— eaten above ground level	**Cabbage moth** (see page 29)
	— eaten at ground level	**Cutworm** (see page 157) or **Wireworm** (no cure)
	— diseased	7 or 8 or 11
	— yellow, drooping	1 or 13 or 14
	— green, drooping	2
	— white tipped	10
	— swollen, distorted	4
Plants	— abnormally thick-necked	9
	— run to seed	3
Bulbs in the garden	— tunnelled, maggots present	1
	— split at base	5
	— mouldy at base	13
	— soft, not evil-smelling	4 or 11 or 13
	— soft, evil-smelling inside	14
Bulbs in store	— soft, mouldy near neck	15
	— soft, evil-smelling	**Soft rot** (see page 85)

TUNNELLED BULBS

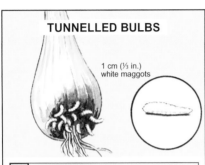

1 cm (⅓ in.) white maggots

1 | ONION FLY

Tell-tale signs are yellow drooping leaves. Worst attacks occur in dry soil in midsummer. The maggots burrow into the bases of the bulbs — young plants are frequently killed, older ones fail to develop properly.

Treatment: Lift and burn badly affected plants.

Prevention: No chemical for soil treatment before planting is available. Destroy all thinnings, damaged leaves and infested bulbs — firm the soil around the plants. If onion fly is a regular problem grow onions from sets rather than seeds.

TWISTED, SWOLLEN LEAVES

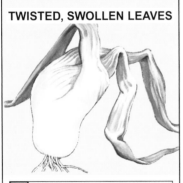

4 | STEM & BULB EELWORM

Swollen, distorted foliage indicates attack by this microscopic soil-living pest. Young plants are killed; older ones produce soft bulbs which cannot be stored.

Treatment: Lift and burn infected plants.

Prevention: Do not grow onions, peas, beans or strawberries, for several years, on land affected by stem and bulb eelworm.

2 | DROOPING LEAVES

Leaves sometimes droop even though neither pest nor disease is present. If foliage is darker green than normal, then the usual cause is either too much fresh manure before planting or too much nitrogen in the soil. Watering with a potash-rich fertilizer, such as a tomato or rose fertilizer, will help.

BULBS SPLIT AT BASE

5 | SADDLEBACK

Harvested onions are found to be split at the base. This disorder affects crops grown from sets, and it is always associated with heavy rain or watering after a prolonged period of drought.

Treatment: None. Use affected onions as soon as possible as they will not keep in store.

Prevention: Never keep the plants short of water during dry spells in summer.

3 | BOLTING

Onions occasionally bolt (premature production of flower heads). When this happens cut off the flower stalks and lift bulbs in the usual way. Use as soon as possible as they will not store satisfactorily. Common causes are early sowing or planting in a cold spring and planting in loose soil.

6 | SET DIVISION

Onions grown from sets may produce twin bulbs. The cause of this splitting is usually planting at the wrong time or growing the plants in poor soil. Prolonged dry weather can also induce set division.

7 SMUT

Black spots and blotches appear on leaves and bulbs. Only young plants are affected — the leaves become thickened and twisted. Leeks are more susceptible than onions.

Treatment: None. Lift and burn diseased plants.

Prevention: Do not grow leeks nor onions on infected land for at least 8 years.

SPOTS ON LEAVES

8 RUST

Orange spots and blotches appear on the surface of leaves. Uncommon, but effect can be fatal in a severe attack in summer. Leeks are more susceptible than onions.

Treatment: Remove and burn diseased leaves.

Prevention: Do not grow leeks nor onions on land affected by rust in the previous season.

WHITENED LEAVES

10 WHITE TIP

Leaf tips of leeks turn white and papery in autumn. Disease spreads downwards and growth is stunted.

Treatment: No fungicidal spray is approved for this use. Lift and burn badly diseased plants.

Prevention: Do not grow leeks on land affected in the previous season.

9 BULL NECK (Thick Neck)

The production of abnormally thick necks is a serious complaint as the bulbs will not store properly. Bull-necked onions are often associated with the overmanuring of land and the use of too much nitrogen. Use a liquid feed during the growing season — choose one such as tomato fertilizer which contains more potash than nitrogen. Another possible cause is sowing seed too deeply.

MOULD ON LEAVES

11 DOWNY MILDEW

Downy grey mould covers leaves, which slowly die back and shrivel from the tips. Bulbs are usually soft and not suitable for storage. A serious disease in cool, damp seasons.

Treatment: No fungicide spray is available for controlling this disease.

Prevention: Grow onions on a different site each year. Avoid badly-drained areas.

TUNNELLED LEAVES

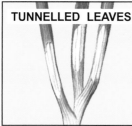

12 LEEK MOTH

Pale green 2 cm ($^2/_3$ in.) caterpillars feed inside young onion leaves so that only outer skin remains. The foliage of leeks may also be attacked.

Treatment: Spray with a contact insecticide at the first signs of attack. Destroy badly affected leaves.

Prevention: No practical method available.

ROTTING BULBS IN STORE

15 NECK ROT

Grey mould appears near neck in store; bulbs turn soft and rotten.

Treatment: None. Examine stored bulbs frequently and remove rotten bulbs immediately.

Prevention: Do not apply a fertilizer late in the season. Follow all the rules for correct storage — dry bulbs thoroughly and store only hard, undamaged ones in a cool well-ventilated place. Don't store onions with fleshy, green necks.

ROTTING BULBS IN THE GARDEN

13 WHITE ROT (Mouldy Nose)

Foliage turns yellow and wilts. Fluffy white mould appears on the base of the bulbs, and round black bodies appear in this fungus. White rot is a serious disease, and is always worst in hot, dry summers.

Treatment: None. Lift and burn diseased plants.

Prevention: There is no chemical treatment you can use. Do not grow onions on infected land for at least 8 years.

14 SHANKING

Centre leaves turn yellow and collapse; outside leaves soon follow. Cut open a bulb; the tell-tale sign is evil-smelling slime within the scales. This disease is much less common than white rot.

Treatment: None. Lift and burn diseased plants.

Prevention: No practical method available. Do not grow onions on infected land for several years.

Parsnip

Boiled parsnips are not popular and they occupy the ground for a long time, so it is not surprising that parsnips are not in the seed best-sellers list. However, do think before rejecting this vegetable. They need very little attention and a catch-crop of radish or lettuce can be grown between the rows. The roots can be left in the ground over winter, and lifted as required. Finally, parsnips appear in many appetising recipes. A short variety is usually the best choice.

IN A NUTSHELL

Seed is very light — sow on a still day. Germination is slow in cold weather.

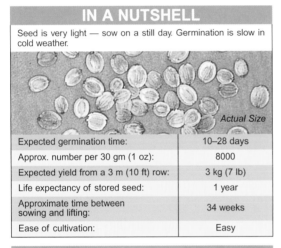

Actual Size

Expected germination time:	10–28 days
Approx. number per 30 gm (1 oz):	8000
Expected yield from a 3 m (10 ft) row:	3 kg (7 lb)
Life expectancy of stored seed:	1 year
Approximate time between sowing and lifting:	34 weeks
Ease of cultivation:	Easy

SOIL FACTS

- If you want to grow long and tapering parsnips you will need a deep, friable and stone-free soil which has been well-manured for a previous crop.
- Any reasonable soil in sun or light shade will grow a good crop of one of the shorter varieties. Dig deeply in autumn or early winter and refrain from adding any fresh manure or compost. Lime if necessary. Break down clods and rake in fertilizer when preparing the seed bed.

SEED SOWING

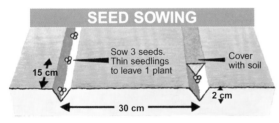

Sow 3 seeds. Thin seedlings to leave 1 plant

Cover with soil

15 cm

2 cm

30 cm

- Use fresh seed every year. February is the traditional month for sowing parsnips, but it is better to wait until March when the weather will be warmer or even April if you are growing one of the shorter-rooted varieties.

CALENDAR

	JAN	FEB	MAR	APR	MAY	JUN	JUL	AUG	SEP	OCT	NOV	DEC
Sowing Time												
Lifting Time												

For key to symbols — see page 7

LOOKING AFTER THE CROP

- Parsnips seldom produce satisfactory roots after transplanting, so throw thinnings away.
- Hoe regularly to keep down weeds. Take care — never touch the crowns of the developing plants. The crop requires very little attention and it is not usually attacked by pests. The leaf-mining celery fly is occasionally a nuisance — squash the blisters between the fingers.
- The soil should not be allowed to dry out, but it will be necessary to water when there is a prolonged dry spell.

HARVESTING

- The roots are ready for lifting when the foliage begins to die down in autumn. It is claimed that the flavour is improved after the first frosts.
- Lift the crop as required, using a fork to loosen the soil. Leave the remainder in the soil for later harvesting. It is a good idea to lift some in November and store as for carrots (see page 40). In this way you will have a supply of parsnips when the soil is frozen or covered with snow. Lift and store any remaining roots at the end of February.

IN THE KITCHEN

Before the potato came to Britain from the New World it was the parsnip which accompanied roasts, game and fish. Nowadays it is regarded as too sweet and too strongly flavoured as an everyday dish, but part of the problem is due to the common habit of boiling it for 25–30 minutes and serving as a straight substitute for boiled potatoes. Parsnips deserve better treatment.

FREEZING: Trim, peel and wash —cut into cubes and blanch for 5 minutes. Freeze in polythene bags.

STORAGE: Store them in a polythene bag in the refrigerator — parsnips will stay fresh for up to 2 weeks.

COOKING: Top and tail with a knife and remove any damaged or diseased parts. Scrub — avoid peeling if you can. Remove central hard core if roots are old. Parboil for 2 minutes and then place around a joint of meat for roasting. Alternatively cut into strips and fry as chips or cut into rings and fry as fritters after dipping in batter. Boil and mash with butter, nutmeg and carrots or go American and glaze them with brown sugar.

VARIETIES

GLADIATOR: An F$_1$ hybrid which has become popular — the wedge-shaped roots are smooth and white-skinned. Resistant to canker.

TENDER AND TRUE: Still the most popular long variety, widely recommended for exhibition. There is very little core and the resistance to canker is high.

COUNTESS: A smooth-skinned maincrop variety noted for its high yields — a winner of the RHS Award of Garden Merit. Resistant to canker. Flavour is rated very highly.

ALBION: Another RHS Award of Garden Merit winner. The roots are long and slender with smooth skin, and the flavour is highly praised. Outstanding resistance to disease.

WHITE GEM: Similar to the old variety Offenham but resistant to canker. Easy to lift, excellent flavour — taking over from Offenham in the catalogues.

STUDENT: Medium-sized — thick and tapering. The one to choose for flavour.

TROUBLES

See pages 42–43

Pea

Home-grown peas are a delight at dinner time. Some of the sugar content of shop-bought peas will have turned to starch at the time of purchase, but there will be no sugar loss with grow-your-own peas if you pick and cook within 10 minutes. Unfortunately peas can be disappointing as a garden crop. The yield can be quite small for the area occupied, and if the soil is poor or the weather is cold you may feel that the effort was not worthwhile. If you do, then remember the taste and remember to follow the golden rules. Grow in fertile soil and never sow when it is cold and wet. Water and hoe when necessary, and keep the birds away. With the right varieties you can then pick peas from May to October.

TYPES

ROUND GARDEN PEA (dried)

WRINKLED GARDEN PEA (dried)

MANGETOUT

PETIT POIS

ASPARAGUS PEA

IN A NUTSHELL

Treat with a fungicidal seed dressing if seed is to be sown in early spring.

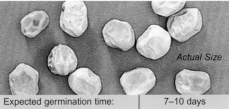

Actual Size

Expected germination time:	7–10 days
Approx. number per ½ litre (1 pint):	1400
Amount required for a 3 m (10 ft) row:	50 cc (¹/₁₂ pint)
Expected yield from a 3 m (10 ft) row:	5 kg (11 lb)
Life expectancy of stored seed:	2 years
Approximate time between autumn sowing and picking:	32 weeks
Approximate time between spring sowing and picking:	12–16 weeks
Ease of cultivation:	Not easy— support, thorough soil preparation and regular picking are all essential

SOIL FACTS

- Under poor soil conditions the yield will be very disappointing. The need is for good structure, adequate humus and enough lime to ensure that the soil is not acid. Avoid adding too much fertilizer — a heavy nitrogen dressing will do more harm than good.

- Choose an open spot which has not grown peas for at least 2 seasons. Dig the soil in autumn or early winter, incorporating 2 bucketsful of well-rotted manure or compost into each sq. m (10 sq. ft) of soil. Apply a light dressing of a general-purpose fertilizer shortly before sowing time.

SEED SOWING

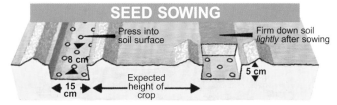

Press into soil surface · 8 cm · 15 cm · Expected height of crop · Firm down soil *lightly* after sowing · 5 cm

LOOKING AFTER THE CROP

- Immediately after sowing you must protect the row from birds. Do not rely on a chemical deterrent — use black cotton stretched between short stakes or plastic netting. You can place twiggy branches over the surface, but best of all are wire-mesh guards.

- Hoe to keep weeds under control. When the seedlings are about 8 cm (3 in.) high insert twigs alongside the stems to provide support. Do not delay this operation — leaving the stems to straggle over the soil surface is likely to result in severe slug damage. Medium- and tall-growing varieties will need extra support — place a strongly erected screen of plastic netting at the side of each row.

- Water during dry spells in summer. Apply a mulch of weedkiller-free grass clippings between the rows in order to conserve moisture.

- Spray the plants with pyrethrins 7–10 days after the start of flowering to avoid maggoty peas.

HARVESTING

- A pod is ready for picking when it is well filled but while there is still a little air space between each pea. Start harvesting at this stage, beginning at the bottom of the stem and working upwards. Use two hands, one to hold the stem and the other to pick off the pod.

- Pick regularly — pods left to mature on the plant will seriously reduce the total yield. If you harvest too many to cook immediately, place the excess in the refrigerator or you can deep freeze them.

- When all the pods have been picked, use the stems for making compost. Leave the roots in the soil.

- To dry peas, allow the pods to mature on the stems — in wet weather lift the plants and hang in bundles indoors until the pods are ripe.

- Pick mangetout when they are about 8 cm (3 in.) long and the peas within are just starting to develop. Asparagus peas are ready when they are 3–5 cm (1–2 in.) long.

IN THE KITCHEN

As the textbooks will tell you, this vegetable has been popular since prehistoric times. An interesting fact which is not usually mentioned is that it was *dried* peas which were part of our staple diet in the old days. Pease pudding, made from dried peas, butter and eggs, was the traditional accompaniment to boiled bacon or pork. It was not until the 17th century that the wealthy and fashionable in Britain adopted the Continental idea of cooking *fresh* peas. Today, of course, almost all of us prefer fresh peas. Pick before maturity and cook as soon as possible after picking. Do not overcook (10 minutes should be enough) and do not use too much water. The rule for shop-bought peas is different — you may need to boil them for 15 minutes.

FREEZING: Use young peas. Shell and blanch for 1 minute. Cool, drain and freeze in polythene bags or rigid containers. Use within 12 months.

STORAGE: Keep in a polythene bag in the refrigerator — peas will stay fresh for up to 3 days.

COOKING: The standard method of boiling peas is given above — for a change you can try *petit pois a la francaise*. A petit pois variety is used, or an ordinary garden variety picked when the peas are small. These are gently cooked with lettuce and shallots or salad onions for about 10 minutes in a covered pan with a tablespoon or two of water, a little butter and a sprinkling of sugar. Boiled peas are usually served as a hot vegetable but they are also a useful salad ingredient when cold. For the thrifty, you will find a recipe for pea pod soup in many cookery books — the soup is mixed in a blender and then sieved to remove the fibre. With mangetout the pods are not a problem. You eat them pods and all — raw when small and fresh or boiled for 3 minutes and then tossed in butter. Asparagus peas, like mangetout, are not shelled before eating — boil or steam for 5 minutes.

CALENDAR

		JAN	FEB	MAR	APR	MAY	JUN	JUL	AUG	SEP	OCT	NOV	DEC
For a May/June Crop: Choose a sheltered site — expect some losses if the site is cold and exposed. Grow a round variety — Feltham First is reliable for both early spring and late sowing. Meteor has an excellent reputation for hardiness. Cover seedlings and plants with cloches.	Sowing Time		▓	▓							▓	▓	
	Picking Time					▓	▓						
For a June/July Crop: For a mid March sowing choose a round variety or a First Early wrinkled variety such as Kelvedon Wonder or Early Onward. For late March or April sowing pick a Second Early wrinkled type — Onward is the usual choice but Hurst Green Shaft is a good alternative.	Sowing Time			▓	▓								
	Picking Time						▓	▓					
For an August Crop: Use a Maincrop wrinkled variety — be guided by the height on the back of the packet rather than the pretty picture on the front. If space is limited choose a medium-height pea such as Ambassador — leave Alderman for the people who can spare 1.5 m (5 ft) between the rows.	Sowing Time					▓							
	Picking Time							▓	▓				
For an Autumn Crop: Fresh peas are especially welcome in September and October when the main picking season is over. June-July is the sowing season and you must choose the right type — a First Early wrinkled variety with good mildew resistance. Neither Kelvedon Wonder nor Pioneer will let you down.	Sowing Time						▓	▓					
	Picking Time									▓	▓		
Mangetout & Petit pois: Sow seed when the soil has started to warm up in April — sowing can be delayed until May. Neither mangetout nor petit pois have become popular like garden peas — you may have to send off for seeds if your local garden shop does not carry them.	Sowing Time				▓	▓							
	Picking Time							▓	▓				
Asparagus Pea: Sow seed in mid or late May so that the seedlings will appear after the last frosts have gone. Make 3 cm (1 in.) deep drills about 40 cm (16 in.) apart and sow seeds at 15 cm (6 in.) intervals. The harvest period usually starts at the beginning of August.	Sowing Time					▓							
	Picking Time								▓				

For key to symbols — see page 7

VARIETIES

ROUND varieties

The seeds of these varieties remain smooth and round when dried. They are all First Earlies — hardier and quicker maturing than other types and more able to withstand poor growing conditions than the wrinkled types. Round varieties are used for late autumn and early spring sowing.

FELTHAM FIRST: 45 cm (18 in.). An old favourite which requires little support, producing 10 cm (4 in.) long pointed pods 11–12 weeks after sowing.

METEOR: 30 cm (1 ft). The baby of the group with a high reputation for succeeding in cold and exposed sites.

PILOT: 1 m (3 ft). Once popular but now very hard to find. It combines earliness with a heavy crop. It is a good choice for a May/June crop.

DOUCE PROVENCE: 45 cm (18 in.). Perhaps you are looking for maximum sweetness rather than maximum yield. Douce Provence is the one to choose — it has all the robustness of Feltham First but the flavour is superior.

FORTUNE: 45 cm (18 in.). Similar to Feltham First, but matures later and yields are higher. Hard to find.

Feltham First

WRINKLED varieties

Kelvedon Wonder

The seeds of these varieties are distinctly wrinkled when dried. These 'marrowfat' peas are sweeter, larger and heavier cropping than the round ones, and are therefore much more widely grown. They are, however, less hardy and should not be sown before March. These wrinkled varieties are classified in two ways. Firstly by height (there are the 45–60 cm/1½–2 ft dwarfs and the 1.5 m/ 5 ft tall varieties) and secondly by the time taken from sowing to first picking. First Earlies take 11–12 weeks, Second Earlies 13–14 weeks and Maincrop 15–16 weeks. In catalogues and garden centres you will find a large choice from each group.

First Earlies
KELVEDON WONDER: 45 cm (1½ ft). An excellent choice if you want to buy just one variety for successional sowings. A good one to pick for early sowing or for sowing in June for an autumn crop. Mildew resistance is high.

LITTLE MARVEL: 45 cm (1½ ft). All the catalogues list it, but Little Marvel is not as popular as Kelvedon Wonder. The flavour is good and the blunt-ended pods are borne in pairs.

EARLY ONWARD: 60 cm (2 ft). Look for its more famous brother in the Second Earlies section. This one has all the Onward characteristics, but matures about 10 days earlier.

TWINKLE: 45 cm (1½ ft). A March sown crop will be ready for picking in May. Shows good resistance to both wilt and mildew.

EXZELLENZ: 60 cm (2 ft). Long, pointed pods bearing up to 10 sweet-tasting peas.

PIONEER: 45 cm (1½ ft). A useful variety for early sowing and also for June sowing as, like Kelvedon Wonder, it resists mildew. Unfortunately, you will have to search for it these days.

Second Earlies
HURST GREEN SHAFT: 75 cm (2½ ft). All the catalogues sing its praises — pods with 10 peas borne in pairs at the top of the plant to make picking easier, pods which can win prizes at the show and peas to win praise in the dining room. Resistant to both mildew and fusarium wilt.

ONWARD: 75 cm (2½ ft). The most popular garden pea. It crops heavily and has good disease resistance. The pods are plump, blunt-ended and dark green.

LINCOLN: 60 cm (2 ft). The pods are small, but yields are good and the peas are very sweet. The plants are bushy and compact so little support is needed.

ALEXANDRA: 1.5 m (5 ft). This variety is the giant among the Second Earlies. Crops are heavy and each large pod contains 10 peas or more. Too big for most people, so suppliers are hard to find.

Maincrops
RONDO: 1 m (3 ft). It is claimed that this variety outperformed its rivals in trials. The long straight pods contain about 10 peas — good wilt resistance.

ALDERMAN: 1.5 m (5 ft). Quite a giant — popular with exhibitors. The large pods contain 11 large peas. Yields are high and the picking season is prolonged.

ZEPHYR: 60 cm (2 ft). This variety has a good reputation for performing well on heavy soil and for resisting mildew and wilt. Few leaves — so picking is easy.

AMBASSADOR: 75 cm (2½ ft). Another semi-leafless variety with high resistance to wilt and mildew. Stands up well to poor weather — an RHS Award of Garden Merit winner.

MANGETOUT varieties

Oregon Sugar Pod

There are several names for this group — Chinese peas, snow peas, sugar peas and eat-all. They are rather easier to grow than garden peas — pick before the seeds swell and cook the pods whole.

OREGON SUGAR POD: 1 m (3 ft). A popular variety listed in many catalogues — pods can reach 10 cm (4 in.), but pick at the 8 cm (3 in.) stage.

DELIKATA: 60 cm (2 ft). Harvest young pods as mangetout or leave to mature for podding. Highly rated.

SUGAR SNAP: 1.5 m (5 ft). A dual-purpose pea — when the pods are young they are cooked like a true mangetout variety. More mature pods with peas inside can be 'stringed' and then cooked like French beans or shelled and cooked like peas.

SUGAR ANN: 75 cm (2½ ft). The favourite snap pea variety. Early maturing and very productive — the flavour is excellent.

PETIT POIS varieties

Waverex

Petit pois are not immature peas gathered from small pods of any garden pea variety — they are a small number of dwarf varieties which produce unusually small peas which are uniquely sweet.

PEAWEE 65: 75 cm (2½ ft). The usual choice for petit pois fans. They obtain an abundant supply of pods, each one containing about 10 small peas which are full of flavour. Good resistance to mildew and wilt.

WAVEREX: 60 cm (2 ft). The petit pois you are most likely to find. Eat raw in salads or cook the French way described on page 78.

CALIBRA: 75 cm (2½ ft). A petit pois variety which was launched as an improvement on Waverex. Sow in March-June for a May-September crop.

ASPARAGUS PEA variety
This variety is also known as the winged pea. It is not really a pea at all — it is a vetch which produces sprawling bushy plants. It is not frost-hardy, so sowing must be delayed until May. The red flowers which appear in summer are followed by curiously shaped winged pods — these must be gathered whilst they are still small or they will be fibrous and stringy. The small pods are cooked whole like mangetout.

TROUBLES
See pages 20–22

Potato

Early varieties give you 'new' potatoes in summer — Maincrops provide you with tubers for eating in autumn and for storing over winter for later use. Where the plot is large you can grow both Earlies and Maincrops to ensure a long harvesting period — where space is limited make an Early variety your choice. The yield will be lower than from a Maincrop, but the plants will take up less space, miss the ravages of blight and provide new potatoes when shop prices are high. It may be that the vegetable area in the garden is too small for even Early potatoes — you can then turn to container growing. Place a layer of soil at the bottom of a large tub or bucket (drainage holes are essential) and place seed tubers of a First Early variety on top. Cover with more soil, and add more soil when shoots appear — keep adding soil to keep the tubers covered. Now for the rules for growing in the garden. Buy certified seed and grow the crop on land which has been dug in autumn — liming is rarely necessary. The ground should not have been used recently for growing potatoes. Earthing-up will be necessary to keep tubers covered.

IN A NUTSHELL

Seed should be the size of a small hen's egg (30–55 gm / 1–2 oz). Do not plant diseased or soft seed potatoes. Large seed should not be cut in half.

rose end
most eyes occur in this area

½ Actual Size

Amount required for a 3 m (10 ft) row:	700 gm (1½ lb)
Expected yield from a 3 m (10 ft) row:	5 kg (11 lb) (Early varieties) 9 kg (20 lb) (Maincrop varieties)
Approximate time between planting and lifting:	13 weeks (Early varieties) 22 weeks (Maincrop varieties)
Ease of cultivation:	Not difficult — but high yields call for watering and spraying

SOIL FACTS

- Potatoes can be grown in practically every soil type. It is the best crop to grow in grassland or wasteland which is to be turned into a vegetable plot — earthing-up and the dense leaf canopy help to clean up new ground. In the established vegetable plot potatoes should not be grown on land which has been used for this crop within the past 2 seasons.

- Choose a sunny spot if possible and avoid frost pockets. Dig the soil in autumn and add compost if the soil was not manured for the previous crop.

- Wireworms are likely to be a problem in newly-dug grassland, but pesticides to control this pest are no longer available. Break down any clods and sprinkle a compound fertilizer over the surface.

PLANTING

- When you obtain your seed potatoes in February set them out (rose end uppermost) in egg boxes or in wooden trays containing a 3 cm (1 in.) layer of sand. Keep them in a light (not sunny) frost-free room and in about 6 weeks there will be several sturdy 1–3 cm (½–1 in.) shoots. Do not remove any of these sprouts. Chitting is vital for Earlies and useful for Maincrops.

30 cm (Early varieties)
40 cm (Maincrop varieties)
Cover tuber with fine soil
Replace earth carefully. Make a low ridge with a rake
12 cm
60 cm (Early varieties)
75 cm (Maincrop varieties)

LOOKING AFTER THE CROP

- If there is a danger of frost when the shoots have begun to emerge draw a little soil over them for protection.

- When the haulm is about 25 cm (10 in.) high it is time for earthing-up. First of all, break up the soil between the rows with a fork and remove weeds. Use a draw hoe to pile the loose soil against the stems to produce a flat-topped ridge about 15 cm (6 in.) high. Some people like to earth-up a little at a time, but there is little evidence that such a procedure gives better results than the one-step method.

- Water liberally in dry weather — this is most important once the tubers have started to form.

HARVESTING

- With Earlies wait until the flowers open or the buds drop. Carefully remove soil from a small part of the ridge and examine the tubers. They are ready for harvesting as new potatoes when they are the size of hens' eggs — insert a flat-tined fork into the ridge well away from the haulm and lift the roots forward into the trench.

- With Maincrops for storage cut off the haulm once the foliage has turned brown and the stems have withered. Remove the cut haulm and wait 10 days — then lift the roots and let the tubers dry for several hours. Place them in a wooden box and store in a dark, frost-free shed — they should keep until the spring.

- When harvesting remove all tubers from the soil, however small, to avoid problems next year.

IN THE KITCHEN

We cook potatoes every day and so the experienced cook will probably not bother to read this section. Certainly a short summary cannot begin to describe the 500 ways of serving potatoes, but there are a few rules for the everyday methods which are frequently ignored. New potatoes are earlies lifted before the plant has reached maturity and before the skins of the tubers have set. Rub the skin of a raw potato gently — if it does not come off readily then it doesn't deserve the title 'new'. Serve them boiled — hot, or cold in salads. Use old potatoes (maincrops which have been allowed to set their skins) for the multitude of other uses — chipped, mashed, creamed, baked, sautéed, roasted and so on.

FREEZING: Blanch whole new potatoes in water and chips in oil — blanching time 3 minutes. Cool and drain — then pack and freeze in rigid containers.

STORAGE: Store in a cool, dark place. In the kitchen you can keep new potatoes in a polythene bag in the refrigerator — potatoes will stay fresh for up to 2 weeks.

COOKING: First of all, new potatoes. Wash under running water and either leave skins on or rub off with your fingers. Boil for 12 minutes with a sprig of mint. Drain, and then toss in a little butter. Now for old potatoes — scrub under running water and scrape off the skin if you can — peeling removes much of the vitamin C which is just below the surface. For boiling, cut into chunks and cook for 15–20 minutes; for roasting parboil for 5 minutes and put around the roast for 45 minutes. Cooking the perfect chip is an art — cut 2 cm (⅔ in.) thick strips and wash in ice-cold water to remove the surface starch. Drain and dry thoroughly in a cloth, then fry until golden as a shallow layer in a frying basket in a pan one-third full of oil at 180ºC (350ºF). Drain and serve. Baking is much easier — wash, dry and prick the surface all over with a fork. Brush lightly with oil and bake for 1 hour at 200ºC (400ºF). In a microwave oven you will only have to wait for about 10 minutes. Potatoes *duchesse, anna, château, rösti, pont-neuf, dauphine* … you'll find them all in a good cookery book.

- **First Early varieties**: Plant seed potatoes in late March — a week or two earlier in southerly areas and a couple of weeks later in the north. Harvest in June or July.
- **Second Early varieties**: Plant in early-mid April and lift in July or August.
- **Maincrop varieties**: Plant in mid-late April. Some of the tubers can be lifted in August for immediate use but potatoes for storage should be harvested in September or early October.

CALENDAR

	JAN	FEB	MAR	APR	MAY	JUN	JUL	AUG	SEP	OCT	NOV	DEC
Planting Time			▓	▓								
Lifting Time						▓	▓	▓	▓	▓		

For key to symbols — see page 7

VARIETIES

FIRST EARLY varieties

Potatoes are available in a wide range of shapes, sizes, colours and textures. The skin may be red, yellow or white and the flesh pale cream or yellow. Texture may be waxy or floury and the shape is round, oval or long. Variety is the basic deciding factor with regard to shape and quality but both soil type and weather play a part.

Round

Oval

Long

Duke of York

ARRAN PILOT: Long; white flesh. An old favourite, now being replaced by modern varieties. A heavy cropper which does best in light soil in southern counties.

DUKE OF YORK: Oval; yellow flesh. This variety will succeed in nearly all areas and soil types, and is reputed to have the finest flavour among the First Earlies.

ROCKET: Round; white flesh. A variety of the 1980s bred in Cambridge. It has become popular — the yields are good and the egg-sized tubers have waxy flesh. Tuber blight can be a problem.

MARIS BARD: Oval; white flesh. The earliest of all, producing heavy crops of waxy, well-flavoured tubers. Scab resistance is slight, but resistance to virus is high.

FOREMOST: Oval; white flesh. Value in the kitchen is its selling point — good flavour and stays firm when boiled.

EPICURE: Round; white flesh. An old variety which is chosen by people seeking an 'old-fashioned' flavour. Hardier than most on cold, exposed sites.

SHARPE'S EXPRESS: Long; white flesh. Once available everywhere — now pushed aside by the new varieties. Still a good choice for heavy soil. Rather late, but tubers store well.

CASABLANCA: Oval; creamy flesh. A heavy-cropping variety producing lots of exhibition quality tubers. Good for boiling.

SWIFT: Oval; white flesh. Low-growing and very early — ideal for growing under fleece or cloches.

PENTLAND JAVELIN: Oval; white flesh. One of the modern varieties which is later than most First Earlies but produces heavy crops which are resistant to scab and some strains of eelworm. The texture is waxy.

Pentland Javelin

Wilja

Desiree

Pentland Crown

SECOND EARLY varieties

NADINE: Round; white flesh. An attractive potato which has replaced a number of old favourites. The tubers are smooth and uniform, making this variety a good exhibition potato. Flavour rating is high. An added benefit is its high resistance to eelworm and scab.

CHARLOTTE: Long-oval; creamy flesh. A favourite salad potato at the supermarkets, and an RHS Award of Garden Merit for its qualities as a grow-your-own vegetable. Waxy flesh.

KESTREL: Oval; white flesh. Considered by many as the best Second Early. White smooth skin and violet eyes make it a popular show variety. Good for roasting and chips.

WILJA: Oval; pale yellow flesh. According to many experts this variety, Nadine and Estima are the ones to choose. High yields, excellent cooking qualities and reliability are the reasons for its popularity.

ESTIMA: Oval; pale yellow flesh. Another modern Dutch variety which is a popular choice because of its attractively-shaped tubers and heavy crops. Scab can be a problem.

MARIS PEER: Oval; white flesh. Good yields and some resistance to both scab and blight — but it will fail miserably in dry soil which is not irrigated.

ANYA: Long; white flesh. Pink-skinned and knobbly with waxy flesh — a salad potato bred from the old favourite salad Maincrop Pink Fir Apple.

MAINCROP varieties

MARIS PIPER: Oval; creamy flesh. One of the varieties which has taken over from the once popular Majestic. It has its problems — scab, slug and drought resistance are low, but it gives excellent yields and its cooking qualities are rated highly.

MAJESTIC: Long; white flesh. Now about 100 years old, it is less vigorous than it used to be. It has been pushed out of the recommended lists by modern varieties, but it still keeps its reputation as a fine potato for making chips.

DESIREE: Oval; pale yellow flesh. The combination of good characteristics found in this pink-skinned variety makes it hard to beat. It is a very heavy cropper and succeeds in all soil types. It has good drought resistance and the waxy-textured tubers have an excellent flavour.

PENTLAND CROWN: Oval; white flesh. This late Maincrop is claimed to produce higher yields than other popular varieties — grow it for its good resistance to blight, scab and virus but not for its keeping and cooking qualities, which are only moderate.

LADY BALFOUR: Oval; creamy flesh. A white-skinned potato splashed with pink. It has several selling points — good yields in all sorts of conditions and good resistance against both blight and eelworm.

INTERNATIONAL KIDNEY: Oval; creamy flesh. Can be grown as a Second Early if chitted — sold as Jersey Royals. Waxy flesh with a buttery taste — recommended for boiling and salads.

KING EDWARD: Oval; creamy flesh. This red-blotched variety is one of the best known of all potatoes and is still grown by gardeners who are looking for cooking quality rather than quantity.

CARA: Round; creamy flesh. This high-yielding potato stores well and the pink-eyed tubers are excellent for baking. There is some blight resistance but it has a drawback — it is a late maturing variety.

VALOR: Oval; white flesh. This heavy-cropping variety is recommended for poor-quality soils. There is some resistance to blight and eelworm. A general-purpose potato.

GOLDEN WONDER: Long; yellow flesh. The best-flavoured of all potatoes according to many books, but it is rarely a good choice. It needs well-manured soil and is susceptible to both drought and slugs. Tubers are small and yields are low.

PINK FIR APPLE: Long; yellow flesh. This peculiar variety is over a century old and is worth trying, although the yields may disappoint you. The long, irregular tubers are waxy and have a new-potato flavour — serve hot or cold.

PICASSO: Round-oval; creamy flesh. A general-purpose variety which stores well. It has a good reputation for both drought and eelworm tolerance. Bright red eyes.

ROMANO: Oval; white flesh. A red-skinned variety with waxy-textured tubers. It stores and cooks well but you must water when the weather is dry.

CHRISTMAS POTATOES

New potatoes for Christmas Dinner — something of a gamble but worth trying if you want to beat the Jones's. When lifting your crop of First Earlies in July set a few tubers aside. Plant them in a warm spot in the garden and look after them in the normal way. In late September cover the plants with large cloches and then get busy with a fork on Christmas Eve.

POTATOES UNDER PLASTIC

The practice of growing potatoes under plastic saves you the chore of earthing-up. After planting, the row is covered with a sheet of black plastic — before putting down the sheet scatter slug pellets along the mounded ridge. Push the edges of the plastic sheet into the soil with a spade. As the haulm emerges it will push against the plastic sheet — at this stage cut a slit and pull through the young stems.

There are many advantages with this method of growing — the soil is warmer and moister, and potatoes can be harvested a few at a time simply by lifting up a section of the sheet. Weeds are suppressed and the chore of earthing-up is removed, but there are drawbacks. There is the cost of the plastic and the menace of slugs.

POTATO TROUBLES

Many diseases, pests and disorders can attack potatoes and reduce yields, but only four are likely to be a serious threat. Three of these are pests — potato cyst eelworm, slugs and wireworm. The other one is a disease — potato blight. The virus diseases can be a menace and you should therefore buy seed which is known to be virus-free.

	Symptom	Likely Causes
Seed potatoes	— thin, long sprouts	[2]
	— no sprouts	[11]
Leaves	— pale green or yellow	[6] or [12] or [14] or Drought
	— pale green or yellow mottling	[4] or [9]
	— yellow or brown between veins	[10]
	— rolled, brittle	[3]
	— torn	[9]
	— brown patches	[1]
	— many small holes	[7]
	— tiny brown spots	[7]
	— greenfly clusters	[6]
Stems	— tunnelled	[13]
	— blackened at base	[12]
Roots	— covered with tiny cysts	[14]
Tubers	— abnormally small	[3] or [4] or [12] or [14] or Drought
	— contain narrow tunnels	[21]
	— contain wide tunnels	[15] or Millepede (see page 157) or Cutworm (see page 157)
	— hollowed out	[23] or [26]
	— split	[22]
	— scabby spots on surface	[16] or [18]
	— wrinkled area, small woolly growths	[20]
	— brown lines in flesh	[17]
	— brown areas under skin	[19]
	— flesh slimy, evil-smelling	[25]
	— sunken brown area on surface	[26]
	— cauliflower-like warty outgrowths	[24]
	— black at centre	[8]
	— poor flavour or texture	[8]
	— soft at lifting time	[5]

BROWN-BLOTCHED LEAVES

1 POTATO BLIGHT

Blight is the most serious potato disease, capable of destroying all the foliage during August in a wet season. The first signs are brown patches on the leaves. Look on the underside of the leaflets — each blight spot has a white mould fringe in damp weather.

Treatment: None, once the disease has firmly taken hold.

Prevention: Plant healthy seed tubers. Spray with Copper in July and repeat at fortnightly intervals if the weather is damp. If blight spots are already present, spraying will slow down the spread of the disease to other plants.

2 SPINDLY SPROUTS

By far the most common cause of spindly sprouts is keeping the tubers too dark or too warm prior to planting. If threadlike shoots form despite standing the tubers in a light, cool place then virus infection is a possible cause. Alternatively the tubers may have been slightly frosted. Always buy good quality seed potatoes and sprout them in a light, frost-free location.

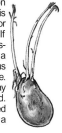

5 SOFT TUBERS

Some of the tubers lifted after an extremely dry summer may appear to be perfectly sound on the outside but are soft and rubbery to the touch. This is not a disease; it is a disorder caused by the plant withdrawing water from the developing tubers. It can be prevented by watering thoroughly during drought.

ROLLED LEAFLETS

3 LEAF ROLL VIRUS

Leaf roll is one of the most serious virus diseases which attack potatoes. Leaflets roll upward and become hard and brittle. Affected plants are stunted and the yields are poor.

Treatment: None.

Prevention: Use virus-free seed. Spray with insecticidal soap to control the virus-carrying aphids.

MOTTLED LEAVES

4 MOSAIC VIRUS

There are several mosaic diseases, and the symptoms vary with the potato variety grown. The usual tell-tale sign is yellow or pale green mottling over the whole leaf surface. Brown streaks may also appear.

Treatment: None.

Prevention: Use virus-free seed. Spray with insecticidal soap to control the virus-carrying aphids.

POTATO TROUBLES continued

6 | APHID (Greenfly)

In a dry warm season the foliage may be heavily infested with greenfly. Plants are weakened and leaflets turn brown and may die. The most serious effect is the spread of virus diseases by these sap-sucking pests.

Treatment: Spray with insecticidal soap.

Prevention: No practical method available.

INSECTS ON LEAVES

1 cm (⅓ in.) greenish insects

7 | CAPSID BUG

Small brown spots which later turn into holes appear on the foliage. Young shoots may be distorted and the crinkling of small leaflets may be severe.

Treatment: Damage is usually too slight to affect yield. Spray the plants with insecticidal soap if attack is severe.

Prevention: No practical method available.

YELLOW-BLOTCHED LEAVES

9 | FROST

Late spring frosts can severely damage the young shoots, delaying the development of early varieties. A severe frost can turn the stems black; less severe frosts cause yellow patches and torn leaflets on the older foliage.

Treatment: None.

Prevention: Cover shoots of Earlies with newspaper if frosts are expected.

8 | POOR QUALITY

The cooking and eating qualities of tubers can sometimes be disappointing. Obviously all the tuber troubles described on the next page make kitchen use difficult or impossible, but several disorders do not show up until the potatoes are being cooked or eaten. A **soapy texture** is usually due to lifting the tubers before they are mature. It can also be caused by growing potatoes on chalky soil. A **sweet taste** is usually due to keeping the tubers too cold during storage. An **earthy taste** is caused by the presence of powdery scab. Potatoes sometimes have a **black heart** or turn **black when cooked**. The major causes are storage at over 38°C (100°F) and potash deficiency.

11 | GAPPING

The failure of seed potatoes to develop sprouts is usually due to the presence of disease in the tuber. Another possible reason for this failure is the frosting of the seed tubers in transit or during storage. If such faulty seed is planted then a gap will occur where a plant should be.

BROWNING BETWEEN VEINS

10 | MAGNESIUM DEFICIENCY

The first symptom is a yellowing of the tissue between the veins of the leaflets. These yellow areas then turn brown and brittle. Growth is stunted.

Treatment: Apply a trace element spray. Repeat if necessary.

Prevention: Feed regularly during the growing season with a fertilizer, which contains magnesium as well as nitrogen, phosphates and potash.

BLACKENED STEMS

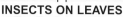

12 | BLACKLEG

Tell-tale sign is the blackening of the stems at and below ground level. The leaves turn yellow and wilt; eventually the haulm withers. This disease attacks early in the season and is worst in heavy soils and rainy weather.

Treatment: None. Lift and burn affected plants.

Prevention: Never plant seed tubers which are soft and rotten. The practice of making seed potatoes go further by cutting them increases the risk of attack.

TUNNELLED STEMS

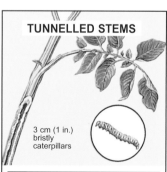

3 cm (1 in.) bristly caterpillars

13 | ROSY RUSTIC MOTH

Potatoes grown in new gardens may have their stems hollowed out by these caterpillars. Affected plants die down earlier than normal.

Treatment: None. Dig out and destroy infested plants.

Prevention: No practical method available.

WITHERED LOWER LEAVES

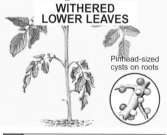

Pinhead-sized cysts on roots

14 | POTATO CYST EELWORM

Plants appear weak and stunted. Lower leaves wither away; upper leaves are pale green and wilt during the day. Haulm dies down prematurely. Marble-sized tubers are produced.

Treatment: None. Destroy infected plants and tubers.

Prevention: Practise crop rotation. Do not grow a susceptible variety on infected land for at least 6 years — grow a resistant variety instead.

TUBER TROUBLES

15 | SLUGS

Attacks begin in August — Maincrop potatoes grown in heavy soil can be ruined.

Treatment: None.

Prevention: Avoid susceptible varieties. Apply slug pellets in July. Lift the crop as soon as the tubers are mature.

Large holes eaten in flesh

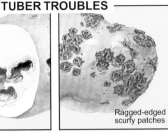

Ragged-edged scurfy patches

16 | COMMON SCAB

Disease is only skin deep; eating qualities unaffected. Most severe on light soils under dry conditions.

Treatment: None.

Prevention: Dig in compost but do not lime before planting. Grow a resistant variety (e.g Wilja).

17 | SPRAING

Tubers are normal on the surface — discoloured inside. There are several causes — viruses, trace element deficiency or water shortage.

Treatment: None.

Prevention: Practise crop rotation. Do not grow Pentland Dell, which is very susceptible.

Curved lines in flesh

Round patches with raised margins

18 | POWDERY SCAB

Much less frequent than common scab. Most severe on heavy soils under wet conditions. Scabs are powdery on the surface.

Treatment: None.

Prevention: Practise crop rotation. Do not grow susceptible varieties (e.g Cara, Estima and Pentland Crown).

19 | POTATO BLIGHT

Caused by blight spores from the leaves reaching the tubers. Affected potatoes rot in store.

Treatment: None. Do not store.

Prevention: Keep haulm well earthed-up. If there is blight on the leaves then cut off and destroy stems 10 days before lifting.

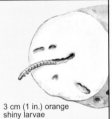

Grey patches, reddish brown below skin

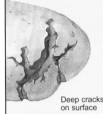

Shrunken area, whitish pustules

20 | DRY ROT

Dry rot occurs in store. Careless handling when lifting makes tubers more susceptible.

Treatment: None. Destroy tubers.

Prevention: Practise crop rotation. Store only sound, healthy tubers and keep them in a cool but not over-dry atmosphere.

21 | WIREWORM

Wireworm is a serious pest in new gardens, especially in wet summers. Tubers are riddled with narrow tunnels.

Treatment: None.

Prevention: No insecticide for use below ground is available.

3 cm (1 in.) orange shiny larvae

Deep cracks on surface

22 | SPLITTING

Deep cracks make the tubers difficult to peel. The affected potatoes are also very susceptible to rotting in store and so should be used immediately.

Treatment: None.

Prevention: Keep plants well watered during dry spells.

23 | HOLLOW HEART

Affects large tubers. Caused by a prolonged wet spell after dry weather. Hollow-hearted potatoes may rot in store.

Treatment: None.

Prevention: Keep plants well watered during dry spells.

Hollow centre

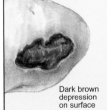

Black warty outgrowths

24 | WART DISEASE

Once very serious, now uncommon as nearly all modern varieties are immune.

Treatment: None. Destroy affected tubers. DEFRA must be informed of the outbreak.

Prevention: Plant only immune varieties on infected land.

25 | SOFT ROT

Soft rot is an infection which attacks damaged tubers. Affected tubers soon become slimy and putrid and are quite unusable.

Treatment: None. Destroy tubers.

Prevention: Store only sound, healthy tubers and make sure they do not become damp.

Soft, evil-smelling flesh

Dark brown depression on surface

26 | GANGRENE

Gangrene occurs in store. Inside of tuber becomes decayed and hollow.

Treatment: None. Remove from store.

Prevention: Store only sound, healthy tubers and make sure the store is airy and frost-free.

Radish

The summer or salad radish is an ideal starter vegetable for children — it is practically trouble-free and the round or long roots are ready for salads or sandwiches in about a month. On the vegetable plot the well-known red and white-and-red varieties are used to fill the space between rows of peas or carrots, or mixed with slow-germinating seeds such as parsley, parsnips and onions to grow and so mark out the row before the main vegetable needs the space. It is a pity that so many people don't take their interest in radishes beyond this point. There are a number of unusual varieties for you to grow — small yellow roots, large Japanese types for pulling in winter or summer, and even a radish which is grown for its pods rather than its roots (see page 122).

IN A NUTSHELL

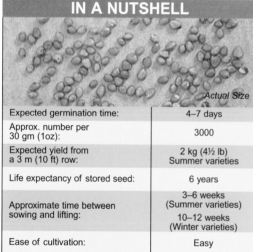

Actual Size

Expected germination time:	4–7 days
Approx. number per 30 gm (1oz):	3000
Expected yield from a 3 m (10 ft) row:	2 kg (4½ lb) Summer varieties
Life expectancy of stored seed:	6 years
Approximate time between sowing and lifting:	3–6 weeks (Summer varieties) 10–12 weeks (Winter varieties)
Ease of cultivation:	Easy

SOIL FACTS

- All the textbooks will tell you that radishes relish a reasonably fertile, well-drained soil which is adequately supplied with humus and free from stones, but summer radishes usually have to put up with an odd corner without any thought about soil preparation.

- Despite this lowly status, they should be given some soil preparation so as to ensure the quick growth which is essential for tenderness and flavour. Dig leaf mould or well-rotted compost into the soil if it was not manured for a previous crop — apply a general-purpose fertilizer before sowing and rake to a fine tilth.

- Choose a sunny spot for spring sowing but the summer crop needs some shade — sow between other vegetables.

- **Summer varieties:** Sow under cloches in January or February or outdoors in March. For a prolonged supply sow every few weeks or try 'Mixed Radish' seed which contains varieties which mature at different times. Sowing after early June often gives disappointing results.

- **Winter varieties:** Sow in July or early August. Lift roots from late October onwards.

SEED SOWING

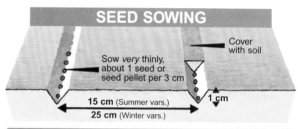

Cover with soil

Sow *very* thinly, about 1 seed or seed pellet per 3 cm

15 cm (Summer vars.)
25 cm (Winter vars.)

1 cm

LOOKING AFTER THE CROP

- With the summer varieties little or no thinning should be necessary — if there is any overcrowding then thin immediately so that the plants are spaced at 3 cm / 1 in. (small radishes) or 5–10 cm (2–4 in.) intervals (larger and Japanese radishes). With the winter varieties thin to leave the plants 15 cm (6 in.) apart — thin before the plants are overcrowded.

- Protect the crop against birds if they are a nuisance in your area. Spray with pyrethrins if flea beetles begin to perforate the leaves.

- Hoe to keep down weeds. Water if the soil is dry — rapid and uninterrupted growth is essential for top quality. Summer radish is not an easy crop to grow in July or August when the weather is hot and dry. Swelling is often unsatisfactory and the roots may be woody and peppery.

HARVESTING

- Pull the summer varieties when the globular ones are the diameter of a 10p coin and the intermediates are no longer than your thumb. They can, of course, grow much longer but overgrown specimens would be woody and hollow.

- Japanese varieties are best when pulled at the 15 cm (6 in.) stage but can be grown longer if required for cooking.

- The winter varieties can be left in the soil and lifted as required, provided that you cover the crowns with straw or bracken. It is better to lift them in November and store as for carrots (see page 40).

CALENDAR

	JAN	FEB	MAR	APR	MAY	JUN	JUL	AUG	SEP	OCT	NOV	DEC
Sowing Time												
Lifting Time												

IN THE KITCHEN

Thinly-sliced summer radishes may be a satisfactory way of decorating a salad plate but they are not a suitable way of savouring this vegetable. The proper way was described hundreds of years ago — wash and trim each root, then cut off the foliage so as to leave the bottom 3 cm (1 in.) of the stalks to serve as a handle. You hold the handle and eat with coarse bread, butter, salt, cheese … and alcohol. Radishes have been used as an appetiser since the dawn of history and the Ancient Egyptians fed them to the pyramid-makers. Despite this long history of the radish as a health-giver and sustainer of the poor, it will remain primarily a garnish for salads. To make radish roses, cut off the stalk end and make a number of cuts from the stalk end to the root. Place the cut radishes in iced water for ½ hour and the 'petals' will open.

STORAGE: Keep in a polythene bag in the refrigerator — radishes will stay fresh for up to 1 week.

COOKING: Summer radishes are for eating raw and the Winter varieties are for cooking or pickling, according to the general rule. After peeling, boil the sliced or cubed radish in lightly salted water for about 10 minutes. Drain thoroughly and serve with parsley sauce or tossed in butter. This is not the only or even the best way to cook radish — thin slices or strips of a winter variety or one of the larger summer types can be stir-fried. This means that despite the general rule the Japanese-type of summer radish is suitable for cooking — and to break the rule still further the winter radishes can be peeled and then grated or sliced for eating raw in salads. The texture is somewhat coarse and the flavour is rather pungent, but how else can you enjoy fresh radishes from the garden with your Christmas Dinner?

VARIETIES

  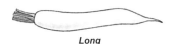

SUMMER varieties

Globular *Intermediate* *Long*

This is by far the more popular group — the radishes which garnish the salad plate. Most (but not all) are small and the usual colour is all-red or a red/white mixture. There are variations — the Japanese types which can grow 30 cm (1 ft) long and the yellow and all-white varieties which have never become really popular.

CHERRY BELLE: Globular; all-red. A very popular radish — cherry-coloured on the outside and white, crisp and mild inside. It will remain in the ground for a considerable time without going pithy.

SCARLET GLOBE: Globular; all-red. Another popular round radish with bright red skin. A quick-maturing variety for early spring sowing.

PRINZ ROTIN: Globular; all-red. One of the radishes for which it is claimed that the roots remain crisp and mild even when they are double or treble the diameter of a normal round radish. A good choice if you plan to sow in the difficult midsummer period.

GIANT OF SICILY: This one is for cutting between spring and autumn — roots measure about 5 cm (2 in.) across.

FRENCH BREAKFAST: Intermediate; red/white. One of the most popular of all radishes. The cylindrical roots are crisp and mild when pulled at the proper time but hot and woody if harvesting is delayed.

ROUGETTE: A quick-growing variety with red globular roots. On open ground it can be sown for an April-October harvest — its low growth habit means it can be grown under cloches.

LONG WHITE ICICLE: Long; white. An excellent choice, producing in a few weeks 8 cm (3 in.) long roots which are crisp and nutty-flavoured. It has never become popular as we expect radishes to be red.

MINOWASA SUMMER: A Mooli or Japanese-type radish producing roots up to 30 cm (1 ft) long. Sow in May and begin pulling when the roots are 15 cm (6 in.) long — harvesting can continue for about a month.

Scarlet Globe

French Breakfast

WINTER varieties

The Cinderella group, rarely grown and only a few varieties are listed in the catalogues. The roots are large — some reaching 30 cm (1 ft) or more. They have white, black or pink skins and a flavour which is usually stronger than the summer varieties.

CHINA ROSE: Not really a giant — the oval roots are about 15 cm (6 in.) long and 5 cm (2 in.) wide. The skin colour is deep rose, the flesh is white.

BLACK SPANISH ROUND: A large globular variety, black-skinned and white-fleshed. Like China Rose it appears in some catalogues — others are not as easy to find.

BLACK SPANISH LONG: Similar to Black Spanish Round apart from its shape — 30 cm (1 ft) long and tapered like a parsnip.

MINO EARLY: Cylindrical roots with a flavour which is milder and perhaps more acceptable for salads than the other winter varieties. Hard to find.

TROUBLES

See page 107

China Rose

Rhubarb

We usually regard rhubarb as a fruit, but it gets into vegetable books because it is so often grown on vegetable plots and allotments. It is usually neglected, but it will repay a little care by producing a succession of succulent stalks from February to midsummer. Divide the roots every five years. The stalks ('sticks') can be left to develop naturally for pulling in spring, or the plants can be forced by covering in late winter for an early spring crop. The leaves are dangerous — put them on the compost heap.

IN A NUTSHELL

Can be raised from seed sown in April, but results are sometimes disappointing. Much better to lift mature roots ('crowns') and divide into pieces ('sets') bearing one or more buds.

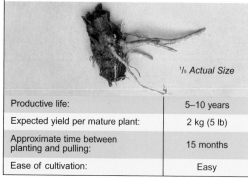

¹/₅ Actual Size

Productive life:	5–10 years
Expected yield per mature plant:	2 kg (5 lb)
Approximate time between planting and pulling:	15 months
Ease of cultivation:	Easy

SOIL FACTS

- Not fussy at all, provided that the soil is not subject to prolonged waterlogging in winter.
- Pick an open site which is not shaded. Dig deeply in autumn, incorporating a liberal amount of compost or well-rotted manure. Rake in a general-purpose fertilizer shortly before planting.

PLANTING

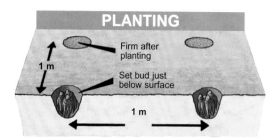

Firm after planting

1 m

Set bud just below surface

1 m

CALENDAR

	JAN	FEB	MAR	APR	MAY	JUN	JUL	AUG	SEP	OCT	NOV	DEC
Planting Time												
Pulling Time												

For key to symbols — see page 7

LOOKING AFTER THE CROP

- Keep the plants well watered. Remove any flowering shoots which may appear.
- Feed the plants with a liquid fertilizer during the summer. If this is not done, sprinkle a general-purpose fertilizer around the crowns once the harvesting season is over.
- Place a mulch of compost or well-rotted manure over the crowns in January or February.

HARVESTING

- Begin pulling the sticks in April — hold the stalk close to the ground and then pull upwards with a twisting motion. Never strip a plant — always leave at least 4 stalks. Do not remove any stalks after July.
- Allow new plants to become established during the first year — pulling can begin 12–18 months after planting.
- Force one or two plants for a February or March crop — cover each crown in January with an upturned bucket or plastic bin which should be covered with compost or straw. The forced sticks will be ready in about 6 weeks — do not force these plants again for at least 2 years

IN THE KITCHEN

The thin, pale sticks of forced rhubarb need less preparation and less sugar than the stalks gathered later in the season. Stewing with or without water is the usual method of cooking and custard is the usual accompaniment, but there are many other ways of using the crop. Pies, crumbles, jams, chutneys, fools, mousses … there is a long list of traditional recipes.

FREEZING: Place a layer of rhubarb sections in an open freezer tray and freeze for an hour. Pack into polythene bags — store for up to 1 year.

COOKING: Simply cut off the leaves of forced rhubarb, wash and cook slowly with sugar (no water) in a pan until the flesh is tender. Do not overcook. Older sticks should be peeled to remove the stringy skin. Improve the flavour by adding orange juice and cinnamon.

VARIETIES

CHAMPAGNE EARLY: Deep red stems make this one of the most attractive varieties. Reliable and early — sometimes listed as Early Red.

GLASKIN'S PERPETUAL: In more seed catalogues than the others because it can be cut in the first year.

VICTORIA: A very popular variety although it is the last one to produce its stalks in late spring.

TIMPERLEY EARLY: The opposite to Victoria — thin stems which are ideal for forcing in early spring.

TROUBLES

CROWN ROT

The terminal bud rots and the tissue below the crown decays. The sticks are spindly and dull-coloured. There is no cure, so badly infected plants should be dug out and burnt. Do not re-plant the affected area.

HONEY FUNGUS

Tell-tale sign is the presence of white streaks in the brown, dead tissue of the crown. Orange toadstools appear around the affected plants. Dig out and burn diseased roots.

Salsify & Scorzonera

These vegetables have been around for centuries but they still remain rarities in the garden. Salsify looks quite like a poorly-grown parsnip — long, rather thin and with a slightly corky skin. The flavour, however, is delicate — likened by some to asparagus or oysters. Scorzonera is its black-skinned relative — its flavour is delicious.

IN A NUTSHELL

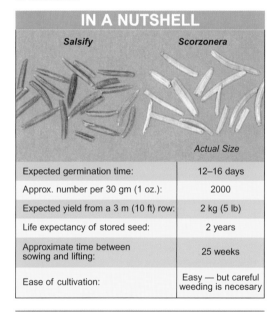

	Salsify	Scorzonera
		Actual Size
Expected germination time:		12–16 days
Approx. number per 30 gm (1 oz.):		2000
Expected yield from a 3 m (10 ft) row:		2 kg (5 lb)
Life expectancy of stored seed:		2 years
Approximate time between sowing and lifting:		25 weeks
Ease of cultivation:		Easy — but careful weeding is necesary

SOIL FACTS

- These vegetables grow best in deep, friable and stone-free soil which has not been recently manured.
- Dig deeply in autumn or early winter and refrain from adding any fresh manure or compost. Lime if necessary. Break down clods and rake in Growmore fertilizer when preparing the seed bed.

SEED SOWING

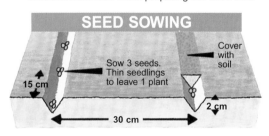

Cover with soil

Sow 3 seeds. Thin seedlings to leave 1 plant

15 cm

2 cm

30 cm

CALENDAR

	JAN	FEB	MAR	APR	MAY	JUN	JUL	AUG	SEP	OCT	NOV	DEC
Sowing Time												
Lifting Time												

LOOKING AFTER THE CROP

- Salsify and scorzonera will not produce satisfactory roots after transplanting, so throw thinnings away.
- Weed carefully around each plant. If using a hoe, avoid at all costs touching the crown of the plant.
- The crop requires very little attention and is rarely attacked by pests. Water in dry weather and apply a mulch in summer.

HARVESTING

- The roots are ready for lifting from mid October onwards. They are hardy and can be left in the soil until April.
- Lift as required, taking great care not to snap the brittle roots. You will not be able to harvest them in frosty weather, so lift some in November and store as for carrots (see page 40).
- Some books recommend that the tops should be cut off some of the roots in autumn and the fresh shoots which appear in spring used as greens in May. This is not really advisable — these vegetables produce superior-tasting roots but only average-flavoured leaves.

IN THE KITCHEN

Salsify and scorzonera can be cooked in a variety of ways — baked, puréed, dipped into batter and fried, or served *au gratin* (with cheese and breadcrumbs). According to some culinary experts the delicate flavour should not be masked — simple boiling is recommended. The young shoots ('chards') can be blanched like chicory and served raw in salads.

STORAGE: Keep in a polythene bag in the refrigerator — roots will stay fresh for up to 1 week.

COOKING: The secret for top flavour appears to be peeling after and not before boiling. Scrub the roots thoroughly under the tap and trim the ends. Cut into 5 cm (2 in.) lengths and cook for 25 minutes in boiling salted water to which lemon juice has been added. Drain and squeeze off skins — toss with a little melted butter and chopped parsley.

VARIETIES

There are only 2 or 3 varieties of salsify and there are no particular merits to help you make your choice. Just buy the one you are offered.

MAMMOTH-SANDWICH ISLAND: Some suppliers call it Mammoth — in other catalogues it is listed as Sandwich Island. This variety of salsify has been around since the beginning of the 20th century.

GIANT: The only other salsify you are likely to find — just as reliable as Mammoth-Sandwich Island.

RUSSIAN GIANT: The most popular variety of scorzonera — you might be offered Long Black instead but there is little to choose between them.

TROUBLES

WHITE BLISTER

Shiny white blisters on the leaves; growth is stunted and root development is limited. Cut off and burn diseased foliage.

Seed sprouts

Many of us gained our first practical experience in growing things when we sowed mustard and cress on damp blotting paper. Unfortunately our involvement with sprouting seeds for kitchen use generally ended there, despite the fact that they are a rich source of vitamins, minerals, protein and polyunsaturated fats. Even if nutritional values don't interest you, there is still something appealing about vegetables easily raised indoors to provide flavours ranging from bland to peppery. Mung beans are the most popular choice — 'bean sprouts' are to be found in Chinese restaurants everywhere. There are many other seeds which can be sprouted for table use — see page 91. Some seeds of outdoor vegetables can be used, such as broccoli and peas, but don't experiment. Many sprouts are tasteless, some are bitter and a few (e.g tomato) are harmful. All you require is a jar or tray and a few days' patience. There are instructions for each type of seed on page 91.

BEFORE YOU START

Weigh out the amount of seeds you propose to sprout and wash them in cold water. Drain thoroughly and then let them soak overnight in a bowl of tepid water. Next day allow the seeds to drain and then use the appropriate sprouting technique.

IN THE KITCHEN

Wash and dry the harvested sprouts, and then use as quickly as possible — do not store for more than 2 days. They can be served raw in salads — some are soft (e.g mustard and cress) and others, such as mung beans, are crunchy. Bean sprouts are, of course, a basic ingredient in Oriental cooking and are used in a variety of ways. The basic method of preparing them is by stir-frying. Heat a little vegetable oil in a pan and add the bean sprouts — stir quickly for about 2 minutes and serve immediately.

SPROUTING TECHNIQUES

Jar Method

- Place soaked seeds in a clean jam jar — remember that their volume will increase four or five times by harvest time. Cover the top with a square cut from a pair of old tights and secure with a rubber band. Fill the jar with water and pour off.

- Put the jar in a bowl, propped up as shown below to ensure that the seeds will not stand in water.

- If the seeds require **forcing**, place the bowl in a cupboard from which all light is excluded. A temperature of 13°–21°C (55°–70°F) is required — an airing cupboard is often ideal. If the seeds require **greening**, place the bowl in the dark until the seeds have germinated. Move to a well-lit spot away from direct sunlight 1-2 days before harvesting.

- It will be necessary to rinse the seeds twice daily. To do this, half fill the jar with water and then drain it away through the cloth at the top. Replace the jar in the bowl when the rinsing process has been completed.

Tray Method

- Place several sheets of kitchen paper towelling at the bottom of a shallow waterproof tray. Dampen this absorbent layer thoroughly, pour off any excess water and then scatter the soaked seeds evenly over the surface.

- If the seeds require **forcing**, put the tray inside a polythene bag and place in a cupboard from which all light is excluded — an airing cupboard is often ideal. If the sprouts require **greening**, place the tray in the dark until the seeds have germinated. Move to a well-lit spot away from direct sunlight 1-2 days before harvesting.

- It will be necessary to inspect the tray regularly to ensure that the absorbent layer remains damp. Moisten as necessary, but make sure that there is no free water standing at the base of the tray.

ADZUKI BEAN

The Japanese form of the Chinese bean sprout. The adzuki (or aduki) bean is chestnut brown and the short white sprouts have a crisp, nutty flavour. Eat raw or use as directed in Oriental recipes.

Propagation: Requires forcing by the tray or jar method. Harvest when sprouts are 3 cm (1 in.) long — this will take 3–6 days.

FENUGREEK

Smell the seeds and you will know that they are a constituent of curry powder. All sorts of medicinal properties have been ascribed to them, but the sprouts are now used solely for their spicy flavour in salads, soups or stews.

Propagation: Requires greening by the jar method. Harvest for a strong curry flavour when the sprouts are 1 cm (½ in.) long — for a mild flavour leave until they are 8 cm (3 in.) long. This will take 4–8 days.

MUSTARD AND CRESS

The old favourites for salads, garnishing and sandwiches. There are two types of cress — curly-leaved and plain, and the mild-flavoured rape seed is sometimes substituted for the rather peppery white mustard.

Propagation: Requires greening by the tray method. Sow cress seed evenly and thickly and 3 days later sprinkle mustard seed over or alongside the emerging cress seedlings. Move to a well-lit spot when the leaves start to unfold. Harvest when 5 cm (2 in.) high — this will take 10–15 days. Remove by cutting the base of the stems with scissors.

MUNG BEAN

The familiar Chinese bean sprout, now widely available in supermarkets. The green beans produce long and plump sprouts which can be eaten raw with a suitable dressing or cooked in a variety of ways. Soya beans are sometimes used as a substitute but the flavour is inferior.

Propagation: Requires forcing by the tray or jar method. Harvest when sprouts are 5 cm (2 in.) long — this will take 4–6 days.

ALFALFA

Grown to maturity by farmers for cattle food, but the young sprouts have a sweet, pea-like flavour and crisp texture when served raw in salads. Rich in minerals and Vitamin B.

Propagation: Requires greening by the jar method. Harvest when sprouts are 3–5 cm (1–2 in.) long — this will take 3–5 days.

RADISH

Radish is present on nearly every vegetable plot but a rarity on the seed sprouter's list. Strange, because radish seeds readily sprout and provide a pleasant and peppery taste to sandwiches and salads. Any variety is suitable.

Propagation: Requires greening (½ day) by the jar method. Harvest when sprouts are 1–3 cm (½–1 in.) long — this will take 3–4 days.

TRITICALE

A hybrid of wheat and rye. The protein-rich sprouts can be used in several ways — salads, soups, stews or as a constituent of bread dough.

Propagation: Requires forcing by the tray or jar method. Harvest when 5 cm (2 in.) long — this will take 2–3 days.

Spinach

Grow this vegetable only if the family likes it. This calls for learning how to cook it properly — it really doesn't have to be slimy, strong-tasting mush. There are two types of true spinach — they are both annuals which are either picked in summer (round-seeded varieties) or during autumn, winter and spring (mostly prickly-seeded varieties). It is possible to pick spinach from your garden almost all year round. For maximum flavour and tenderness grow one of the summer varieties. You can add raw spinach leaves to a salad — harvest the leaves when they are about 8 cm (3 in.) long. For cooking you can wait until leaves are twice this size, but they should still be young, outer leaves. The New Zealand variety is not a true spinach — it is a half hardy annual. Perpetual spinach is a type of leaf beet — see page 93.

IN A NUTSHELL

Spinach seed is either round (smooth-surfaced) or prickly (rough-surfaced).

Actual Size

Expected germination time:	12–20 days
Approx. number per 30 gm (1oz):	1500
Expected yield from a 3 m (10 ft) row:	2–5 kg (4–11 lb)
Life expectancy of stored seed:	4 years
Approximate time between sowing and picking:	8–14 weeks
Ease of cultivation:	Not easy to grow well — rich soil and regular watering are required

SOIL FACTS

- Spinach is sometimes described as an easy vegetable to grow, but it will not succeed if the soil and position are poor. The ground must be rich and contain plenty of organic matter — starved spinach produces a bitter-tasting crop.
- The ideal place for summer spinach is between rows of tall-growing vegetables — the dappled shade will reduce the risk of running to seed. Sow winter spinach and New Zealand spinach in a sunny spot.
- Dig deeply in winter and apply lime if necessary. Apply a compound fertilizer about 2 weeks before sowing time.

- **Summer varieties:** Sow every few weeks from mid March to the end of May for picking between late May and the end of October.
- **Winter varieties:** Sow in August and again in September for picking between October and April.
- **New Zealand variety:** Sow in late May for picking between June and September.

SEED SOWING

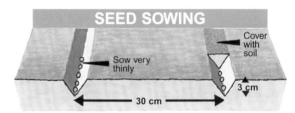

Sow very thinly • Cover with soil • 30 cm • 3 cm

- New Zealand spinach needs more space. Sow 3 seeds about 3 cm (1 in.) below the surface, spacing the groups 60 cm (2 ft) apart. Thin to 1 plant per station.

LOOKING AFTER THE CROP

- The seedlings of summer and winter varieties should be thinned to 8 cm (3 in.) apart as soon as they are large enough to handle. A few weeks later remove alternate plants for kitchen use — do not delay thinning.
- Hoe to keep down weeds. Water copiously during dry spells in summer.
- Winter varieties will need some sort of protection from October onwards unless you are lucky enough to live in a mild area. Use cloches or straw to cover the plants.

HARVESTING

- Start picking as soon as the leaves have reached a reasonable size. Always take the outer leaves, which should still be at the young and tender stage.
- The secret is to pick continually so that fresh growth is encouraged. With summer varieties you can take up to half the leaves without damaging the plants — with winter varieties pick much more sparingly. Take care when harvesting. Pick off the leaves with fingernails — don't wrench them off which could damage the stems or roots.
- The rules for New Zealand spinach are different — pull off a few young shoots from the base of the plant at each harvesting session. A single sowing will last throughout the summer if you pick little and often.

CALENDAR

	JAN	FEB	MAR	APR	MAY	JUN	JUL	AUG	SEP	OCT	NOV	DEC
Sowing Time												
Picking Time												

For key to symbols — see page 7

IN THE KITCHEN

Young spinach leaves can be used for salad making but this vegetable is usually cooked before serving. A boiled or steamed mound between the potatoes and meat on the dinner plate should not be its only role — try it for filling an omelette or quiche, as a base for poached eggs (eggs florentine) or as an ingredient in soup. The summer varieties are the most tender and delicately flavoured — winter spinach is darker and coarser.

FREEZING: Use young leaves. Wash well and drain, then blanch for 2 minutes. Cool and press out all excess moisture. Pack into polythene bags and squeeze out air before sealing.

STORAGE: Try to cook spinach on the same day as picking — the flavour deteriorates rapidly with age. If you must store it, place washed leaves in a polythene bag in the refrigerator — spinach will stay fresh for up to 2 days.

COOKING: Thorough washing to remove grit is the first essential step. Place the leaves in a large bowl of cold water, shake them and then remove. Change the water in the bowl and repeat the process — once or twice depending on the amount of grit and sand present. Trim the leaf bases of summer varieties — the coarser winter types should have the midribs removed. The best way to cook the leaves is to steam and not boil them. Place the washed leaves in a large pan and sprinkle with salt, pepper plus a small knob of butter or margarine. Add no extra water. Steam for 5–10 minutes and then squeeze out as much water as you can with a potato masher. Add grated nutmeg or chopped mint, say the culinary experts.

VARIETIES

SUMMER varieties

These varieties have round seeds and will grow quickly under good conditions to provide an early and tender crop. The major problem is their dislike of hot and dry weather, and some varieties rapidly run to seed during a prolonged warm spell in summer.

MEDANIA: This popular variety has several plus points — vigorous growth, good mildew resistance and it is slow to bolt.

MATADOR: An RHS Award of Garden Merit winner. A good variety for early sowing — large, medium-green leaves.

BLOOMSDALE: A deep green variety which has earned a good reputation for resistance to bolting. Certainly worth a trial.

BORDEAUX: The stalks and leaf veins are wine red — the leaves are dark green. The variety Reddy has similar colouring.

WINTER varieties

Most of these varieties have prickly seeds but there are exceptions, such as Sigmaleaf, which have smooth seeds. These plants provide a useful harvest of greens from October to April. Pick regularly and use only young leaves for cooking — pick old leaves and keep them in the kitchen for a few days and you will soon discover just how unpleasant spinach can taste!

BROAD-LEAVED PRICKLY: The name refers, of course, to the seeds and not the leaves. A standard winter variety — the foliage is dark and fleshy and the plants are slow to bolt.

GIANT WINTER: Winter spinach is hard to find in the seed catalogues and garden centre racks — this one is perhaps the most popular. It produces large, dark green leaves on spreading plants. Sow the seeds in summer or autumn for spinach leaves all winter and spring.

PERPETUAL variety

If you like spinach but find the standard varieties hard to grow then perpetual spinach is the type to choose. It is not really spinach at all — it is a variety of leaf beet and you may find it listed as spinach beet. The plants are very hardy and are less likely to run to seed than true spinach.

NEW ZEALAND variety

This is not a true spinach. It is a dwarf and rambling plant with soft, fleshy leaves which are used as a spinach substitute. It is sensitive to frost and so it should be raised indoors and planted out in May or sown outdoors when the danger of frost has passed. Soak seed overnight before sowing and pinch out the tips of young plants to induce bushiness. The flavour is milder than true spinach.

Bloomsdale

New Zealand Spinach

SPINACH TROUBLES

There are only three troubles which are likely to affect spinach, but they can make this a difficult crop to grow. Downy mildew, bolting and spinach blight are the major troubles, and if you have had problems with annual spinach in the past then try the much easier types — New Zealand or perpetual Spinach (page 93).

	Symptom	Likely Causes
Seedlings	— eaten	**Birds** or **Millepede** or **Slugs & Snails** (see page 157)
	— toppled over	**Damping off** (see page 157)
Leaves	— yellow between veins; acid soil	**Magnesium deficiency** (see page 31)
	— yellow between veins; chalky soil	2
	— holed	**Slugs & Snails** (see page 157)
	— spotted	4
	— infested with blackfly	**Black bean aphid** (see page 20)
	— infested with greenfly	**Aphid** (see page 157)
	— rolled	5
	— blistered	**Mangold fly** (see page 26)
	— yellow patches above	1
	— greyish purple mould below	1
	— inner leaves narrow, yellow	5
Plants	— run to seed	3
	— early death, leaves deformed	5
	— early death, leaves not deformed	**Too hot and dry** or **Overcropping**

YELLOW PATCHES

1 DOWNY MILDEW

Watch for downy mildew if the weather is wet and cold. It begins on the outer leaves — yellow patches above and greyish purple mould below. As the disease progresses affected patches turn brown.

Treatment: Pick off diseased leaves. No fungicidal spray is available for tackling this disease.

Prevention: Practise crop rotation. Make sure the soil is well drained and avoid overcrowding by thinning the crop promptly.

2 MANGANESE DEFICIENCY

YELLOWED LEAVES

Yellow blotches appear between the veins, and the margins tend to curl up slightly. The symptoms are most pronounced in midsummer. Manganese deficiency is associated with poorly-drained soils, which can make successful spinach growing difficult in such areas.

Treatment: Apply a trace element spray containing manganese to the soil. Spraying with a foliar feed may help.

Prevention: Avoid growing spinach in poor soil. Do not overlime.

3 BOLTING

The commonest spinach trouble in home gardens is bolting, which results in the premature flowering of the plants. The danger is greatest in hot, settled weather and it will occur if the plants have been kept short of either water or nutrients. Avoid trouble by preparing the soil properly by digging in compost and raking in a general purpose fertilizer. Choose a variety which is described as bolt-resistant. Thin the seedlings early, and water in dry weather. In some soils bolting occurs year after year, and the best plan here is to grow New Zealand spinach.

SPOTTED LEAVES

4 LEAF SPOT

Numerous 1 cm (⅓ in.) spots appear in the foliage — in a bad attack the spots join up and the leaf is destroyed. Central area of each spot is pale brown and may drop out — outer ring is dark brown or purple.

Treatment: Pick off and burn diseased leaves.

Prevention: Practise crop rotation. Apply a balanced fertilizer before sowing seed.

ROLLED LEAVES

5 SPINACH BLIGHT

Young leaves are affected first. The tell-tale signs are narrow and small leaf blades, inrolled margins and a puckered, yellow surface. The cause of this serious disease is the cucumber mosaic virus.

Treatment: Destroy infected plants — there is no cure.

Prevention: Keep down weeds. Spray with insecticidal soap to control greenfly, which carry the virus.

Swede

Swedes are related to turnips (the name is an abbreviation of Swedish turnip) but the flesh is generally yellow and the flavour is sweeter. Swedes have a number of advantages — they are hardier and the yields are higher. Few other crops are easier to grow — sow in late spring or early summer, thin a few weeks later and lift as required from autumn until spring. The introduction of disease-resistant varieties has made them even easier to grow.

IN A NUTSHELL

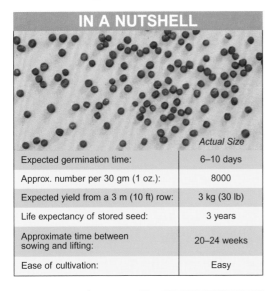

Actual Size

Expected germination time:	6–10 days
Approx. number per 30 gm (1 oz.):	8000
Expected yield from a 3 m (10 ft) row:	3 kg (30 lb)
Life expectancy of stored seed:	3 years
Approximate time between sowing and lifting:	20–24 weeks
Ease of cultivation:	Easy

SOIL FACTS

- Swedes are brassicas (see page 27) and like other members of the family need a firm, non-acid soil which has reasonable drainage.
- Pick a sunny spot and dig in autumn. Lime if necessary. In spring apply general-purpose fertilizer — prepare the seed bed about a week later. Apply a nematode-based insecticide if cabbage root fly is known to be a problem.

SEED SOWING

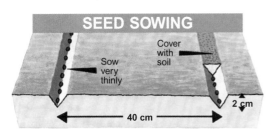

Sow very thinly

Cover with soil

40 cm

2 cm

CALENDAR

	JAN	FEB	MAR	APR	MAY	JUN	JUL	AUG	SEP	OCT	NOV	DEC
Sowing Time												
Lifting Time												

For key to symbols — see page 7

LOOKING AFTER THE CROP

- Thin out the crop as soon as the seedlings are large enough to handle. Do this in stages until the plants are 25 cm (10 in.) apart.
- Keep the soil hoed and remember to water in dry weather — failure to do so will result in smaller and woodier roots. Rain following a dry spell can cause roots to split.
- Spray with pyrethrins at the first signs of flea beetle damage.

HARVESTING

- Begin lifting as soon as the roots are large enough to use. This will be from early autumn onwards, and there is no need to wait until they reach their maximum size. You can leave them in the soil and lift with a fork as required until spring, but it may be more convenient to lift and store them indoors in December for later use.
- The storage technique is to twist off the leaves and place the roots between layers of dry sand in a stout box. Store in a cool shed.

IN THE KITCHEN

Swede is generally acceptable as an ingredient for stews, casseroles and soups, but for many people the memory of the yellow mush from schooldays has outlawed this vegetable as an accompaniment to meat or fish. Give it another try — lift some roots when they are the size of a large grapefruit and make the swede and potato mixture described below.

STORAGE: Keep unpeeled in a cool and dry place — swedes will stay fresh for up to 5 days.

COOKING: Remove the tops and roots — peel thickly until the yellow flesh is reached. Boiling and mashing is the traditional method of cooking — the 'bashed neeps' of Scotland. Cut the flesh into slices or cubes and boil for 30 minutes. Drain, and then mash with butter, cream, pepper and either ginger or nutmeg. This dish is a little watery for some palates — mixing it with an equal quantity of leftover potatoes at mashing time makes it more acceptable to English swede-haters. You can use swede fingers instead of parsnips for roasting around the joint.

VARIETIES

MARIAN: This is the swede to buy. It has all the plus points — high yields, good flavour and texture with the bonus of resistance to club root and mildew.

BEST OF ALL: You will find this purple-skinned, yellow-fleshed variety in many catalogues. Very hardy and reliable.

INVITATION: A purple-topped variety which heralded a breakthrough. It introduced resistance to both club root and mildew.

RUBY: This red-skinned variety is noted for its extra sweetness, ease of cultivation and good resistance to mildew.

TWEED: One of the first F₁ swede hybrids. Cream-coloured with purple tops, this hybrid has the extra vigour you would expect, and is the one to choose if your soil is rather poor.

HELENOR: An all-purple variety which is noted for its mild, sweet flesh.

TROUBLES

See page 107

Sweet corn

The flavour of home-grown sweet corn cooked within an hour of picking is so much better than the taste of shop-bought corn. Some gardeners still believe that sweet corn cannot be grown in northern counties, but this is no longer true. Choose one of the F_1 hybrids listed on page 97 — these varieties have revolutionised the reliability of this crop in our climate. The older open pollinated varieties produce heavier crops but are a risky venture in Britain. In April raise the seedlings indoors in fibre pots for planting outdoors once the danger of frost has passed. The tassels at the top of the plant are the male flowers — the female flowers ('silks') are above the immature cobs.

IN A NUTSHELL

Use a seed dressing before sowing outdoors. A minimum soil temperature of 10°C (50°F) is required for germination.

Actual Size

Expected germination time:	10–12 days
Amount required for a 3 m (10 ft) row:	2 gm (1/12 oz)
Expected yield from a 3 m (10 ft) row:	10 cobs
Life expectancy of stored seed:	2 years
Approximate time between sowing and picking:	14 weeks
Ease of cultivation:	Not difficult if you can provide the necessary growing conditions

SOIL FACTS

- There are two basic soil requirements — good drainage and enough humus to ensure that the ground will not dry out too quickly. Ideally it should be slightly acid, reasonably fertile and deep, but the situation is more important than the soil type.

- Choose a spot in full sun which is sheltered from the wind. Dig in winter, incorporating old compost if the previous crop was not manured. Rake in a compound fertilizer about 2 weeks before sowing or planting.

- **Southern counties:** Sow outdoors in mid May — the cobs should be ready for picking in late August or September. For extra reliability and an earlier crop (late July onwards in mild areas) sow under glass as described below.

- **Other counties:** Sow seeds under glass in mid April–early May and plant out in late May–early June. Alternatively sow outdoors under cloches in mid May — place cloches in position about 2 weeks before sowing.

SOWING & PLANTING

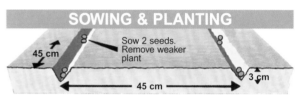

45 cm · Sow 2 seeds. Remove weaker plant · 45 cm · 3 cm

- Sweet corn must be sown or planted in rectangular blocks, not as a single row. This will ensure effective wind pollination of the female flowers.

- Outdoor sowing may be reliable in the south but in other areas sow under cloches or preferably in pots indoors. Root disturbance must be avoided so use 8 cm (3 in.) fibre pots — not clay or plastic ones. Sow 2 seeds about 3 cm (1 in.) deep in seed compost — remove weaker seedling. Harden off before planting outdoors — leave 45 cm (18 in.) between transplants.

LOOKING AFTER THE CROP

- Remove cloches when the foliage touches the glass. Protect seedlings with black cotton if birds are a nuisance. Keep down weeds but do not hoe close to the plants.

- Roots will appear at the base of the stem — cover them with soil or a mulch of old compost. The side shoots ('tillers') which may develop should not be removed.

- Water in dry weather — this is especially important at flowering time. Stake if the plants are tall and the site is exposed.

- Tapping the tassels at the top of each stem when they are fully developed in late June or July will help pollination. Liquid feed when the cobs begin to swell.

HARVESTING

- Each plant will produce 1 or 2 cobs. Test for ripeness when the silks have turned chocolate brown. Pull back part of the sheath and squeeze a couple of grains between thumbnail and fingernail. If a watery liquid squirts out then the cob is unripe. If the liquid is creamy then the cob is just right for picking but if the liquid is thick and doughy you have waited too long.

- Carefully twist off the ripe cob from the stem. Do this just before it is required for cooking.

CALENDAR

	JAN	FEB	MAR	APR	MAY	JUN	JUL	AUG	SEP	OCT	NOV	DEC
Sowing Time (outdoors)					⇕							
Sowing Time (indoors)				⊔	⧯							
Picking Time								▮	▮			

For key to symbols — see page 7

IN THE KITCHEN

Country sayings emphasise the need to cook sweet corn as soon as possible after picking. According to the Americans, "walk slowly to pick it, run back to the kitchen to cook it". Nearer home, the advice is to "take a pan of boiling water with you when you pick the cobs". Freshness, then, is all-important for top flavour and so are two other tips — never add salt to the water and never boil for more than a few minutes if the cobs have been freshly picked. To prepare the cob, strip off the outer leaves, cut off the stalk and pull off the silks.

FREEZING: Blanch prepared cobs for 4–6 minutes, depending on their size. Cool and drain thoroughly, then wrap individually in foil or cling film before freezing.

STORAGE: If storage is unavoidable, place cobs in the refrigerator — sweet corn will stay fresh for up to 3 days.

COOKING: Place the cobs in a pan of boiling unsalted water for 5–8 minutes. They are ready when a kernel can be easily detached with a fork from the cob. Drain thoroughly and serve with melted butter and coarse salt. If you want to do things properly, serve each cob in a long dish with corn holders inserted at each end. It may be more satisfying to the viewer (but less satisfying to the eater) to serve the separated kernels in a dish — they can be easily stripped off the cooked cob for this purpose. Boiling is not the only cooking method — if you are having a barbecue wrap the cobs in buttered foil and place amongst the ashes for 10 minutes. Corn fritters are an American favourite but it would be a pity to waste home-grown sweet corn on them — use tinned corn instead. Deep fry spoonfuls of a mixture of mashed corn, salt, flour, milk and egg for 1–2 minutes or until golden brown.

VARIETIES

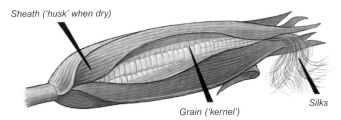

Sheath ('husk' when dry)

Grain ('kernel')

Silks

Only one or two of the best Open-pollinated varieties have survived in the catalogues as they are not as reliable in our climate as the F_1 hybrids. These hybrids have been bred for northern conditions so that a mild climate is no longer essential. There are early-midsummer and late-maturing varieties — the late ones are tall with large cobs, but choose an early-maturing type if the climate in your area is not a favourable one.

The latest development has been the Supersweet and Tendersweet varieties. These contain more sugar than standard varieties and are extra tender, but these benefits do not extend to their ease of cultivation. They are less vigorous than the older ones and sowing before the end of June is not recommended for many areas. Still, their flavour and tenderness have made them the favourite sweet corn varieties. Do not grow the Supersweet varieties near older traditional varieties — cross-pollination will result in starchy kernels.

KELVEDON GLORY: The Open-pollinated variety which can still be found in some catalogues. A mid-season variety — cobs are large and well-filled.

LARK: An F_1 hybrid and an RHS Award of Garden Merit winner. A popular mid-season Tendersweet variety with better-than-average performance in cold conditions.

SWIFT: Like Lark it is a Tendersweet variety which is popular and extra sweet, but the cobs appear earlier.

EARLY EXTRA SWEET: A Supersweet variety with shortness as its selling point. The sturdy plants stand up well to wind and cold conditions.

SUNDANCE: This Supersweet sweet corn is an RHS Award of Garden Merit winner. It is highly recommended for growing in northern areas.

SWEET NUGGET: Another of the Supersweet varieties which is ready for cutting in early September. Performs well in our climate.

MINIPOP: Something different. Minipop has been bred to produce baby cobs — they are cut when they are about 10 cm (4 in.) long. Can be used for cooking or eating raw.

HONEYDEW: This RHS Award of Garden Merit winner is claimed by some to be one of the sweetest and tenderest of all.

SUGAR BUNS: Two advantages here — the sweet and tender cobs are the earliest of all, according to the catalogues, and they can be harvested over a long period.

MIRAI M130: One of the much praised Mirai varieties, noted for reliability. Can be eaten straight from the plant.

Kelvedon Glory

TROUBLES

SMUT

Large galls ('smut balls') appear on the cobs and stalks in hot and dry weather. These galls should be cut off and burnt as soon as they are seen, or they will burst open and release a mass of black spores. Burn all plants after harvesting and do not grow sweet corn on the site for at least 3 years.

FRIT FLY

Frit fly maggots bore into the growing points of corn seedlings which then develop twisted and ragged leaves. Growth is stunted and undersized cobs are produced. Control measures are not generally worthwhile — grow the seedlings in pots under glass until they reach the stage when they are not susceptible to frit fly attack.

Sweet Nugget

Tomato, Greenhouse

Tomatoes are the main greenhouse crop in this country. A succession of fruit all summer long which is always in demand is probably the main reason for its popularity. There may be additional reasons such as the fascination of watching a small cluster of green pinheads develop into a large truss of tomatoes. Popular, but not an easy choice — there is a lot of work for the reward obtained. The plants need constant care — in summer it is necessary to water growing bags and pots every day, and pests and diseases find the plants an ideal host. Greenhouse tomatoes are cordon varieties which are single-stemmed and can reach 2 m (7 ft) or more if not stopped.

IN A NUTSHELL

Actual Size

Expected germination time:	8–11 days
Expected yield per plant:	4 kg (9 lb)
Life expectancy of stored seed:	3 years
Approximate time between sowing and picking:	16 weeks
Ease of cultivation:	Not easy — growing tomatoes under glass is time-consuming

SOIL FACTS

- Tomatoes can be grown in border soil — raised beds give better results than beds at ground level. Prepare the soil in winter — dig in a small amount of compost or manure. Rake in a compound fertilizer shortly before planting. Unfortunately border soil soon becomes infested with soil pests and root diseases, so the soil must either be sterilised or changed after a couple of seasons.

- Because of the difficulties with border soil, other growing systems have been evolved. Ring culture and growing on straw bales have lost their popularity as they can be tricky, but growing in 25 cm (10 in.) pots filled with soilless potting compost is simple.

- Growing bags have taken over as the most popular growing system with both the professional nurseryman and amateur gardener. Good and reliable ... if you master the watering technique.

- In a heated greenhouse kept at a minimum night temperature of 10º–13ºC (50–55ºF), tomato seed is sown in late December and planed out in late February or early March for a May-June crop.

- Most gardeners, however, grow tomatoes in an unheated ('cold') house. Sow seed in early March and plant out in late April or early May. The first fruit will be ready for picking in July.

SOWING & PLANTING

- If you need a large number of plants, then follow the conventional technique of sowing thinly in trays or pans filled with seed and cutting compost. Cover lightly with compost — keep moist but not wet at about 18ºC (65ºF). When the seedlings have formed a pair of true leaves prick them out into 8 cm (3 in.) fibre pots filled with potting compost.

- If only a few plants are required, it is easier to sow a couple of seeds in each 8 cm (3 in.) fibre pot of compost, removing the weaker seedling after germination. Alternatively, buy plants from a reputable supplier.

- Plant out into growing bags, pots or border soil when the seedlings are 15–20 cm (6–8 in.) tall and the flowers of the first truss are beginning to open. Water the pot thoroughly before planting. In border soil plant 45 cm (1½ ft) apart.

LOOKING AFTER THE CROP

- Tie the main stem loosely to a cane or wind it up a well-anchored but slack vertical string. Side shoots will appear where the leaf stalks join the stem. Cut or pinch them out when they are about 3 cm (1 in.) long.

- When the plants are about 1.2 m (4 ft) tall, remove the leaves below the first truss. Remove yellowing leaves below fruit trusses as the season progresses, but never overdo this deleafing process. Use a sharp knife to remove this unwanted foliage.

- Water regularly to keep the soil moist — irregular watering will cause blossom end rot or fruit splitting. Feed with a soluble tomato fertilizer every time you water. If using growing bags you *must* water frequently.

- Mist plants and tap the supports occasionally to aid pollen dispersion and fruit set. Ventilation is essential in summer — shade the glass with Coolglass when temperature reaches 25ºC (78ºF). When plants have reached the top of the greenhouse or when 7 trusses have set, remove the tip at 2 leaves above the top truss.

HARVESTING

- Follow the rules set out for outdoor tomatoes — see page 100.

CALENDAR

	JAN	FEB	MAR	APR	MAY	JUN	JUL	AUG	SEP	OCT	NOV	DEC
Sowing & Planting (Heated greenhouse)	🪴	🌱 🌱										🪴
Sowing & Planting (Cold greenhouse)			🪴 🪴	🌱 🌱								
Picking Time												

VARIETIES

CHERRY varieties

Most or all of the round fruit on the trusses are less than 3 cm (1 in.) in diameter. Sweetness is a general but not universal character. This is the type to grow outdoors if the plot is not mild and sunny.

GARDENER'S DELIGHT: This favourite variety is in most of the catalogues. Its tangy taste beats most standard varieties, but it has its rivals among the cherry types. Trusses are long and yields are outstanding.

ORANGE PANACHE: Sungold wears the orange cherry crown, but this one is a worthy rival. Both taste and yields are rated very highly.

SAKURA: Another winner of the RHS award. Its resistance to both virus and fusarium wilt, the sweet taste of the fruit and the vigour of the plants must have impressed the judges.

SUN CHERRY PREMIUM: An F₁ hybrid which has given outstanding results in both tasting and yield trials. It is an early variety with a long cropping season.

SUNGOLD: An RHS Award of Garden Merit winner — very popular because of its outstanding taste. The fruit is gold-coloured and growth is vigorous.

SWEET MILLION: An early variety which is easy to grow. The fruit is sweet and thin-skinned.

MASKOTKA: see
RED ALERT: page 101

Sweet Million

STANDARD varieties

This is the 'ordinary' tomato you find at the supermarket. Most or all of the round fruit are more than 5 cm (2 in.) in diameter. They are the multipurpose type for cooking and eating raw.

HERALD: This variety has been around a long time and has a great reputation for sweetness and flavour. Some experts love it, but it is in very few catalogues.

MONEYMAKER: An old timer like Ailsa Craig, and even more famous. It keeps its place because of its reliability and high yields, but there are better-tasting varieties.

SHIRLEY: Winner of several awards and a popular choice for many years. It can be grown outdoors, but it really flourishes best in a cold greenhouse. Yields are high.

VANESSA: An F₁ hybrid which has been given an RHS Award of Garden Merit. The firm flesh of the fruits and their excellent storage properties are the outstanding features.

GRENADIER: A heavy-cropper which produces fairly large fruits.

AILSA CRAIG: Varieties come and go, but this old favourite has kept its place in the catalogues. The flavour of the medium-sized fruits is good and yields are high.

ALICANTE: Sometimes described as an improved version of Moneymaker — the flavour is better. Heavy crops are produced — good resistance to greenback.

COSSACK: An F₁ hybrid of the Moneymaker type — heavy crop of large fruit can be expected and they are resistant to greenback.

HARBINGER: Yet another oldie. It is an early variety for growing in an unheated house or outdoors. Thoroughly reliable but without any outstanding features.

GOURMET: Another Moneymaker type of tomato, but it is more prolific and it has better disease resistance. Medium-sized fruit. Hard to find.

Shirley

BEEFSTEAK varieties

These are the large tomatoes used for sandwiches, grilling etc. Most or all of the fruit are more than 8 cm (3 in.) in diameter. They are generally smooth-skinned. Stop the plants when the fourth truss has set, and provide support for the fruit if necessary. The Marmande group are flattened and ribbed and are recommended for growing outdoors and not under glass.

BRANDYWINE: This variety has been around for more than 100 years. Not the prettiest of Beefsteaks, but its flavour has not been equalled.

COUNTRY TASTE: The experts heap praise on this one. It crops early and the meaty fruit can grow to 250 gm (½ lb) or more if trusses are restricted to 3 fruits. One for the show bench.

BEEFMASTER: Another extra large Beefsteak. Not in many catalogues, but it is brightly coloured, and the size of the fruit can rival Country Taste.

BEEFEATER: Produces large meaty toms under glass like the other Beefsteak varieties — this one claims good disease resistance and also a place on the patio if it is unshaded.

Country Taste

PLUM varieties

Oval tomatoes have become more popular because of their taste and the increased interest in Mediterranean cookery — these are the ones for making tomato sauces and pestos. There are both Cherry and Standard varieties.

ROMA: The fleshy fruits of this variety have the classic plum shape but differ from the others by being almost seedless. It is recommended as a cooking variety rather than a salad ingredient.

RED PEAR: Shaped like a pear. The two key features are the exceptional sweetness and the large trusses of small fruits.

SAN MARZANO: The classic Italian Plum tomato. It matures rather late, producing oval fruits with a strong flavour — perfect for cooking rather than the salad bowl.

BRITAIN'S BREAKFAST: A lemon-shaped variety which is recommended for the show bench. The fruits are borne on large trusses.

San Marzano

Tomato, Outdoor

Outdoor tomatoes are not for everyone — in many areas the crop is unreliable and there the plants need the protection of a greenhouse. But if you live in an area with a mild climate you can expect a satisfactory crop in most summers provided you choose a protected spot in full sun — see Soil Facts below. The outdoor crop is basically easier to grow than the indoor one, but it is not really an easy crop. Attention has to be more regular than with many other outdoor crops. Remember to choose a variety which is recommended for outdoor growing and make sure the soil is rich in humus. Bush varieties are the easier ones to grow — with cordon types the tips must be removed while the plants are still quite small.

IN A NUTSHELL

Actual Size

Expected germination time:	8–11 days
Expected yield per plant:	2 kg (4 lb)
Life expectancy of stored seed:	3 years
Approximate time between sowing and picking:	20 weeks
Ease of cultivation:	Not easy — tomatoes in growing bags need regular attention

SOIL FACTS

- Outdoor tomatoes are a tender crop, so choose a warm spot in front of a south-facing wall if you can. During the winter dig thoroughly and incorporate garden compost. Shortly before planting rake in a general fertilizer.

- If you are growing only a few plants or if you have no land available, then outdoor tomatoes can be grown in 25 cm (10 in.) pots or in compost-filled growing bags. These can be placed on the open ground or on balconies and patios. Remember that container growing will call for much more frequent watering. Regular feeding will be essential.

- The standard time for sowing seed under glass is in late March or early April. The young plants are hardened off during May and planted out in early June, or late May if the weather is favourable and the danger of frost has passed. Plants to be grown under cloches are planted out in the middle of May.

- Under average conditions the first tomatoes will be ready for picking in mid August.

SOWING & PLANTING

- If you want to raise your own seedlings, follow one of the techniques described on page 98. Alternatively, you can buy tomato seedlings for planting out. Look for ones which are dark green, sturdy and about 20 cm (8 in.) tall. These young plants should be pot grown.

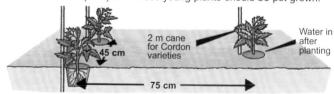

2 m cane for Cordon varieties — 45 cm — 75 cm — Water in after planting

- Plant out into growing bags, pots or the vegetable plot when the flowers of the first truss are beginning to open. Water the pot before planting out and ensure that the top of the soil ball is set just below the soil surface.

- You will get a better crop if you spread black polythene sheeting over the soil surface and plant the tomato seedlings through X-shaped slits.

LOOKING AFTER THE CROP

- If a cordon variety is grown, loosely tie the stem to the cane. Make the ties at 30 cm (1 ft) intervals as the plant grows.

- Side shoots will appear where the leaf stalks join the stem. Pinch them out when they are about 3 cm (1 in.) long. Remove yellowing leaves below fruit trusses as the season progresses, but never overdo this deleafing process.

- Water regularly in dry weather to keep the soil moist — alternating dryness with flooding will cause blossom end rot or fruit splitting. If using growing bags you *must* water frequently as noted on the instructions. Feed regularly with a tomato fertilizer. When small tomatoes have developed on the 4th truss remove the tip at 2 leaves above this truss.

HARVESTING

- Pick the fruits when they are ripe and fully coloured. Hold the tomato in your palm and with your thumb break off the fruit at the 'knuckle' (swelling on the flower stalk).

- At the end of the season the stems can be removed from the canes and laid under cloches on a bed of straw. An easier way to ripen green fruit is to place them as a layer in a tray and put them in a drawer. Next to the tray set a couple of ripe apples to generate the ripening gas ethylene.

CALENDAR

	JAN	FEB	MAR	APR	MAY	JUN	JUL	AUG	SEP	OCT	NOV	DEC
Sowing & Planting Time			▪	▪	▪							
Picking Time												

IN THE KITCHEN

It is true that a tomato picked from the plant will taste better than the fruit of the same variety bought in the supermarket, but a home-grown Moneymaker will have none of the 'real' tomato taste of shop-bought Gardener's Delight. Variety is all-important and you should check that your choice is recommended for its flavour. Most garden tomatoes are used for salads or for grilling and frying — simple methods of preparation for one of our favourite vegetables. Bite-sized tomatoes should be served whole but slicing or quartering are the usual methods of presentation on the salad plate. Simply add French dressing or else make a tomato salad fit for a gourmet — sprinkle salt and freshly ground pepper over the slices, add a little sugar and then cover with chopped basil or a mixture of parsley and chives.

FREEZING: Skin and remove core of ripe fruit. Simmer for about 5 minutes and then sieve through a nylon strainer. Cool, pack in a rigid container and freeze.

STORAGE: Keep in a polythene bag at the bottom of the refrigerator — tomatoes will stay fresh for up to 1 week.

COOKING: For grilling, cut in half and coat exposed surface with oil, pepper and sugar — grill for 5 minutes. Stuffed tomatoes are delicious and may be served hot or cold — use a large, meaty variety rather than a small juicy one. Many recipes call for skinned tomatoes — peeling is simple if you first put the fruits in a bowl and cover with boiling water for about a minute. Tomatoes are used in many, many ways such as stews, omelettes, sauces, soups, sandwiches and so on. However, the tomato juice and the tomato soup you make at home will not taste like the canned versions — these commercial products are made from special varieties grown in sunny climes.

VARIETIES

CORDON varieties

These varieties are grown as single stems and they have to be trimmed and supported. As described on page 100, the stem is stopped after the 4th truss has set so as to hasten ripening before the autumn frosts. There are many red varieties, varying in size from giants to bite-sized fruits, and there are also yellow, orange and striped tomatoes.

AILSA CRAIG:	HARBINGER:	SWEET MILLION:	see
MONEYMAKER:	COSSACK:	ORANGE PANACHE:	page
ALICANTE:	SUNGOLD:	GARDENER'S DELIGHT:	99

ST. PIERRE: This is a French variety with medium-sized bright red fruit which are just right for salads and sandwiches rather than cooking. It is a late variety.

YELLOW PERFECTION: Perhaps the most highly rated of all the yellow tomatoes. High yields, beautiful golden fruit, early cropping and excellent flavour.

MARMANDE: The other end of the scale to Gardener's Delight and Sweet Million — the irregular-shaped fruits are very large and fleshy with few seeds. These are the well-known Continental tomatoes, but the full flavour does not develop under our cooler conditions.

ORKADO: An F_1 hybrid which produces trusses filled with bright red large fruit noted for their resistance to splitting.

GOLDEN SUNRISE: This medium-sized variety is an RHS Award of Garden Merit winner and appears in several popular catalogues. It crops early and the fruit is sweet.

CHERROLO: An early variety which produces Cherry tomatoes on vigorous plants. Yields are high, but its main selling point is its moderate resistance to blight.

FANDANGO: Resistance to blight and wilt are the key features of this vigorous variety. The deep red fruit are larger than the average standard.

Yellow Perfection

Marmande

BUSH varieties

These varieties make outdoor tomato growing much easier. They are either bushes 30–75 cm (1–2½ ft) high or creeping plants less than 20 cm (8 in.) tall. They do not require supporting, trimming or stopping, and are excellent for cloche culture. One drawback is that the fruits tend to be hidden, which makes harvesting more difficult than with cordon varieties. Straw or plastic sheeting must be laid around the plants as many fruits are at ground level.

RED ALERT: Most experts agree that this popular variety has the best flavour among the Bush varieties. It is very early — the fruit are bite-sized.

AMATEUR: Once in all the catalogues but not any more. It is an old variety noted for good yields and reliability rather than flavour.

TUMBLER: A trailing Cherry variety which is a good choice for a hanging basket or patio container. It is an extra early variety, producing bright red tomatoes.

MASKOTKA: You will find this Cherry variety in a number of the popular catalogues. The bush is small — the fruit is sweet-flavoured.

INCAS: Consider this one if you want to grow a bush outdoors which produces large Plum tomatoes. Early cropping — tolerant of wilt.

SWEET OLIVE: Choose Incas for large fruit, but this is the one for bite-size Plum tomatoes growing on cascading branches.

TUMBLING TOM RED: This was the first true trailing tomato. Grow it in windowboxes, tubs or hanging baskets for a plentiful supply of Cherry tomatoes.

TUMBLING TOM YELLOW: The plant grows like and looks like Tumbling Tom Red and so do the fruit, but they are golden-yellow, not red.

GARDEN PEARL: Yet another trailing type — this time the Cherry tomatoes are pink rather than red or yellow.

LOSETTO: An F_1 hybrid Cherry tomato which has good blight resistance.

Tumbling Tom Red

TOMATO TROUBLES

Diseases and disorders are much more important than insect pests — outdoor tomatoes are much less susceptible than crops grown under glass. Keep a careful watch and treat plants immediately symptoms appear. Tomatoes require regular feeding with a specific fertilizer which is rich in potash in order to prevent undersized fruit on the upper trusses. Don't over-feed — little and often is the secret.

	Symptom	Likely Causes
Seedlings	— eaten or severed	**Woodlice** or **Slugs** or **Cutworm** (see page 157)
	— toppled over	**Damping off** (see page 157)
	— gnawed roots	**Millepede** (see page 157)
Stems	— tunnelled	22 or **Wireworm** (no cure)
	— grey mouldy patches	4
	— brown zone near soil level	6 or 7
Leaves	— blue tinged	**Too cold** or **too dry**
	— yellow between veins	12
	— grey mould	4
	— papery patches	17
	— brown patches on upper surface	13
	— yellow patches on upper surface	3
	— mottled	1 or **Red spider mite** (see page 56)
	— curled	1 or 2 or 8 or 9
	— wilted	5 or 6 or 7 or 10 or 11
	— fern-like	1 or 8
	— infested with greenfly	**Aphid** (see page 157)
	— tiny moths, sticky surface	9
	— holed, caterpillars present	22
Roots	— brown, corky	5
	— covered with cysts or galls	10
Fruits	— flowers drop before fruits form	16
	— form, but drop before maturity	4
	— form, but remain tiny	19
	— sticky, covered with black mould	9
	— soft rot	23
	— discoloured spots or patches	14 or 15 or 17 or 18 or 20 or 25
	— hollow	8 or 21
	— split or tunnelled	22 or 24

DISTORTED OR DISCOLOURED LEAVES

Fern-leaf virus

Mosaic virus

1 | VIRUS

There are several important virus diseases which affect tomatoes. Leaves may be mottled and curled, stems may bear dark vertical streaks, foliage may be thin and distorted and growth may be stunted. Affected fruit is often mottled and bronzed.

Treatment: None. Destroy affected specimens. Feed remaining plants.

Prevention: Try to buy virus-free plants. Spray to control greenfly. Do not handle immediately after smoking.

2 | LEAF ROLL

Unlike potatoes, rolled tomato leaves do not indicate disease. The inward curling of young leaves is usually taken as a good sign if they are dark green. The rolling of older leaves is usually due to excess deleafing or a wide variation between day and night temperatures. Provided that pests and disease are absent, there is no need to take action.

5 | ROOT ROT

Poor drainage can lead to root disease. Below ground the roots become brown and corky, above ground the plants tend to wilt in hot weather. Rots cannot be cured once they have taken hold — mulch around the stems with moist garden compost to promote the formation of new roots. Next year grow plants in bags, fresh compost or sterilised soil.

BROWN MOULD PATCHES

3 | TOMATO LEAF MOULD

Purplish brown mould patches appear on the underside of the foliage — the upper surface bears yellowish patches. Lower leaves are attacked first.

Treatment: Remove some of the lower leaves. No systemic sprays are available.

Prevention: Ventilate the greenhouse, especially at night.

GREY FURRY PATCHES

4 | GREY MOULD (Botrytis)

Grey mould usually starts on a damaged area of the stem. Other parts of the plant may then be infected — diseased flower stalks cause fruit drop.

Treatment: Cut out diseased areas and remove all rotting parts.

Prevention: Reduce humidity by adequate ventilation. Remove decaying leaves and fruit. Avoid overcrowding. No systemic sprays are available.

6 | FOOT ROT

Foot rot is generally a disease of seedling tomatoes, but mature plants can be attacked.

Treatment: None if diseased area is large. Lift plant and burn. If plant is only slightly affected mulch stem base with moist garden compost and water with Cheshunt Compound; some fruit may be obtained.

Prevention: Use sterilised soil or compost for raising seedlings. Avoid overwatering. Never plant into infected soil.

BROWN STEM BASES

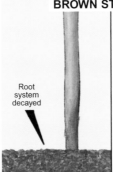

Root system decayed

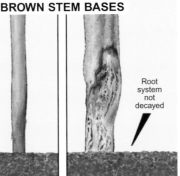

Root system not decayed

7 | STEM ROT (Didymella)

Stem rot is a disease of mature plants. Lower leaves turn yellow and a sunken brown canker appears at the base of the stem. Black dots develop in this cankered area. Disease may spread to other parts of the stem.

Treatment: None. Lift and destroy badly affected plants. If the plant is only slightly affected cut out the diseased area. Fungicidal sprays are no longer available for treating this disease.

Prevention: Sterilise greenhouse and equipment between crops.

FERN-LIKE LEAVES

8 | HORMONE DAMAGE

Traces of lawn weedkiller can cause severe distortion. Leaves are fern-like and twisted, stems and leaf stalks are also twisted. Similar in appearance to a virus disease, but spiral twisting is more pronounced. Fruit is plum-shaped and hollow. Avoid trouble by treating the lawn on a still day and by never using weedkiller equipment for other plants.

TINY MOTHS UNDER LEAVES

9 | GREENHOUSE WHITEFLY

The most widespread of all tomato pests. Both the adults and larvae suck sap from the leaves which become pale and curled. Foliage and fruit are rendered sticky — black mould grows on this honeydew, thereby disfiguring the surface.

Treatment: Not easy to control. Spray with pyrethrins at 3 day intervals until the infestation has been cleared. Spray in the morning or evening.

Prevention: Hang yellow Flycatcher Cards above the plants.

SWELLINGS ON ROOTS

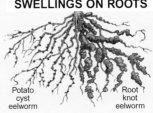

Potato cyst eelworm

Root knot eelworm

10 | EELWORM

Growth is stunted and leaves are discoloured and wilted. Foliage may be purplish on the underside. Roots bear either tiny white cysts (potato cyst eelworm) or large brown swellings (root knot eelworm).

Treatment: None. Destroy plants.

Prevention: Do not grow tomatoes or potatoes in infested soil for at least 6 years.

BROWN-STREAKED TISSUE

11 | VERTICILLIUM WILT

Leaves wilt in hot weather, appearing to recover on cool evenings. Lower leaves turn yellow. If you cut open the lower stem the tell-tale signs of wilt are revealed. Brown streaks run through the stem tissue.

Treatment: There is no chemical treatment — mulch around stem so new roots can form. If possible keep at 25ºC (77°F) for about 2 weeks.

Prevention: Do not grow tomatoes in infected soil — grow in compost.

YELLOWING BETWEEN VEINS

12 | MAGNESIUM DEFICIENCY

Discoloration begins on lower leaves and moves upwards until all foliage is affected. Yellow areas may turn brown. A common and serious disorder which is made worse, not better, by standard feeding.

Treatment: Spray with Epsom Salts (15 gm/½ litre,½ oz/pint) or use a foliar spray containing magnesium.

Prevention: Use a fertilizer which contains magnesium (Mg).

DARK BROWN BLOTCHES

13 | POTATO BLIGHT

Blight can be a devastating disease of outdoor tomatoes in wet weather. The first signs are brown areas on the edges of the leaves. The patches spread until the leaves are killed. Stems show blackened patches.

Treatment: None, once the disease has firmly taken hold.

Prevention: Systemic fungicides are no longer available for this disease. Use a copper-based spray. It is essential to spray at intervals as instructed.

TOMATO TROUBLES continued

FRUIT TROUBLES

14 BLOSSOM END ROT
Leathery dark-coloured patch occurs at the bottom of the fruit. It is a frequent problem where growing bags are used.

Treatment: None.

Prevention: Never let the soil or compost dry out, especially when the fruit is swelling.

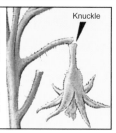

15 BLOTCHY RIPENING

Parts of the fruit remain yellow or orange and fail to ripen. The cause is usually too much heat or too little potash.

Treatment: None.

Prevention: Apply Coolglass and control heat. Feed with a potash-rich fertilizer. Water regularly.

16 BLOSSOM DROP
Flowers sometimes wither and break off at the knuckle. Pollination has not taken place, and the cause is usually dryness at the roots and in the air.

Treatment: None.

Prevention: Water regularly and spray flowers in the morning. Tap plants to aid pollination.

Knuckle

17 SUN SCALD
Pale brown, papery-skinned depression on the side of fruit facing the glass. Papery patches on leaves. Exposure to bright sun is the cause.

Treatment: None.

Prevention: Paint glass with Coolglass. Damp down adequately, but do not spray the plants at midday.

18 GHOST SPOT
Grey mould spores fall on or splash on to fruit. Small, transparent rings ('water spots') are formed.

Treatment: None. Affected fruit can be eaten.

Prevention: Provide good ventilation. Do not splash developing fruit when watering. Control grey mould.

19 DRY SET
Growth of the fruitlet ceases when it reaches the size of a match-head. The trouble is due to the air being too hot and dry when pollination is taking place.

Treatment: None.

Prevention: Spray the plants daily with water in the morning or evening.

20 GREENBACK
Area around the stalk remains hard, green and unripe. The cause is too much sunlight or too little potash.

Treatment: None.

Prevention: Apply Coolglass. Control heat of greenhouse. Feed regularly with a potash-rich fertilizer. Resistant varieties are available.

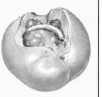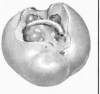

21 HOLLOW FRUIT

There are several causes of hollow fruit — poor conditions for pollination (air too hot, too cold or too dry), too little potash in the soil or damage by a hormone weedkiller.

Treatment: None.

Prevention: Avoid factors listed above.

22 TOMATO MOTH
Large green or brown caterpillars tunnel into fruit and stems. Young caterpillars eat holes in leaves.

Treatment: Too late for effective treatment at this stage. Destroy fruit.

Prevention: Spray with insecticidal soap when small caterpillars and holes appear on leaves.

23 POTATO BLIGHT
Brown, shrunken area appears on fruit. The affected tomato is soon completely rotten. Infection may develop during storage.

Treatment: None. Destroy fruit.

Prevention: Protect fruit by spraying against potato blight as soon as it appears on the leaves (page 103).

24 SPLIT FRUIT
A common complaint, both outdoors and under glass. It is caused by heavy watering or rain after the soil has become dry around the roots. The sudden increase in size causes the skin to split.

Treatment: None.

Prevention: Keep roots evenly moist.

25 BUCKEYE ROT
Brown concentric rings around a grey spot on unripe fruit. Spores splash up from soil on to trusses.

Treatment: None. Remove and destroy infected fruits.

Prevention: Tie up lower trusses to prevent splashing. Apply a mulch. Water carefully.

Turnip

The large and woody roots bought from the greengrocer or supermarket have a limited use in the kitchen — they are used as one of the ingredients in casseroles and stews. So this easy-to-grow and quick-maturing crop does not appear in the best-selling seed list. This is unfortunate, because home-grown turnips have much more to offer. There are Early (bunching) varieties which are sown in spring and then pulled when they are the size of golf balls for eating raw in salads or boiled for the dinner plate. Round is not the only shape for Early turnips — there are flat and cylindrical ones. The tops of Maincrop varieties sown in summer can be cut in spring for use as an alternative to spinach. An easy crop, but Earlies are more demanding than Maincrops.

IN A NUTSHELL

Actual Size

Expected germination time:	6–10 days
Approx. number per 30 gm (1oz):	8000
Expected yield from a 3 m (10 ft) row:	3 kg (7 lb) (Early varieties) 5 kg (11 lb) (Maincrop varieties)
Life expectancy of stored seed:	3 years
Approximate time between sowing and lifting:	6–12 weeks
Ease of cultivation:	Easy

SOIL FACTS

- Turnips are brassicas (see page 27) and like other members of the family need a firm, non-acid soil which has reasonable drainage.
- Early varieties require fertile soil — choose another crop if your soil is sandy or shallow.
- Pick a reasonably sunny spot and dig in autumn. Lime if necessary. In spring apply a compound fertilizer and prepare the seed bed about a week later. You will have to take preventative measures (page 28) if cabbage root fly is known to be a problem.

- **Early turnips:** Sow Purple-top Milan under cloches in February and other Early varieties outdoors during March-June for a May-September crop.
- **Maincrop turnips:** Sow Maincrop varieties in mid July-mid August for cropping and storage from mid October onwards.
- **Turnip tops:** Sow a Maincrop variety in August or September for spring greens in March and April.

SEED SOWING

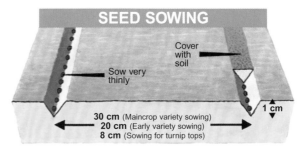

Sow very thinly

Cover with soil

1 cm

30 cm (Maincrop variety sowing)
20 cm (Early variety sowing)
8 cm (Sowing for turnip tops)

LOOKING AFTER THE CROP

- Thin out turnips grown for roots as soon as the seedlings are large enough to handle. Do this in stages until the plants are 25 cm / 10 in. (Maincrop varieties) or 15 cm / 6 in. (Early varieties) apart. Do not thin turnips grown for their tops.
- Keep the soil hoed and remember to water in dry weather — failure to do so will result in smaller and woodier roots. Rain following a dry spell can cause roots to crack if the soil has not been watered.
- Spray with pyrethrins at the first signs of flea beetle damage.

HARVESTING

- The roots of Early varieties are pulled like radishes rather than levered out with a fork like swedes. Pull whilst the roots are still small — golf-ball size if they are to be eaten raw or between golf-ball and tennis-ball size if they are to be cooked.
- Begin lifting Maincrop turnips as soon as they are large enough to use — remember that tenderness and flavour decrease with age. Harvesting normally begins in October and in most areas you can leave the turnips in the soil and lift them out with a fork as required. In cold and wet areas it is preferable to lift in early November — twist off the leaves and place the roots between layers of dry sand in a stout box. Store in a cool shed.
- Turnips grown for spring greens should have their tops cut in March or April when they are about 15 cm (6 in.) high. Leave the plants to resprout — several cuts should be obtained.

CALENDAR

	JAN	FEB	MAR	APR	MAY	JUN	JUL	AUG	SEP	OCT	NOV	DEC
Sowing Time												
Lifting Time				TOPS ONLY								

IN THE KITCHEN

Early turnips can be eaten raw — merely wash, remove the tops and roots, and peel thinly. Cut into slices or grate before adding to your favourite summer salad. Some people find raw turnips rather indigestible — in that case boil them whole for about 25 minutes and toss in butter and chopped parsley before serving. Maincrop turnips are more fibrous and need to be treated rather differently, as described below.

FREEZING: Use small turnips — wash, trim off the tops and roots, and cut into slices or cubes. Blanch for 3 minutes, cool and then drain thoroughly. Freeze in a rigid container.

STORAGE: Keep in a polythene bag in the refrigerator — turnips will stay fresh for up to 2 weeks.

COOKING: After trimming maincrop turnips the outer fibrous layer should be removed by peeling thickly. Cut the roots into chunks and boil for about 30 minutes. Drain thoroughly and decide on your method of serving this hot vegetable. You can toss the chunks in melted butter and parsley or you can mash them with butter, cream, pepper and a little lemon juice. Some people prefer to mix them with boiled carrots or potatoes before mashing. Stews, casseroles and soups are the usual home for turnips, but you can also parboil them for roasting around the Sunday joint. Turnip tops are cooked in the same way as spinach — place the leaves in a pan and add salt, pepper and a small knob of butter or margarine. Add no water — simply steam for about 10 minutes in the water left on the leaves after washing. Drain thoroughly in a strainer, squeeze out excess water with the back of a spoon.

VARIETIES

EARLY varieties

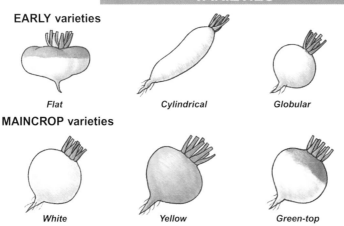

Flat   *Cylindrical*   *Globular*

MAINCROP varieties

White   *Yellow*   *Green-top*

Snowball

The Early varieties mature quickly and should be pulled when the roots are still small and tender. They are not suitable for storing — use within a few days of harvesting. Spring and early summer are the usual sowing times, although Tokyo Cross is recommended for sowing from spring to autumn. A globe is the usual shape, followed by the flat ones. Cylindrical turnips are out of favour, and you will have to search to find a supplier.

The Maincrops are larger and slower to mature than the Early varieties. They are also hardier with good keeping qualities — they can be lifted and stored in November for use throughout the winter and spring.

SNOWBALL: A quick-growing, globular turnip with white flesh. A popular variety, considered by many to be the best Early for both table and exhibition use. It is a good choice for growing under cloches to provide a May-June crop.

SWEETBELL: White globes with a purple top. This one is a multipurpose variety. You can cook the roots in the usual way, or you can grate them for eating raw in salads. Use the leaves as a spinach substitute.

PURPLE-TOP MILAN: Something different — a flat white turnip which is capped with purple. Very early.

WHITE-TOP MILAN: Similar in shape, taste etc to Purple-top Milan apart from its all-white colouring.

TINY PAL: An RHS Award of Garden Merit winner. Matures extremely quickly — pull when golf-ball size is reached. There is a long sowing season — the supplier claims that you can sow as late as August and get a Christmas crop.

MARKET EXPRESS: It is claimed that this white turnip can be ready in 30–40 days after sowing for pulling at golf-ball size.

RED GLOBE: The medium-sized roots are globular — the flesh is white and the skin is white with a red top. Leaves can be used in place of spinach.

TOKYO CROSS: Another Early variety which can be sown in late summer. A sowing between May and August produces small, white globes ready for harvesting in about 6 weeks.

SCARLET QUEEN: An Early variety which makes a change from the all-whites and part-whites. This one is bright red — lift when the roots are about 5 cm (2 in.) across.

GREEN-TOP WHITE: The roots of this Maincrop are large and green-topped if left in the ground to mature. There are very similar (or identical) varieties such as Marble-top Green, Green Top and Green Globe, but they are very hard to find these days.

GREEN-TOP STONE: The globe-shaped roots are pale green with a white base. They are sown in autumn for a winter crop.

GOLDEN BALL: The flesh is yellow and tender — the skin is golden. It is sown in the spring or autumn — a very hardy variety with good keeping qualities.

Green-Top White

TURNIP, SWEDE & RADISH TROUBLES

The brassica family is notorious for the frightening number of pests and diseases which can attack the plants. The root-producing members are no exception, as the extensive table on the right clearly shows, but in practice the troubles you are likely to encounter in the garden are very few. Flea beetle is the only serious problem of the radish crop — turnips and swedes have to face a few additional ones, including club root, powdery mildew and soft rot. Gall weevil and cabbage root fly are occasionally a nuisance, but the root brassicas are generally much healthier than the leafy ones such as cauliflower and Brussels sprouts.

	Symptom	Likely Causes
Seedlings	— eaten	**Birds** or **Slugs** (see page 29) or **Flea beetle** (see page 30) or **Cutworm** (see page 31)
	— toppled over	**Damping off** (see page 157)
	— peppered with small holes	**Flea beetle** (see page 30)
	— severed at ground level	**Cutworm** (see page 31)
Leaves	— swollen, distorted ('Crumple leaf')	**Swede midge** (see page 30)
	— white floury coating	**Powdery mildew** (see page 21)
	— greyish mould on underside	**Downy mildew** (see page 28)
	— white spots	**White blister** (see page 29)
	— yellowing; black veins	4
	— dark green, raised spots	1
	— infested with greenfly	**Mealy aphid** (see page 30)
	— holed	**Cabbage caterpillar** (see page 29) or **Slugs** (see page 29) or **Flea beetle** (see page 30) or **Diamond-back moth** (see page 31)
Roots	— tunnelled, maggots present	**Cabbage root fly** (see page 28)
	— swollen outgrowths	**Club root** or **Gall weevil** (see page 28)
	— covered with purple mould	**Violet root rot** (see page 43)
	— scabby patches	**Common scab** (see page 85)
	— side shoots around crown ('Many neck')	**Swede midge** (see page 30)
	— split	**Splitting** (see page 43)
	— bitter, stringy	3
	— woody	**Short of water or fertilizer** or **Delayed harvesting**
	— inner black ring	4
	— wet rot starting at crown	2
	— brown markings in flesh	3

DARK GREEN SPOTS

1 | TURNIP MOSAIC VIRUS

An infectious and damaging disease of turnips, which is fortunately uncommon. Young leaves are twisted and mottled; it may be fatal to young plants. Tell-tale sign is the presence of dark green, raised spots on the leaves.

Treatment: There is no cure. Destroy affected plants, as this disease can lead to soft rot.

Prevention: Spray with insecticidal soap to control the greenfly which are the carriers of the disease.

2 | SOFT ROT

A wet and slimy rot, beginning at the crown, can occur in both the growing crop and in stored roots. The outer skin of the roots remains firm. A tell-tale sign is the collapse of the foliage. Soft rot can be serious, especially in a wet season. It is essential to remove affected plants immediately. To avoid trouble next season make sure the soil is well drained, avoid over-manuring, be careful not to injure roots when hoeing and never store damaged turnips or swedes. Practise crop rotation.

BROWN MARKINGS

3 | BROWN HEART

Greyish-brown rings run through the flesh. Affected areas become water-soaked. This disease is much more likely to attack swedes than turnips, and is usually restricted to light soils in a dry season. Affected roots are bitter. The cause is boron deficiency.

Treatment: None.

Prevention: If soil is known to be boron deficient, apply 30 gm (1 oz) of borax per 16 sq.m (180 sq.ft) before planting — take care not to overdose.

OUTER BLACK RING

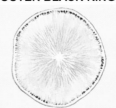

4 | BLACK ROT

Above ground the symptoms of black rot are yellow leaves with black veins (see page 29). If an affected root is cut across a tell-tale ring of black dots can be seen just below the skin. Attacks are worst in a warm, wet summer on poorly drained soil.

Treatment: None. Lift diseased plants and burn.

Prevention: Practise crop rotation. Make sure the soil is well drained.

CHAPTER 3
BABY VEGETABLES

Cauliflowers no larger than a tennis ball and tiny cobs of sweet corn for stir-frying. Bite-sized tomatoes and cucumbers that can fit in the palm of your hand. These baby vegetables have been bred to be genetically undersized varieties.

There is, however, another type of baby vegetable. These are standard varieties which are grown closely together and are then harvested at an early stage. They are generally quick-maturing varieties — good examples are Early carrots such as Amsterdam Forcing and Early turnips like Snowball. The leek Jolant can be widely spaced and left to mature to produce 30 cm (1 ft) thick white shanks, but it can also be grown in close rows and pulled after 12 weeks as a substitute for spring onions.

Thus there are two types of baby vegetable. Both are grown more closely together than ordinary varieties grown in the standard way. The usual distance between rows is 15 cm (6 in.), but you will need more space for larger plants such as courgettes and sweet corn. The distance between the plants after thinning is 3 cm (1 in.) for roots such as carrots, beetroots and turnips, 15 cm (6 in.) for cabbage and lettuce, and 30 cm (1 ft) for sweet corn.

Baby vegetables are extremely useful where space is limited. They make growing food in pots, tubs, tiny beds and window boxes a practical proposition, but there is a golden rule for you to follow. They need to be grown quickly. Humus-rich soil is necessary, and so is regular feeding in addition to thorough watering when the weather is dry.

They are described and illustrated as a separate section in a few catalogues, but it is more usual to find them listed alongside the normal-sized varieties of the vegetable.

Cauliflower Idol

Kale Showbor

Parsnip Lancer

BABY VEGETABLE VARIETIES

Included here are varieties which have been specially bred as baby vegetables, together with some standard varieties which can be harvested at an early stage.

A number of the varieties listed below appear in this book — the remainder can be found either in one or more of the popular seed catalogues or by searching for a supplier on the internet.

VEGETABLE	VARIETY
BEETROOT	Solo Detroit 2 — Little Ball
BRUSSELS SPROUT	Energy Bitesize
CABBAGE (RED)	Primero
CABBAGE (SAVOY)	Protovoy
CAPSICUM	Minibell
CARROT	Amsterdam Forcing Parmex
CAULIFLOWER	Igloo
COURGETTE	Supremo Patriot
CUCUMBER	Petita
FRENCH BEAN	Masai Safari
KALE	Redbor
KOHL RABI	Logo
LEEK	King Richard Jolant
LETTUCE	Blush Minigreen Tom Thumb
ONION	Imai Senshyu
PARSNIP	Arrow Lancer
SPINACH	Teton
SQUASH	Sunburst Peter Pan
SWEET CORN	Minipop
TOMATO	Tumbler Gardener's Delight Sweet Million Red Alert
TURNIP	Tiny Pal Tokyo Cross

Turnip Tokyo Cross

Cabbage Protovoy

Leek King Richard

Brussels sprout Energy

Sweet corn Minipop

Carrot Amini

CHAPTER 4
HERBS

The increase in the number of TV cookery programmes and celebrity cookery books in recent years has led to a growing interest in exotic recipes. One of the results has been a resurgence in the use of herbs.

In bygone days herbs were widely grown for medicinal purposes, but this need has greatly declined with the advent of modern medicines. Once there was a need for sweet-smelling herbs to mask the unpleasant odours, but with modern sanitation they are no longer required.

Neither of these two uses has entirely disappeared, and both are touched on in this chapter and so are herb teas, but almost all the plants described here are culinary (pot) herbs which are grown for adding to food. They differ from vegetables by adding flavour or serving as a garnish rather than being a dish in their own right.

This culinary use of adding flavour is shared with spices. We might feel that we know how to tell a herb from a spice, but surprisingly there is no clear-cut dividing line. One book says that 'herbs grow in temperate areas and spices grow in sub-tropical and tropical areas' but that won't do. The definition in this book is a very simple one — a herb is a flavouring and/or a garnishing plant which is traditionally thought of as a herb and not a spice.

Growing herbs is for everyone. Pots of parsley, thyme, mint etc can be grown on the windowsill. If there is a balcony or patio you can be more expansive with a herb trough or growing bags, but for those of us blessed with a garden we can create a herb bed.

In the following pages the most popular home-grown types are described. Nearly all are quite easy to grow, and the standard requirements are for some sun, a well-drained soil and fairly regular picking to keep the plant compact. Weeding will be necessary, and so will watering when the weather is dry.

Site the bed as close to the house as possible and wherever possible grow each type in a separate pocket. Most types can be raised from seed, but you may find it more practical to buy small plants from the garden centre if your needs are modest.

Most herbs can be dried for winter use. Hang them in bunches in a warm airing cupboard or greenhouse for several days and then move to a room with an ordinary temperature until they are cornflake crisp. Crush and store in an airtight tin.

The ice-cube method has revolutionised the preservation of soft-leaved herbs. Fill each cup of an ice-cube tray with the chopped and blanched herb, and top up with water. Place in the freezer, and then bag up the cubes in a plastic bag before returning to the freezer. Use cubes to replace the fresh chopped leaves called for in the recipe.

Herb Gardens

A group of pots containing herbs is well worth considering if you use only a few different types and the amount you require to pick is small. Site the pots near the kitchen. ▷

Some herbs (sage, thyme, mint, etc.) are ◁ available in different colours so that you can make an attractive bed in various shades. A problem here is that the invasive types soon spread and swamp the more restrained ones.

△ *The best way to grow herbs is to create a system of pockets into which a single variety is sown or planted. You can create your own scheme in a paved area by removing some slabs or you can buy a preformed herb wheel as illustrated above.*

Herb Uses

BOUQUET GARNI

A bunch of several sprigs of parsley, a sprig of thyme and a bay leaf tied with fine thread. Tarragon or marjoram may be added. Place the bouquet garni in stock, stews or casseroles during cooking — remove before serving. If dried herbs are used it is necessary to place them in a muslin bag before putting in the pan.

FINES HERBES

A mixture of finely-chopped herbs with a delicate flavour. Three or more are required — popular ingredients are parsley, chives, chervil and tarragon. The mixture is used fresh or dried and is mainly associated with egg dishes.

HERB BUTTER

Butter in which finely-chopped herbs have been incorporated. The herbs should have a strong flavour — examples include garlic, thyme, chives, rosemary and sage. Mix about a tablespoon of herbs to 100 gm (4 oz) of softened butter — beat until they are evenly mixed. Let the herb butter stand for a day or more before serving and then put into a mould or place in the refrigerator before cutting into cubes. Cream cheese can be flavoured in the same way.

HERB OIL

Oil in which one or more herbs have been steeped. Olive oil, sunflower oil, etc. are being increasingly used for salad dressings, marinading and stir-frying, etc. these days and these oils can be given a flavour boost by adding sprigs of herbs. Leave the mixture to stand for about a month and then strain before bottling the oil. A favourite herb oil for Italian cooking is basil-flavoured olive oil, but there are others to try — fennel, marjoram, savory, etc.

HERB PILLOW

With modern sanitation the need for herb pillows is less than it used to be, but a sachet of sweet-smelling herbs inside the pillow case can still be a welcome and soothing touch. The favourite plant materials are the ones which smell of newly-mown hay when dried — examples include woodruff and melilot. Hops are another popular material as they are reputed to have sleep-inducing properties.

HERB TEA

A drink made by steeping herb leaves, flowers or fruits in hot water to produce a tisane (tea made with unfermented plant material). Mint and chamomile are the favourite herbs — use fresh or deep frozen leaves (see page 110) rather than dried ones if you can. Pour boiling water over the leaves and allow to stand for 5–15 minutes before serving. Use 3 teaspoons of chopped fresh herbs (1 teaspoon if dried) per cup of water.

HERB VINEGAR

Vinegar in which one or more herbs have been steeped. Bruise the leaves of a few sprigs of the chosen herb and place in a jar — pour 500 cc (1 pt) of tepid wine vinegar over them. Cover tightly and place the jar in a warm place for about 2–3 weeks — shake occasionally. Strain the vinegar and then bottle — include a sprig of the herb. Suitable herbs include mint, dill, rosemary, chervil, bay, basil and thyme — use alone or in combination.

MIXED HERBS

A mixture of chopped herbs with a stronger flavour than *fines herbes*. Popular ingredients include sage, thyme, marjoram and parsley. The mixture is used fresh or dried and is recommended for fish and meat dishes.

PESTO

An Italian sauce which has become popular for use with pasta, steak and poultry. It is a blend of two herbs (basil and garlic) with parmesan cheese, pine nuts and olive oil.

POT-POURRI

A mixture of dried flowers and leaves which remains fragrant for a long time. There are many recipes — below is a typical example. Collect petals from colourful flowers (marigold, rose, delphinium, cornflower, etc.) and place on a mesh-bottomed rack together with leaves from aromatic herbs — mint, lavender, pineapple sage, geranium, bergamot, etc. Place in an airing cupboard for a week or two, stirring occasionally until cornflake-crisp. You now need to add a mixture of spices (to enrich the fragrance) and a fixative (to stop the fragrance from disappearing in a short time). A basic recipe is 30 gm (1 oz) dried orris root, ½ teaspoon allspice and ½ teaspoon cinnamon to 1 lt (1 qt) of dried flowers and leaves. Keep in a tightly-closed container for about 3 weeks before placing in bowls around the house. Add a few drops of flower oil (rose or violet) when fragrance fades.

SALAD FLOWERS

Flowers from herbs and a few other plants which can be used to both decorate and add flavour to salads and other cold dishes. Examples include rose, chives, nasturtium, basil, thyme and pot marigold.

TUSSIE MUSSIE

A small nosegay or posy made with fragrant herbs surrounding a central flower. This central flower is usually a rose bud with a ring of other flowers (e.g violets, honeysuckle, pinks) round it. The outer leafy ring is composed of lavender, scented geranium, thyme, etc. Ribbon is tied around the leaf stalks to keep the posy in place.

BASIL

This herb has become a favourite in recent years and there are now green, red and purple varieties in a range of flavours. Sow under glass in spring and plant out in early June — space plants about 30 cm (1 ft) apart. During the summer months gather leaves as required — preserve by the ice-cube method (see page 110). For fresh leaves in winter pot up a plant and keep on the windowsill. Basil is an essential ingredient alongside tomatoes in many Italian recipes.

BAY

The sweet bay is an evergreen, laurel-like shrub or small tree. It may suffer in cold winters, but new growth appears from the base in spring. Pick a sheltered spot and plant a pot-grown specimen in spring. Water during dry spells in summer. Pick young leaves for kitchen use and dry some at room temperature for winter. Bay leaves are a basic ingredient of a *bouquet garni*, and are also used in stews and fish dishes. Caution — never use laurel leaves by mistake.

BERGAMOT

You will find this herb in the perennial flowers section of your garden centre. It is the well-known border plant Monarda, and not the bergamot used in Earl Grey tea. Plant pot-grown specimens 60 cm (2 ft) apart. It will grow 60 cm–1 m (2–3 ft) high — cut back to soil level in autumn. The mint-like leaves are orange-flavoured and are used in desserts. The flower-heads can be used to decorate trifles etc, and a herb tea (see page 112) can be made with the leaves.

BORAGE

The leaves and flowers are used where a cucumber-like flavour is required. The plants grow about 60 cm–1 m (2–3 ft) and small blue flowers appear in summer. Choose a sunny spot and sow seeds in the herb garden in April-July — borage hates transplanting. Thin seedlings to about 45 cm (1½ ft). Staking will be necessary. The main use is as a garnish/flavouring for cold drinks — wine, fruit juice etc. Use leaves or flowers. Finely-chopped leaves can be added to salads or sandwiches.

CARAWAY

A biennial herb which bears small pink flowers on 60 cm (2 ft) stems. It hates transplanting — sow seeds where it is to grow. Partial shade is preferred and autumn is the best time for sowing. Thin to about 15 cm (6 in.). Cut leaves during the growing season — the flavour is more like parsley than 'caraway'. The caraway flavour is obtained from the seeds. Harvest when brown — leave to dry in a paper bag. Use in coleslaw, soups, baking rye bread etc.

CHAMOMILE

Several types are available — the one to choose is the English chamomile *Anthemis nobilis Flore Pleno*. This creeping perennial grows about 15 cm (6 in.) high and produces yellow-centred flowers above the feathery leaves. Plant clumps in spring or autumn — leave 20 cm (8 in.) between plants. Lift and divide the plants every 3 years. Chamomile is not used in food preparation but it does have several other uses. The most popular is for making a herb tea.

CHERVIL

Chervil grows quickly — the first leaves can be picked about 8 weeks after sowing. It is hardy, so you can pick the parsley-like leaves in winter when many other herbs have died down. Sow where it is to grow, thin to about 15 cm (6 in.) apart and water regularly when it is dry. Always remove outer leaves first — remove most of the flowers at the same time. The aniseed flavour is short-lived, so add to soups, fish dishes and salads just before serving.

CHIVES

The mild member of the onion family — the grass-like leaves are cut between March and October. Use the ice-cube method (page 110) to preserve for winter use. Plant pot-grown specimens in spring or autumn — leave 20 cm (8 in.) between the clumps. Water regularly. Cut leaves to about 3 cm (1 in.) above the ground — remove flowers before they open. Many uses — add finely-chopped leaves to potato salad, stuffed eggs, soups, omelettes, salads etc.

CORIANDER

The aromatic leaves are used to give a spicy flavour to soups, salads and meat dishes — the seeds are used in curries. Pick a sunny spot and sow the seeds of this annual in spring. Thin the seedlings to 10 cm (4 in.) apart — keep the row weeded. For seed collection cut the flower-heads when the seeds are brown, cover with a paper bag and hang up to dry in a warm place. Grow the variety 'Leisure' if you are interested in the leaves rather than the seeds.

DILL

Dill has attractive feathery foliage and flat plates of small yellow flowers in summer. The distinct flavour of the foliage is retained after drying, and the seeds when crushed have an even stronger flavour. Sow seeds in April where they are to grow, and thin to 30 cm (1 ft). Pick young leaves for immediate use and for drying. For seed gathering, see coriander. Chopped leaves are used with yoghurt and in meat dishes. Seeds have various uses, including pickling cucumber.

FENNEL

A 1.5 m (5 ft) perennial with blue-green feathery foliage which has an aniseed flavour. Do not confuse with the vegetable Florence fennel — see page 126. Choose a sunny spot in the herb bed or herbaceous border and plant a pot-grown specimen in spring. Pick leaves in summer as required — harvest seeds using the coriander method (see above). In the kitchen fennel is interchangeable with dill — the seeds are highly recommended for cooking with oily fish.

GARLIC

Any well-drained spot will do for this herb. Buy a head of garlic from a supermarket and split it up into individual cloves. Plant these cloves 5 cm (2 in.) deep and 15 cm (6 in.) apart in March. There is little else to do apart from watering in dry weather. In July or August the foliage turns yellow and it is now time to lift and allow the heads to dry under cover. Garlic has an important role in Continental cookery, but there is no point in growing it if you are not a fan.

HORSERADISH

Horseradish sauce is the traditional accompaniment for roast beef. However, you would have to be a horseradish devotee to grow it in your garden, especially as it can spread so rapidly. Make a 15 cm (6 in.) deep hole with a dibber, and drop in a 15 cm (6 in.) piece of root. Set the plants 60 cm (2 ft) apart. Lift the plants in October — store the roots in sand. Grated horseradish can be used as a garnish for fish, but it is generally used to make a sauce for beef or ham.

HYSSOP

This shrubby perennial has narrow, dark leaves and spikes of late summer flowers. Choose a sunny area and sow seeds in spring if you need more than one plant. Set out seedlings or pot-grown plants 60 cm (2 ft) apart. Pinch out growing tips and cut back hard in spring every year. The leaves are used in salads, soups and stews to provide a flavour described as sage-minty. They are also used to flavour pork, and the flowers make a colourful garnish.

LAVENDER

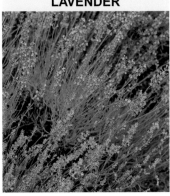

The grey-green needle-like leaves and the spikes of fragrant mauve flowers are known to everyone, but other colours and shapes are available. Plant rooted cuttings in sunny, well-drained soil at 30 cm (1 ft) intervals. Prune once the flowers have faded, but do not cut back into old wood. The plants become leggy with time — replant every 5 years. It is of little or no use in the kitchen — use it to make pot-pourri or sew flower-heads in small muslin bags.

LEMON BALM

A bushy 1 m (3 ft) perennial which like mint can quickly spread. It is grown for its leaves which emit a strong lemon aroma when crushed. Start with small potted plants — it has no special soil or site needs. Remove flowers as they appear — cut back stems at the end of the season. Divide the clumps in spring or autumn if you want more plants. Add chopped fresh leaves to salads and fish dishes — add dried leaves to stuffing mixes and to pot-pourri, or use to make herb tea.

LEMON GRASS

Lemon grass grows wild in many tropical countries, and is an essential ingredient in many Thai dishes. For the adventurous seed is available in a number of catalogues. It is a half-hardy perennial which is raised from seed which is sown indoors and then kept as potted plants in the greenhouse or stood outdoors if you live in a mild area. The swollen stem-bases are crushed or sliced to provide a lemon-like flavour to stir-fries and Oriental dishes.

LOVAGE

One of the giants of the herb world — the stems can reach 2 m (7 ft) or more. Buy plants from a supplier and set them 60 cm (2 ft) apart in spring — a humus-rich soil and thorough watering in dry weather are required. Cut off the greenish flower-heads when they appear. The stalks die down in late autumn — cut them off at ground level. Use the fresh leaves in the kitchen — drying is not advised. Use chopped leaves as a celery-pepper substitute in stews, salads etc.

MARIGOLD

There are few annuals which are easier to grow and not many herbs which can match the pot marigold *Calendula officinalis* for colour. Sow the seeds where the plants are to grow, and thin seedlings to 15 cm (6 in.) apart. Dead-head blooms to prolong active growth and prevent self-seeding. It is the flowers which are used as a herb — use fresh petals or flower-heads to add colour to salads, soups, egg dishes etc. Dried flowers are used as a saffron substitute.

MARJORAM

The easiest variety to grow is pot marjoram. It is a hardy perennial which forms a 30 cm (1 ft) high bush. Sow seeds in March or buy potted seedlings. Set out the plants 20 cm (8 in.) apart in May. Sweet marjoram has a stronger aroma and flavour, and is used in bouquets garni and pot-pourris, but it is killed by winter frosts. The main use of marjoram is for sprinkling over meat or poultry before roasting. Dried marjoram is a stuffing ingredient.

MINT

Mint shares the popularity crown with parsley. Plant pieces of root 5 cm (2 in.) deep and 20 cm (8 in.) apart in autumn or spring. It will thrive in any soil — it usually thrives too well and spreads rapidly. Growing in containers or growing as an annual are easy answers. There are several types — spearmint, Bowles mint, apple mint etc. Sprigs of mint are added to the water when new potatoes or peas are boiled, and chopped mint is the basic ingredient of mint sauce.

OREGANO

Greek oregano has a stronger flavour than other oregano/marjoram varieties — it is an essential ingredient of many Greek dishes. It grows about 60 cm (2 ft) high. Sow seeds in March — set out seedlings 20 cm (8 in.) apart once the danger of frost has passed. The leaves of this perennial are regarded as the stars of the oregano/marjoram group with a wide range of uses — lamb dishes, pizzas, omelettes etc. Use dried leaves as a substitute for sage in chicken stuffing.

PARSLEY

You will find several types in the seed catalogues — the curly-leaved ones are the most decorative and the plain-leaved varieties have the most flavour. Sow seed 1 cm (½ in.) deep in April or August in a semi-shady spot — thin seedlings to 20 cm (8 in.) apart. Remove flowering stems and pick regularly as required. It is our favourite garnish, of course, and is widely used in bouquets garni and fines herbes mixes. Try fried parsley as a vegetable.

ROSEMARY

An attractive evergreen shrub which requires well-drained soil in a sunny, sheltered spot. You can start from seed, but it is better to buy a pot-grown plant in spring. Winter frosts may kill some of the shoots but new growth will appear from the base. Both the needle-like leaves and blue flowers are highly aromatic and are used to flavour meat dishes. Rosemary must be used sparingly. Insert a few sprigs before roasting lamb, veal or pork — remove before serving.

SAGE

The grey-green leaves and spikes of blue flowers are equally at home in the shrub border and herb garden. Plant a pot-grown specimen in a sunny, well-drained spot in spring. Gather leaves regularly — prune lightly after flowering. Collect foliage for drying before the plant has flowered. Sage has a strong flavour and traditionally accompanies onions in the stuffing for goose and duck. It is also used with veal and pork, and in sausages and tomato dishes.

SALAD BURNET

This evergreen perennial with ferny leaves can be used to edge the herb bed. The reddish flower-heads should be removed. Sow seeds in spring and set out the seedlings at 30 cm (1 ft) intervals. Pick leaves as required from the low-growing leafy rosettes. These leaves are odourless, but the chopped foliage has a strong cucumber-like flavour and is used where this taste is required. Examples include summer drinks, sandwiches, soups, salads and yoghurt.

SAVORY

Savory provides an alternative to popular herbs such as sage. There are two types. Summer savory is an annual sown 1 cm (½ in.) deep and thinned to 15 cm (6 in.) intervals. Gather leaves before the flowers appear. Winter savory is a perennial — plant in April and trim back in early spring each year. Both types are used in the same way — summer savory has the better flavour. They are a traditional flavouring for broad beans and lentil soup. Add to salads and egg dishes.

SWEET CICELY

You will need space and humus-rich soil for this perennial — the soft fern-like leaves may grow to 45 cm (1½ ft). Buy one or two pot-grown plants. At the end of the season remove the stems when the leaves have turned brown — new growth appears in early spring. The leaves and the green seeds which follow the white flowers taste of aniseed — brown seeds have no flavour. Chopped leaves and stalks are a natural sweetener for tart fruits. Sprinkle seeds over desserts.

TARRAGON

Make sure you buy French tarragon — the so-called King of herbs. The Russian variety is tasteless. Tarragon spreads like mint — cover the plant with fleece in late autumn. Plant a pot-grown specimen in March. Pick from June to October — remove flowering shoots. Any surplus can be preserved by drying or the ice-cube method (see page 110). Tarragon is used in many classical chicken and fish dishes. Add fresh leaves to omelettes and salads.

THYME

A low-growing evergreen shrub which is delightfully aromatic. Fresh leaves can be picked all year round, so there is no need for drying. Common thyme has the strongest flavour — there is also lemon thyme and caraway thyme. Plant pot-grown specimens 30 cm (1 ft) apart in spring. Pick the leaves as required and divide every 3 years. It is the traditional partner for parsley in the stuffing for poultry. Rub on to meat before roasting and add to fish dishes. Use sparingly.

CHAPTER 5
NOVELTY VARIETIES

'Novelty vegetables' and 'unusual vegetables' are not the same thing. A potato which is fully resistant to blight would be an unusual variety, but not a novelty. To be a novelty variety the vegetable has to have a colour, shape or size which is quite different to the ordinary varieties. In seed catalogues the novelties are included with the ordinary types — in this book the novelty varieties have been grouped together. In this chapter you will find many examples — the white carrot, the ball-shaped cucumber, the purple asparagus and so on. There is a large group of novelties that share the same feature — they are all true dwarfs. These baby vegetables can be found in Chapter 3.

Obviously growing novelty varieties is a good way of surprising your guests around the dinner table, but the general advice is that you should regard novelties in your seed list in the same way as you regard spices in cooking. A little can add interest — too much can be overwhelming.

Asparagus

For details concerning cultivation and cooking see pages 10–11.

PURPLE SPEARS

STEWARTS PURPLE
JACMAR PURPLE
PURPLE PASSION

Purple spears are of course a talking point on the dining room table, but these varieties are much more than coloured novelties. The entire spear is free from fibre, so that young ones can be eaten raw in salads and mature spears need very little trimming before cooking. The sugar content is unusually high. The purple colour is retained when the spears are steamed.

Bean, Broad

For details concerning cultivation and cooking see pages 14–15.

COLOURED BEANS

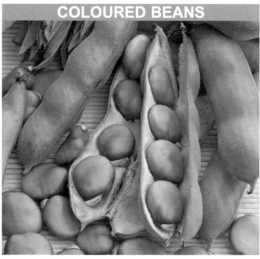

KARMAZYN (pink beans)
RED EPICURE (reddish-brown beans)

There is more to these beans than their novel appearance, the flavour of both of them is rated very highly. In both cases the pods are the usual green of broad beans, but the unusual colour of the beans is retained when steamed. Karmazyn is a compact plant — raw young beans can be used as a salad vegetable. Red Epicure grows to about 1 m (3 ft) — the beans turn yellow if boiled.

Bean, French

For details concerning cultivation and cooking see pages 16–17.

STRIPED PODS

BORLETTO LINGUA DI FUOCO (Climber)
BORLETTO SOLISTA (Climber)
BORLETTO SUPREMO (Dwarf)

The Borletto bean is an Italian type of climbing Flat-pod. Bright red stripes and blotches cover the green pods — unfortunately this colour is lost when they are cooked. The pods can be steamed or boiled whole, or shelled to provide fresh beans (flageolet) for cooking. The pods can also be dried to provide haricot beans for storage.

CURLED PODS

ANELLINO GIALLO

Another Italian novelty. This one is the Shrimp Ring Bean, so called because of the curved shape of its small yellow pods. The recommended cooking method is to steam the uncut pods and serve with an olive oil dressing.

COLOURED PODS

AMETHYST (purple)
PURPLE QUEEN (purple)
PURPLE-PODDED CLIMBING (purple)
SUNGOLD (yellow)

Non-green varieties make picking easier, and are a change from the usual green at the dinner table. Information on these varieties is on page 17.

Beet, Leaf

For details concerning cultivation and cooking see page 23.

VARIETY OF STEM COLOURS

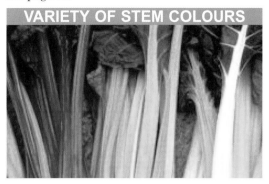

BRIGHT LIGHTS
RAINBOW CHARD

The leaf beets (chards) are attractive plants with showy stems. There are varieties with white, yellow or red stems — the novelty ones bear stems in various colours. For further details see page 23.

Beetroot

For details concerning cultivation and cooking see pages 24–25.

RED & WHITE RINGS

CHIOGGA

Chiogga is an Italian variety which will brighten up the salad bowl. The slices of the pink-skinned root are made up of dark red and white alternating rings to provide a bulls-eye effect. The roots are cooked in the usual way, and the young leaves are used in salads or cooked to provide an excellent spinach substitute.

PALE-COLOURED ROOTS

GOLDEN BEET (yellow)
BURPEE'S GOLDEN (yellow)
ALBINA VEREDUNA (white)
WHITE DETROIT (white)

You will find white and/or yellow varieties of beetroot in most catalogues and garden centres — an interesting change from the standard red colour. This is not the only virtue — staining is less of a hazard, and the flavour is sweeter. For further information see page 25.

Brussels sprout

For details concerning cultivation and cooking
see pages 34–35.

RED SPROUTS

RED BULL
RUBINE

A festive colour for our favourite Christmas-table
vegetable. The colour deepens as the weather turns
colder, and it is retained if the sprouts are steamed. The
flavour is sweeter than most green varieties.

Carrot

For details concerning cultivation and cooking
see pages 40–41.

COLOURED ROOTS

PURPLE HAZE (purple)
YELLOWSTONE (yellow)
WHITE SATIN (white)
RAINBOW (mixed colours)
HARLEQUIN (mixed colours)

Some of the coloured carrots are sweeter than the
average carrot, but their claim to fame is the non-
orange colour of their skin. This colour is retained after
cooking. Purple Haze has the most striking colouring —
it is also the one you are most likely to find.

Cauliflower

For details concerning cultivation and cooking
see pages 44–45.

COLOURED CURDS

GRAFFITI (purple)
VIOLET QUEEN (violet)
TREVI (pale green) — see page 45
SUNSET (orange)

Florets of cauliflower are welcome additions to the
salad or *crudité* bowl, but their white or pale cream
colour adds little interest. In the catalogues and in the
garden centres you can find one or more varieties
which can provide colour to the bowl. Purple Graffiti is
popular — colour needs light in order to darken, so do
not cover the curd.

HEADS OF CONICAL FLORETS

ROMANESCO

The Romanesco varieties bear a pointed head which is
made up of small cone-shaped green florets. These
florets are crunchy when eaten raw, and are strongly
recommended for eating with dips. When steamed the
florets are more tender and better-flavoured than other
cauliflowers. An excellent choice even without its
novelty value.

Courgette

For details concerning cultivation and cooking see pages 68–69.

BI-COLOURED COURGETTES

SUNSTRIPE
ZEPHYR

Zephyr has a standard cylindrical shape and the cream colour of the skin is not unusual. It is the distinct pale green lower section which makes it unique. Sunstripe is yellow with white stripes.

ROUND COURGETTES

GEODE (pale green)
EIGHT BALL (dark green)
ONE BALL (yellow)

This small group of courgettes are quite distinct from the courgettes you will find in the shops. Instead of being cylindrical like small cucumbers they are round like tennis balls.

Cucumber

For details concerning cultivation and cooking see pages 52–53.

ROUND CUCUMBERS

CRYSTAL LEMON

This unique variety of outdoor cucumber is about a hundred years old but it has never become popular — it is present in only a few catalogues. The ball-shaped fruits are small and yellow — the outstanding flavour is free from bitterness.

Onion

For details concerning cultivation and cooking see pages 72–73.

RED SPRING ONIONS

LONG RED FLORENCE
REDMATE
N. HOLLAND BLOOD RED
FURIO

A few of the novelty varieties in this chapter are coloured versions of white vegetables which are used to brighten up the salad bowl — red spring onions belong in this list. The one you are most likely to find is Redmate — other name N. Holland Blood Red.

PERENNIAL ONION

WELSH ONION

This hardy perennial produces clumps of thick hollow leaves which have a strong onion-like flavour. These leaves stay green all-year-round and can be used as a herb — a chive substitute for flavouring, or as a vegetable — a spring onion substitute in recipes or in the salad bowl. It grows about 60 cm (2 ft) high and can be used as an edging plant for the vegetable plot.

Pea

For details concerning cultivation and cooking see pages 77–78.

PURPLE PODS

BLAUWSCHOKKER

When shelled the pods display ordinary-looking peas, but the flowers and the pods are unusual. The flowers are red and violet, and the pods are purple. The weak stems require support.

MULTI-PURPOSE PEA

PEA BEAN

A unique climbing variety which should be grown like a runner bean. The pods can be picked when they are young and cooked whole as mangetout. Mature pods can be shelled, and the peas cooked in the usual way. Finally, the pods can be dried to produce white/brown haricot-style peas for storage.

Potato

For details concerning cultivation and cooking see pages 80–81.

PURPLE POTATOES

PURPLE MAJESTY

An excellent potato for all forms of cooking, but it is its colour which makes it unique. It is deep purple both inside and out, and this colour is retained when the tubers are cooked.

Radicchio (Chicory, Red)

For details concerning cultivation and cooking see pages 50.

WHITE-VEINED RED LEAVES

PALLA ROSSA — see page 50
ROSSA DE VERONA — see page 50
CESARE
ROSSA DI TREVISIO PRECOCE

This Italian type of chicory has become a popular ingredient in shop-bought salad mixes, but it is still a novelty in the vegetable plot. The heads are lettuce-like — the red colour deepens when the weather gets colder and the days get shorter. Cropping starts in autumn — use cloches to extend the season.

Radish

For details concerning cultivation and cooking see pages 86–87.

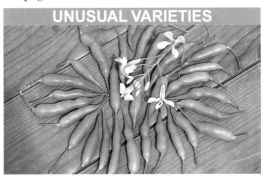

UNUSUAL VARIETIES

AMETHYST
ZLATA
RED MEAT
MANTANGHONG
MUNCHEN BIER

There are several novel varieties to provide a change from the usual red and red/white small types. On page 87 there are details of the giant Japanese varieties and the large winter roots. Other novelties include the purple-skinned Amethyst, the red-fleshed Red Meat, the yellow Zlata and the pink-fleshed Mantanghong. There is even a variety (Munchen Bier) where the seed pods and not the roots are eaten.

Tomato

For details concerning cultivation and cooking see pages 98, 100–101.

see pages 98, 100–101.

UNUSUAL SHAPES

TOMATOBERRY GARDEN
CUOR DI BUE
RED PEAR

The catalogues are filled with round and flattened varieties, but you will also find less usual shapes. The plum-shaped tomatoes were once a novelty, but the increased interest in Mediterranean cookery has seen the introduction of many varieties and an increase in their popularity. But there are novelties — the most popular one is the strawberry-shaped Tomatoberry Garden. You will need to search the catalogues for the heart-shaped Cuor di Bue and the pear-shaped Red Pear. See page 99 for details.

STRIPED FRUITS

TIGERELLA
TUMBLING TIGER
GREEN ZEBRA

Tigerella is a red variety with orange stripes. It has been around for many years and is in a few catalogues, but you will have to search for Tumbling Tiger (an orange-striped version of the popular Tumbling Tom Red) and for Green Zebra (a pale green tomato with dark green stripes).

UNUSUAL COLOURS

BLACK RUSSIAN (purple/brown)
BLACK OPAL (chocolate brown)
BLACK CHERRY (purple/brown)
CHOCOLATE CHERRY (purple/brown)
GREEN GRAPE (green)

The yellow and orange varieties were once a novelty, but now you will find them in all the catalogues. They are not particularly popular, but they are no longer novel. The novelty varieties have skins which are brown, purple or green. You will find the brown and purple ones in a few of the popular catalogues, but you will have to search on the internet to locate suppliers of a green variety.

CHAPTER 6
NON-STANDARD VEGETABLES

Most of this book is taken up by Chapter 2 — the section devoted to the standard or traditional vegetables. This is the group which has appeared in plant and seed catalogues and in textbooks for many years. All the favourites are there, of course, but some are not often seen on the vegetable plot. Artichokes and kohl rabi are examples — unusual choices but they have been in the catalogues and guides for a long time.

There is now a host of vegetables suitable for the grow-your-own gardener which are not included — these are the non-standard vegetables. Some are recent introductions — most Oriental vegetables and some of the salad leaf varieties are examples. There are others which have moved from obscurity to centre stage due to their exposure by TV chefs — you will find rocket and chilli peppers in every supermarket and on every seed rack. There is also a new type of starting point — the grafted vegetable. Finally there are many food plants which have always been an unusual sight in the catalogues and the vegetable garden — okra is an example.

A collection of non-traditional vegetables, both popular ones and rarities, age-old ones and products of the 20th and 21st centuries, appear on the following pages.

Abyssinian cabbage

This member of the cabbage family was discovered growing as a food crop in Ethiopia in 1957. The variety Texsel was developed in Texas as a new vegetable, but it has never become popular despite its several virtues. It is quick-growing and is an excellent cut-and-come-again plant as both the young and mature leaves are tender enough to be eaten raw. The leaves can be cooked like spring cabbage and the flower-heads can be cooked like broccoli. It can be found in the Oriental section of a few catalogues and a number of seed lists as Texsel Greens, although it has no connection with the Orient.

Brokali

A Chinese broccoli/calabrese hybrid — see kaibroc (page 133).

Brukale

This kale/Brussels sprout hybrid can be seen at a few supermarkets. The usual tight buttons we associate with Brussels sprouts have been replaced by frilly-edged purple/green 'flower sprouts'. Grow it in the same way as a traditional Brussels sprout variety — it will look like a sprout when growing, but the flower sprouts will taste more like spring greens when cooked. Sow in April for an October-March crop — it is a very hardy plant and stands well over the winter.

Buck's-horn plantain

This native plant is a major weed in lawns in coastal areas. The cultivated form is very similar, although the leaves are larger. It is grown to provide fleshy leaves for salads or for cooking to provide greens for the dinner table. You won't find it listed in the popular catalogues, but suppliers can be found on the internet. Hard to find, maybe, but extremely easy to grow. Sow thinly in shallow drills in April–June. Do not cover — thin to 15 cm (6 in.). Dense clumps are produced — harvest the narrow, feathery leaves before they are fully grown.

Celtuce

Grow as lettuce — despite the name there is no connection with celery. It is sometimes listed as Chinese stem lettuce. Mature leaves are too coarse to be eaten raw, but young leaves can be used for salads or in stir-fries. The main reason for growing this plant is for its thick, succulent stems. Plant out seedlings 30 cm (1 ft) apart and grow in the same way as lettuce — see page 63. Cut the stems when they are about 45 cm (1½ ft) high. Peel and cut the pale green core into slices for salads or cooking, or into strips for stir-frying.

Cardoon

Cardoons grow to about 2 m (7 ft) and are more suited to the back of the herbaceous border than the vegetable plot. The flower-heads look like small globe artichokes (page 8) and are cooked in the same way, but it is grown for its blanched stems. Sow in April and keep well-watered — leave 60 cm (2 ft) between the plants. In September tie the leaves into a bunch and blanch as for celery — see page 47. Dig up after 5 weeks and cut off roots and outer leaves. Peel, cut the stems into pieces and boil for at least 30 minutes.

Chickpea

Chickpeas are a legume which deserves to be more widely grown. They are a basic ingredient of houmous, and chickpea flour is used to make poppadoms. The dried peas can be roasted like peanuts or popped like corn. It is generally regarded as a tropical plant, but it can be grown in our climate. Sow in April in 3 cm (1 in.) deep drills 30 cm (1 ft) apart. Pick young pods for eating raw — lift plants in autumn before the frosts arrive and allow them to dry indoors for the pods to ripen and produce a supply of dried peas.

Chilli pepper

Until quite recently chilli peppers were regarded as a vegetable to buy rather than to grow. They found little or no space in the catalogues as the wave of interest in cooking exotic dishes had not yet arrived — you will find a range of varieties on the seed racks at your garden centre. They are grown in the same way as sweet peppers — you will need a greenhouse or a sunny and sheltered spot outdoors. Pinch out stem tips occasionally to induce bushiness. These hot peppers can make your throat burn, eyes water and skin sting if you are not used to eating or handling them. As a general rule — the smaller and redder the chilli, the hotter it will be, and removing the seeds plus blanching in hot water before use will remove much of the fire. Use them in cooking to give a spicy taste to potatoes, rice, soups, stews, eggs, sweet corn etc. You will need one chilli per 500 gm (1 lb) of meat or chicken. Popular varieties include **Jalapeno** — harvest at the green or red stage. Hot when ripe. **Hungarian Wax** — long pods which are sweet at first and get hotter as they mature. **Habanero** — very hot tapering orange fruits. **Apache** — dwarf bush with masses of bright red fruit. Can be grown on a windowsill.

Dandelion

Dandelions have no place in the lawn or flower bed but they have had a place in the vegetable garden since mediaeval times. The leaves are blanched by excluding light completely from the plant and they are then cut and used as a salad ingredient. Buy a variety which has been specially bred to produce large and succulent leaves. Sow in April in rows 30 cm (1 ft) apart — thin to 25 cm (10 in.). In the following spring cover each plant with a box or pot which is light-proof. About 10 days later the leaves will be white and ready for use in a salad.

Florence fennel

Florence fennel is grown for its swollen bulb-like base which has a distinct taste of aniseed. The feathery foliage can be used as a substitute for fennel (see page 114). It is not an easy plant to grow — a warm summer is required and any check to growth results in the plant running to seed. Sow 1 cm (½ in.) deep in drills 45 cm (1½ ft) apart in late April and thin the seedlings to 30 cm (1 ft). Earth-up the bulbs when they are the size of golf balls — continue earthing-up and harvest when bulbs are tennis-ball size. Slice for serving raw in salads or boil for 30-40 minutes.

Good King Henry

Good King Henry is a perennial and grows about 60 cm (2 ft) high. Sow the seeds in April in drills which are 6 mm (¼ in.) deep and 45 cm (1½ ft) apart. Thin the seedlings to 30 cm (1 ft) — do not transplant. You must not expect too much in the first season — pick just a few leaves from each plant for cooking. Cut down the foliage in autumn and cover with leafmould or compost. Cropping can begin in the spring — cut some of the new shoots as they appear from April until June and cook like asparagus. Cutting should then cease and all shoots must be allowed to develop. The succulent triangular leaves are picked a few at a time until the end of August and cooked like spinach.

Horseradish

The problem with horseradish is that you cannot just leave it. If allowed to stay in the ground for a few years then a new weed will have appeared in your garden — horseradish. In March make a 15 cm (6 in.) deep hole with a dibber — these holes should be 60 cm (2 ft) apart. Drop a 15 cm (6 in.) piece of root into each hole and fill with soil. The secret of preventing horseradish from swamping the area is to lift all the plants in October. Store the roots in sand. Grating horseradish is an eye-watering job — use the shredder attachment of a food processor.

Hamburg parsley

Leaves which can be used like parsley, roots which taste like well-flavoured parsnips with a hint of celery, and a constitution which allows it to succeed in shade. Sow 1 cm (½ in.) deep in drills 30 cm (1 ft) apart in mid April, thin seedlings to 25 cm (10 in.) apart and in November the first roots will be ready for lifting. They will be about 20 cm (8 in.) long and can be left in the ground over winter or you can lift and store the roots in the same way as parsnips. Remove the stalks and fine roots — scrub thoroughly but do not peel before cooking. Cook them in the same way as parsnips. The tastiest way to cook Hamburg parsley is by roasting or frying them as chips.

Lamb's lettuce

The sole advantage of lamb's lettuce (other name — corn salad) over lettuce is that its small leaves can be picked outdoors between November and January when home-grown saladings are rare. It will grow in nearly all soils and situations. Sow in August or September, 1 cm (½ in.) deep in drills 15 cm (6 in.) apart. Use the thinnings in the kitchen and leave plants at 10-15 cm (4–6 in.) spacings to mature. During winter pick a few leaves from each plant when you harvest. In the kitchen wash the leaves thoroughly to remove grit. Use them as a substitute for lettuce — if you find the flavour a little too bitter, blanch the leaves before the next picking by covering the plants with a box or pot for a few days.

Nasturtium

The use of this flowering plant as a vegetable has greatly declined. It is a pity — the leaves have a peppery taste, rather like watercress, and can add zest to flavourless lettuce. There is, of course, no need to grow nasturtium on the vegetable plot — raise them in the flower bed as usual. Pick young and fresh leaves for salads and sandwiches — flowers can also be added to salads but they have less flavour. Seeds are used for pickling as a substitute for capers. To make nasturtium salad, mix nasturtium leaves with an equal quantity of shredded lettuce in a garlic-rubbed bowl. Add quartered hard boiled eggs, dress with a vinaigrette dressing and garnish with nasturtium flowers.

Okra

With the growth in interest in exotic dishes, okra (other name — lady's fingers) can now be found in most supermarkets and greengrocers, but not in many gardens. It is best treated as a greenhouse crop. Grow it in the same way as indoor tomatoes — soak the seeds overnight before sowing in pots, and pinch out the growing tips when the stems are about 20 cm (8 in.) high. Feed with a tomato fertilizer and pick the pods when they are about 8 cm (3 in.) long. These pods are a feature of many Indian and southern U.S dishes in which they serve as thickening agents. **Clemson's Spineless**, **Pot Luck** and **Cajun Delight** are the main varieties.

New Zealand yam

The South American oca, a tuber-producing plant from the Andes, has been grown in Britain and New Zealand for 200 years or more. In Britain it has aroused little interest, but it is an established vegetable in New Zealand, hence its common name. They differ in a number of ways from potatoes. They are planted later (early June) and do not need earthing-up. They can be eaten raw in salads as well as being baked, boiled or fried like potatoes. The shamrock-shaped leaves can be used as a salad vegetable.

Orache

Orache (other name — mountain spinach) is in very few catalogues and you may have to use the internet to find a source, but growing this spinach substitute is the easy part. There are purple, red, green and gold varieties which are decorative enough for the flower garden. The small leaves are used to add colour to salads, and larger leaves are cooked in the same way as spinach. Sow in May for harvest in summer — leave 8 cm (3 in.) between seedlings and a few weeks later remove alternate ones for salad leaf use. Bolting can be a problem — see page 94.

Sea kale

Use crowns and not seeds for planting — rub off all the buds but one from each crown which should be set 45 cm (1½ ft) apart with a covering of 5 cm (2 in.) of soil. In autumn cut down the yellowing foliage and fork over the ground. In November cover each plant with a pot and surround with leaves for insulation. Cut the blanched shoots in April when they are about 20 cm (8 in.) tall. Cook like asparagus. Apply a mulch and allow growth to develop normally to build up the reserves for next year. You can blanch year after year — a great advantage compared to rhubarb.

Sweet potato

Many American vegetables, from runner beans to tomatoes, have been readily accepted in Britain, but not the sweet potato. Many people find the boiled tubers too sweet with meat and fish, but do try the baked version before rejecting this popular U.S vegetable. Scrub (do not peel) some shop-bought tubers and wrap in silver foil with a little butter and salt. Bake for 1 hour with turkey or pork. Grow it as a greenhouse crop — **Beauregard** is the variety on offer. Plant strips (tuber cuttings) or plugs 8 cm (3 in.) deep in border soil in May, leaving 45 cm (1½ ft) between the plants. Tubers form on the trailing stems. Harvest the sweet potatoes as required — leave to stand for a week before cooking.

Sorrel

The French cannot understand our total disregard for this vegetable — for them it is a basic ingredient in many recipes. It is a perennial, propagated by means of seed or division. Sow seeds in April in drills 6 mm (¼ in.) deep and 45 cm (1½ ft) apart — thin the seedlings to 25 cm (10 in.) spacings. Little attention is needed, but you should water in dry weather and must remove flower-heads as they appear. Pick a few leaves from each plant as soon as they are big enough to use — small leaves are much less bitter than large ones. Once the plants are established the harvesting season lasts from March until November.

Tomatillo

Despite its name and its tomato/lime flavour, this fruit is more closely related to the cape gooseberry than the tomato. The fruit, which may be green, purple, yellow or red when ripe, is surrounded by a paper-like husk. It is a basic of Mexican cuisine. Tomatillo is a greenhouse plant — sow the seeds in February or March and grow in the same way as tomatoes. You will need several plants to ensure successful pollination. The fruits are used to give a tart flavour to salads, sauces and salsas. The cherry tomato-sized fruits will last for several weeks in a refrigerator if the husks are removed.

Oriental vegetables

Oriental vegetables are a group of exotic plants which have come to us predominantly from Japan and China, with a few from other territories such as India. No one can really explain the rapid growth in interest by gardeners in this group. Boredom with the unchanging range of vegetables in the supermarkets is sometimes cited as the cause — so is their use by celebrity chefs in preparing Eastern dishes on TV.

Whatever the cause of this popularity among grow-your-own enthusiasts, you will now find an Oriental vegetable section in most of the popular catalogues and on the seed racks at many garden centres. The use of some of them to produce salad leaves is dealt with on pages 139–145 — in this section we are concerned with the range of types which are harvested as mature plants. As with our standard vegetables each one has its own cultural needs, but there are a few general points to consider.

Most of the Oriental vegetables we grow belong to the Brassica family. With the exception of pak choi and Chinese cabbage they are shallow-rooted, which can mean frequent watering in dry weather. They are generally faster growing than the greens we are used to, and they are prone to bolt if sown early. To avoid this, many are recommended for growing over winter from a late-summer sowing — provide cloche protection if necessary. The main uses are to provide baby leaves, regular salad greens, stir-fries and for steaming or braising as a stand-alone vegetable for the dinner plate. They are also used as ingredients in many Oriental dishes.

All of the vegetables in the A–Z list are to be found in at least one of the popular seed catalogues. Do try one of these non-standard vegetables to provide a taste which your family and guests may never have experienced before.

Amaranth

Amaranth comes to us with several other names — Indian spinach, Chinese spinach, calaloo in the W. Indies, bayan in Malaysia etc. It is best known to us as a source of baby salad leaves (see page 139), but it can be grown outdoors in a sheltered spot if you delay sowing until May or June. Alternatively you can grow it under glass. **Red Army** is a decorative variety with bright red leaves — the most colourful species is the calaloo favourite *Amaranthus tricolor*. Use it as a non-bolting alternative to spinach or remove young leaves to serve raw in salads.

Chinese artichoke

The Chinese artichoke is easier to grow than the Jerusalem artichoke (page 9) as it requires neither staking nor earthing-up. It is, however, less popular with vegetable growers. The reason is the nature of the tubers — they are small, convoluted and indented which make preparation for cooking more difficult. Plant in February-March 15 cm (6 in.) deep at 30 cm (1 ft) intervals in drills 45 cm (1½ ft) apart. Cover with leaves or straw in winter and lift between November and March. Treat as Jerusalem artichoke for cooking.

Chinese broccoli

Sometimes described as Chinese kale, but it is much closer to our Western broccoli in taste and growth habit than it is to kale. **Kailaan** is the variety which is offered. Sow between May and September for cutting from July to November. The leaves and flower-heads can be eaten raw or used in stir-fries — for a steamed vegetable remove the top 8–10 cm (3–4 in.) when the white flowers have begun to open. The stems can be used but may require peeling before steaming.

Chinese celery

You will recognise this vegetable as celery from the aroma and flavour of the leaves, but the plant is thinner and smaller than the celery we buy, or grow in the garden. Another difference is that the time between sowing and cutting is about 10 weeks, and the flavour is unusually strong. The variety **Kintsai** is the only one available — sow between May and September and use the leaves and stalks in stews, soups, stir-fries etc.

Chinese cabbage

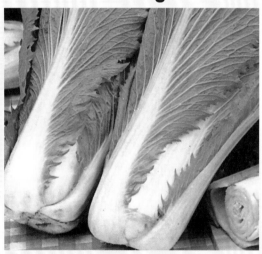

This vegetable which came to us from the Orient has been grown in British gardens for a long time — cultural instructions and variety lists appeared in vegetable guides published during World War II. In addition Chinese cabbage has been sold by greengrocers and supermarkets for many years as Chinese leaves — it has become one of our established vegetables. For this reason it is included in the Standard Vegetables chapter on page 38.

Chinese chives

This perennial plant is often listed in the herb section of the catalogues as garlic chives — a good alternative name as it reveals the two basic features of this vegetable. The flat leaves are used in the same way as chives, and the leaves and stalks have a mild garlic flavour. The blooms can be used as a garnish, but they are attractive enough to be part of a flower arrangement.

Chop suey greens

Chop suey greens are a variety of *Chrysanthemum coronarium* (Crown Daisy) which has been selected for its spicy leaves rather than the beauty of its flowers. The yellow blooms can be used as a garnish in salads or as a stir-fry ingredient, but its main role in the kitchen is as a vegetable for steaming or braising. It doesn't mind a shady location — sow seeds between March and April. The deeply-cut leaves should be ready for cutting after 6 weeks when the plants are 10–15 cm (4–6 in.) high — mature leaves can be bitter. Also known as chrysanthemum greens.

Japanese burdock

Now for something quite different. Pencil-like 30–60 cm (1–2 ft) roots which have a unique flavour — bitter-sweet according to the suppliers. Sow in spring or autumn and follow the cultivation guide for parsnips — see page 76. It is important to harvest the roots while they are still young. After washing and peeling the roots are chopped or cut into strips for cooking. Soaking before preparation is sometimes recommended. Stir-fry, add to stews or roast.

Choy sum

This relative of pak choi is popular in China, but in Britain you will have to search for a supplier. It is grown for its fleshy stalks, which are cut when the yellow flowers are at the bud stage. Sow seeds between May and September for a July-November crop. Unlike most Chinese vegetables it is not an easy plant to grow — its main use in this country is as a salad leaf variety. It is not a cut-and-come-again plant so successional sowing is necessary.

Kaibroc

A hybrid of kailaan (a variety of Chinese broccoli described on page 132) and calabrese (other name — brokali). Grow it in the same way as its Chinese parent, removing the main head first and then cutting side shoots when the yellow flowers are beginning to open. The key feature of this hybrid is the outstanding sweetness and tenderness of the flower-heads and the long stems. You probably already know kaibroc — it is 'Tenderstem' broccoli sold in every supermarket.

Komatsuna

This hybrid brassica may be called mustard spinach on the seed packet — it is one of the Japanese greens, and is noted for its vigour, tolerance of widely varying conditions, and its frost resistance. The dark green leaves are rich in vitamins. Sow it outdoors between March and September — mature plants will be produced in 1-3 months. Cut baby leaves on a cut-and-come-again routine for salads and stir-fries, or leave to mature for fully-grown leaves to use in soups, or steam for a dinner-plate dish.

Mizuna

Packets of mizuna seed is one of the few Oriental vegetables you can expect to find on the seedracks at your garden centre. They are there because the baby leaves of this plant are widely used in salad leaf mixtures. The feathery green leaves are borne on long white stems and have a mild mustard flavour. If protection can be provided it can be grown successively to provide year-round crops. For large plants thin to 30 cm x 30 cm (1 ft x 1 ft).

Mitsuba

You may find this one listed as Japanese parsley as it has a celery/parsley flavour, but it is not related to parsley. It is a hardy perennial, but it is usually grown as an annual by sowing seed in May or August. It can be treated as a cut-and-come-again vegetable rather than lifting the plants at harvest time. Use in salads or soups — blanch like celery for extra length and tenderness.

Oriental bunching onions

This group of salad onions have a number of advantages compared to the standard varieties. They are generally easier to grow with a stronger flavour, they are more tolerant of cold weather and are healthier — mildew and rust rarely occur. See pages 72-73 for cultural and culinary details — one variety (**Ishikura**) is described here, but there are several others to choose from, including **Kyoto Market**, **Savel**, **Hikari Bunching** and **Shimonita**. These salad onions are actually a type of the perennial Welsh onion (page 121), but they are usually grown as annuals.

Oriental mustards

These varieties of *Brassica juncea* play an important part in the cuisine of many Far Eastern countries. They come in a wide range of shapes and colours, and all have an outstanding mineral and vitamin content. Their flavour is described as tangy, peppery, hot and/or mustard-like in the catalogues — this property increases as the plant matures.

Many varieties are available from specialist suppliers, but only five can be found in the popular catalogues. **Red Giant** is the colourful one with green puckered leaves coated with red/purple. **Golden Streaks** has finely-divided leaves and **Green in Snow** is aptly named. It is an all-year-round variety with jagged-edged leaves and a spicy flavour — **Southern Giant** is the mild-flavoured one. All are recommended for stir-frying or steaming. The mild-flavoured **Indian mustard** is the giant among the listed types.

IN THE KITCHEN

Most of the vegetables in this section are 'greens'. In general they contain more vitamins and minerals, and the leaves are more delicate than Western vegetables. The ones we grow are usually boiled or served raw in salads — Oriental vegetables are eaten raw, stir-fried, steamed or braised.

1 **Raw** You have probably eaten Oriental vegetables at home without knowing it. Mizuna, pak choi and tatsoi are ingredients in some supermarket salad leaf packs and they also occur in salad leaf seed mixes at the garden centre.

2 **Stir-frying** We may have been slow in accepting Oriental vegetables as plants to grow and cook for the dinner table, but we have wholeheartedly taken up this Oriental cooking technique. Start with a wok — the basic utensil. Dice or slice the vegetables into even-sized pieces. Turn on the heat below the wok and when it is hot add vegetable oil (1 tablespoonful per 250 gm/8 oz of vegetables). Carefully spread the oil with a spoon or spatula and heat until it is really hot. Now add vegetables — stir continually for 5 minutes. Remove from heat. Add soy sauce if you wish. Serve.

3 **Steaming** Unlike boiling this technique maintains both the vitamins and the full flavour. Use a steamer or place a rack or trivet at the base of a wok. Add water — the level should be below the base of the trivet. Place a layer of vegetables on a plate and stand on the trivet. Cover and keep on medium heat until the recommended steaming time is reached.

4 **Braising** This technique is used for vegetable stems and tough leaves, and also for roots. Cook for a little time in a wok or large pan until cubes or slices of vegetable are hot, and then add stock. Most of the vegetable layer should be above the liquid — cover and allow to simmer.

Oriental radish

Seed packets of the long summer varieties and the round winter ones have been available from larger garden centres and some popular catalogues for many years, but these large radishes have never become popular. See pages 86-87 for details on some of the varieties which are available and how to care for them. A mooli variety such as **April Cross** or **Minowasa Summer** is the one to try.

Pak choi

Like Chinese cabbage this Oriental brassica has become an established supermarket vegetable. Its paddle-like leaves borne on fleshy mid-ribs make it immediately recognisable, and its alternative name (celery mustard) provides some idea of its slightly spicy flavour. It can be grown in a number of ways. It can be treated as a salad leaf vegetable — the plants being lifted when about 10 cm (4 in.) high. This will take about a month from sowing. For mature heads of large flat leaves you will have to wait for about 8–10 weeks — some side leaves can be removed for kitchen use as the plant is growing. After cutting leave the stumps to resprout to provide a supply of new leaves for several months. Eat in salads and stir-fries, or steam for the dinner table. **Joy Choi** is an excellent white-stemmed variety, **Red** bears purple leaves on pale green stems, and **Canton Dwarf** is one of the compact members of the group.

Perilla

In Britain this Japanese herb is a hard-to-find source of salad leaves — see page 143. In its native country it has a much more important role to play — its ground seeds are one of the more important spices and its leaves and flowering shoots are used in a wide range of classic recipes. If you are adventurous it is worth growing a few plants to savour its unique flavour. The attractive saw-edged leaves are available in green or red, and are used to provide colour and/or a novel-shaped leaf for salads or a curry-like flavour for fish.

Tatsoi

The dark leaves form a decorative rosette — each tender spoon-shaped leaf is carried on a pale green stalk. It can be harvested at any stage from baby to fully mature leaf for use in salads, stir-fries, soups and Oriental recipes. Tatsoi may be listed as rosette pak choi — it is slower-growing than the standard types of pak choi, but it has a better flavour. Sow seeds in April-May.

Grafted vegetables

Grafted vegetables for the home gardener made their appearance in 2008, and interest in them has grown steadily in subsequent years. If you grow fruit trees then you will already know something about the concept of grafting. A named **variety** is attached (grafted on) to a **rootstock** which has been taken from a plant which has a benefit or benefits the variety is lacking. Apple trees grow badly on their own roots, and become too tall for a small garden. By grafting a shoot on to a dwarfing rootstock both of these problems are avoided. A grafted vegetable is an established variety which has been attached to the rootstock of a vigorous species of the vegetable which has a number of desirable features. The list of benefits cited in the catalogues is impressive:

- The plants are more vigorous • Good resistance to soil-borne diseases
- Better tolerance to nutritional disorders • Less heating is required
- Cropping starts earlier, and yields are higher

The range of grafted vegetables is quite small — tomatoes, cucumbers, aubergines, sweet peppers and chilli peppers. You can buy them in spring as plugs or potted plants, and they are designed for growing under glass rather than out-doors. Unlike the apple, a grafted vegetable is rather delicate. When you receive it there will be a clip (see below) holding the variety and the rootstock secure until they fuse together. A few cultural notes. Take care not to damage the graft when planting out. Use a high-potash feed during the season, and remove any suckers which may appear below the graft.

Of course a grafted vegetable costs more than a seedling raised from seed in the usual way — the price is about one-third higher. Is it worth paying the extra cost, or is it a new novelty idea which will soon disappear? First of all, it's not new — the first vegetable grafts were made over a hundred years ago. Professional growers started to turn to grafted vegetables in the 1980s and now virtually all of the tomatoes grown in Europe for the supermarkets come from grafted plants.

If the growing conditions are ideal and no cultural problems arise then the benefit may be small, but in some circumstances the benefit can be dramatic. For example, they make it possible for you to grow crops in the greenhouse border year after year without the plants being ruined by soil-borne disease.

TOMATO VARIETY

SUPPORT

CLIP

ROOTSTOCK

Salad leaves

Plastic bags filled with a mixture of baby salad leaves can now be found at every supermarket. The nature of the mix may be stated on the label — sweet, peppery etc. For the home gardener there is an alternative — grow your own.

Buy a pack of a seed mixture from a catalogue or garden centre if you are new to growing baby leaf saladings. You will now have to choose between raising them in the vegetable plot or in containers. The garden would seem to be the better choice. More space, no pots to buy and fill, etc, but there are problems — weeds and slugs can be a menace. As a general rule growing the plants in containers is the better choice.

The mixes made up by the seed houses are based on 'cut-and-come-again' varieties. This means that the first crop of leaves can be cut a few weeks after sowing, and the plant left to recover and to provide a second crop. With some varieties three or four crops may be gathered in this way. Unfortunately there is a problem. Some types grow more vigorously than others, and there are types which do not produce a worthwhile second crop. This means that the composition of the mixture changes over time. Because of this it is recommended that after growing a mixture or two and finding out which salad types you like, you should go over to raising individual varieties in separate pots.

So do try growing baby leaves for a new-style salad or for mixing with traditional large salad leaves such as chicory, Iceberg lettuce etc. You have not much to buy and not much work to do, and you will be gathering your first harvest in just a few weeks time. See page 145 for further details.

Amaranth

Amaranth has a long history as a tropical grain crop, but it is now established as a source of baby salad leaves for the home gardener. Choose a red variety. They are more vigorous than the green types and add colour to the salad — the colour gets stronger as the leaves grow. The flavour is hard to describe — orange-like according to some experts. Sow after the frosts have gone.

Beetroot

One of our favourite root crops has a place here. **Bulls Blood** is the favourite variety. The leaves are green with red veins at first, turning all-over red as they develop. The beetroot flavour is excellent. When growing beetroot in the garden you can earmark a few seedlings in the row to be harvested at the baby leaf stage.

Cress

The salad leaf varieties of cress are cut at a taller stage than the blotting-paper cress we grew as children. The star is the variety **Wrinkled Crinkled** — the parsley-like leaves develop a hot peppery taste.

Kale

Kale does not have many fans as a cooked vegetable, and it therefore seems strange that it should appear in some salad leaf lists. However, there are several varieties which are suitable — **Fizz** was specially bred as a salad leaf vegetable, and red-stemmed kale is an ingredient of some salad leaf mixes.

Endive

Endive is grown in the garden as a salad crop for harvesting at the whole-head stage — see page 57. It can also be grown as a salad leaf vegetable — **Frisée Glory** is one of the varieties recommended for this purpose.

Lamb's lettuce

Lamb's lettuce (other name — corn salad) is an easy-to-grow vegetable which is used as a substitute for lettuce. In this role it has advantages and disadvantages — see page 127. It can be grown as a salad leaf crop for harvesting in the winter when home-grown lettuce is not available.

Land cress

Land cress (other name — American cress) is an excellent substitute for watercress. Sow in succession from early spring to autumn and you can pick the peppery hot leaves from April to November. Easy to grow — all you need do is keep it in a shady spot and make sure that the compost is always moist.

Lettuce

Lettuce has long been the mainstay of almost every green salad — varieties such as **Iceberg** adding crispness to the other ingredients. Lettuce is also used in salad leaf mixtures, but here it is just one more ingredient. Green varieties are sometimes used, but the red-edged frilly types such as **Lollo Rossa** are more popular. Several cuts can be taken from salad leaf lettuce.

Leaf beet

The mature leaves of the varieties of leaf beet (other name — chard) are cooked as a spinach substitute. Baby ones, however, can be used as salad leaves. The stalk and veins provide colour and the leaves provide a crunchy texture to the salad. **Rhubarb Chard** is a popular variety — others include **Oriental Ruby**, **Intense** and **Canary Yellow**.

Mizuna

Mizuna (other name — Japanese greens) is becoming increasingly popular as an ingredient in salad leaf mixes. The finely-cut foliage can be harvested from spring to early winter — the dark green leaves providing a peppery taste to the salad. Choose a lightly shaded spot for the container.

Mustard

An excellent choice but you should sow seeds every few weeks rather than relying on cut-and-come-again. In this way you can have baby leaves from April to November. The varieties come in a range of shapes from simple oval to distinctly feathery, and there are colours from white-veined green to all-over red. Flavours range from a mustard taste to peppery — the strength increasing as the leaves age. Popular varieties include **Golden Streaks**, **Red Giant**, **Green in Snow**, **Red Lion**, **Red Frills**, **Pizzo** and **Ruby Streaks**.

Pak choi

This Oriental vegetable is best known as the green vegetable with unusually thick leaf stalks which is to be found in most supermarkets — see page 136 for further details. Much less well-known is its use as a salad leaf vegetable — lift the young plants when they are about 10 cm (4 in.) high. **Hamakan** is a variety recommended for this use.

Namenia

A salad leaf vegetable with a crunchy texture and a tangy taste, according to the suppliers. A new one which may be hard to find, but it may be worth the hunt as it is claimed that the span between sowing and cutting can be as little as two weeks!

Pea

It may sound an odd choice for a salad leaf, but young pea shoots add a crisp texture and pea-like flavour to the salad bowl. Any variety will do, but **Twinkle** is the one listed in the catalogues. Pick the shoot tips a few weeks after sowing — continue to pick small shoots from this cut-and-come-again vegetable.

Perilla

You can find packets of seed at some garden centres and it is an ingredient in a few salad leaf mixes, but perilla is one of the less common types. This Oriental vegetable is widely used as a garnish and source of salad leaves in China and Japan. Both the red and green varieties have a unique flavour.

Purslane

Winter purslane (other names — claytonia, miner's lettuce) is a useful cut-and-come-again salad leaf as it can be cropped during winter. Remove young leaves as required. **Golden Purslane** is a colourful variety — the yellowish-green leaves have red stems.

Rocket

The unchallenged queen of the salad leaf world. Some of the types in this section are hard to find, but rocket is in all the catalogues. Sow it in the vegetable plot or in containers between March and August — the leaves can be cut after 3–4 weeks as a cut-and-come-again vegetable, but it may be better to sow seed every 2–3 weeks to ensure a regular supply. The basic flavour is peppery, but each variety has its own additional taste. Grow **Wild Rocket** for the strongest flavour, or **Voyager** for vigour — **Sky Rocket** combines the two virtues. **Buzz** is an all-year-round variety.

Sorrel

The mature leaves of sorrel are rather bitter and it is rarely used in British cooking although it is popular in France — see page 129. However, the baby leaves of the variety **Red Veined** have a citrus-like flavour and the red-veined foliage is attractive, and so it is sold as a cut-and-come-again salad leaf vegetable.

Tatsoi

Tatsoi (other name — rosette pak choi) is an Oriental vegetable which bears glossy, deep green leaves which are spoon-shaped. Tatsoi is a very useful ingredient if you are making up a winter mix as it is tolerant of cold weather.

Spinach

The oval-shaped baby leaves of spinach add little to the overall flavour of a salad as the sweetish taste is rather bland, but it does add another shape. Varieties sold for the production of salad leaves include **Lazio**, **Reddy** and **Red Cardinal**. Successional sowing is recommended.

Watercress

The variety **Aqua** does not need running water — it will thrive quite happily in a container filled with compost provided that it is kept really moist at all times. Cut young growth to provide a crunchy and peppery salad leaf vegetable.

Step-by-step Guide

1 If you choose the vegetable plot option: Make sure the area is free from weeds — prepare 1 cm (½ in.) drills leaving 30 cm (1 ft) between the rows. Water the drills before sowing. Sow the seeds thinly — aiming for a distance of 1–3 cm (½–1 in.) between the seeds and cover the drills. Thin the seedlings if necessary to about 4 cm (1½ in.) between the plants.

2 If you choose the container option: Pick waterproof receptacles with drainage holes. Shallow troughs and windowboxes are suitable, but the recommended container is a 25 cm (10 in.) pot. Fill with moist compost. Sow the seeds thinly aiming for a distance of 1–3 cm (½–1 in.) between the seeds. Cover with a sprinkling of compost.

3 The seed packet will give you the recommended timing for sowing. As a general rule salad leaf vegetables are sown between April and August for a May to October harvest. Early-season sowing will benefit from cloche protection.

4 With cut-and-come-again varieties the leaves should be ready for cutting 3–4 weeks after sowing — the leaves should be about 10 cm (4 in.) high. Use scissors, cutting about 2–3 cm (1 in.) above the compost. Leave a few leaves intact. The plant will re-sprout, ready for another cut in a few weeks time. You can expect 1-4 cuts, depending on the variety and conditions.

5 Keep the compost moist at all times. Dryness will encourage bolting — remove plants which have run to seed as the leaves will be bitter.

6 Some of the plants may not re-sprout, and there are others such as pak choi which are pulled up as small plants for their baby leaves. It is therefore highly recommended that you should sow every few weeks to ensure a succession of plants to last the whole season.

7 If a plant on the vegetable plot is new to you it is a good idea to let a few grow on to maturity to see if it appeals to you as a cooked vegetable.

D-I-Y Mixtures

Packets of baby salad leaf mixtures are available in most popular catalogues and you should find a range of them at your local garden centre. You can make up your own mix using seeds from packets of individual varieties. Below are a sample of the types of mixes which are grown. Most of the plants can be found in the A–Z guide on the previous pages — consult the index to find the ones not listed in this section.

Mesclun Mix
This is the most popular of the branded salad leaf mixes. It is listed in several of the main seed catalogues.

ENDIVE	LETTUCE
MIZUNA	CHERVIL
KALE	ROCKET
MUSTARD	SORREL
LAMB'S LETTUCE	

Misticanza Mix
An Italian mix in which varieties of chicory are dominant — the other salad leaf vegetables are optional extras.

CHICORY
RADICCHIO
ENDIVE
ROCKET
WATERCRESS

Spicy Mix
Choose from the following list:

CRESS
ROCKET
MUSTARD
MIZUNA

Herby Mix
Choose from the following list:

MUSTARD	CRESS
WILD ROCKET	LEAF BEET
LETTUCE	CHERVIL
CORIANDER	PARSLEY
MIZUNA	

Oriental Mix
Choose from the following list:

PAK CHOI	PERILLA
MIZUNA	TATSOI
CHOY SUN	
MUSTARD	

French Mix
Choose from the following list:

LETTUCE LOLLO ROSSA
LAMB'S LETTUCE
SORREL
CHERVIL
DANDELION

CHAPTER 7
WHERE TO GROW VEGETABLES

During the Dig For Victory campaign in World War II the gardeners of Britain grew vegetables in just two basic ways. There was the traditional outdoor plot with its long rows of cabbages, peas etc, and also the under-glass area with its tomatoes for people with a greenhouse.

Since then alternative ways of growing vegetables have become increasingly popular for several reasons. For millions of households the garden is too small for a vegetable plot, or the owners want a purely ornamental garden — for them there is the cottage garden approach of growing some vegetables in the beds and borders. Others don't want all the hard work associated with the traditional plot, and so they are increasingly turning to either the bed system in the garden or containers on the patio. The potager is an advance on the simple bed system — a decorative effect is important here as well as the yield of the vegetable. Finally there are the humble pots on the windowsill — so useful where winter rain and cold make a trip to the vegetable plot an unpleasant experience ... or where there is no garden to go into.

THE TRADITIONAL PLOT
page 147

THE BED SYSTEM
page 150–151

VEGETABLES IN CONTAINERS
page 148

VEGETABLES IN THE GREENHOUSE
page 147

VEGETABLES IN THE BORDER
page 149

THE POTAGER
page 149

VEGETABLES ON THE WINDOWSILL
page 148

THE TRADITIONAL PLOT

The traditional plot remains the standard way of
growing vegetables at home. The whole of the area
is cultivated and the plants are grown in rows,
apart from a small patch for permanent plants
such as asparagus or rhubarb. Strips of bare earth
are left between each row or group of rows so that
the gardener is able to walk along for watering,
weeding, feeding, picking, etc. The planting or
final thinning out distance between the seedlings
in the rows and between the rows is sufficiently
large to enable the plant to develop to its full
potential. By this method the longest beans, the
heaviest cabbages and the largest onions are
produced.

Despite its popularity the traditional plot may
not be the best method of growing vegetables for
you, unless you want to grow bigger vegetables
than your neighbour or want to win a prize at the
local show. It is extremely laborious — the
tramping down of the soil along the pathways
means that there is the chore of digging over the
plot every autumn. In addition the bare pathways
and the large spaces left between the plants
encourage weeds and that means regular hoeing.
This is obvious to every gardener who has tended
an allotment or large vegetable plot — less obvious
is the fact that the overall crop yield per sq.m of
growing area is less than the harvest obtained by
using the bed system.

VEGETABLES IN THE GREENHOUSE

The usual reason for growing vegetables in a
greenhouse is the ability to grow those types which
are unpredictable outdoors and even impossible in
some districts — aubergines, capsicum and tomatoes are typical examples. In addition there is the
satisfaction of harvesting produce before the outdoor crop is ready — early potatoes, early carrots
and so on. There is another advantage which is
important but does not appear in the standard
textbooks — the ability to sow, care for the plants
and harvest the crop without having to worry
about wind, rain and snow.

Many ornamentals need a cool (minimum
temperature 7°C/45°F) or a warm greenhouse for
satisfactory development, but all the popular
vegetables can be grown in an unheated greenhouse. This can be more productive than an area
with just a few growing bags of tomatoes —
remember that there are also cucumbers, aubergines, winter lettuce, okra, etc. Early in the season
the space between tomatoes and cucumbers can be
utilised for quick-growing catch crops such as
carrots. Always check that the variety is recommended for greenhouse growing.

The greenhouse has another role to play. It can
be used to give outdoor varieties an early start by
sowing them in a propagator, pricking out into
pots and then planting outdoors to give them
several weeks' advantage over garden-sown ones.

VEGETABLES IN CONTAINERS

Pots, troughs, growing bags, etc are the way to grow vegetables if you have no space in the garden or if you have a balcony but no garden.

Some experts stress the advantages of growing in containers. No poor soil problems if you use shop-bought compost, no weeding and digging worries, and no soil pest problems. Growing bags on the patio can be filled with all sorts of vegetables and tender types can be moved to the most sheltered part of the garden. There are other experts, however, who are not so keen. They point out the amount of produce you can grow by this method is strictly limited and the plants are usually plain or downright ugly if you plan to have the containers close to the house. Perhaps the main drawback is the need for regular watering and feeding.

Any pot, tub or trough deeper than 20 cm (8 in.) will do — make sure that the container is raised above the ground. For most people there is little point in growing 'ordinary' vegetables by this method. You can choose decorative ones (see Vegetables in the Border on page 149 for suggestions) or you can grow tender types such as aubergines, sweet peppers or bush tomatoes against a south-facing wall. Another approach is to raise salad crops in growing bags in order to provide fresh produce without having to walk to the vegetable plot.

VEGETABLES ON THE WINDOWSILL

If you are keen on herbs in cooking then you can have a line of pots on the windowsill in the kitchen and fill them with basil, rosemary, lemon balm, sage, thyme and so on for use during the winter months. You will be able to pick your favourite seasonings without having to trudge through the mud or snow. The kitchen window is an excellent place for plants — the air is often steamy and you can't help noticing if they are in need of watering.

For most people such an extensive herb garden indoors is not a good idea. It is better to restrict your windowsill allotment to just a few herb and salad crops which you eat regularly, because if the plants are left uncut they become leggy and unattractive. So don't be too ambitious at the start. Fill a few pots with seed compost — the pressed-down surface should be about 1 cm (½ in.) below the rim. A typical arrangement consists of a mint pot (plant a rooted clump from the garden), parsley (sow seed), chives (a clump from the garden or garden centre) and spring onions (sow seed). Water in the plants or seeds, and when they are growing water once or twice a week.

Don't forget to mist the leaves once or twice a week. From these simple beginnings you can become more adventurous. Lettuce growing is the next step — raise the seedlings in shallow plastic trays. If you have space for a 15 cm (6 in.) pot you can grow a miniature variety of tomato.

VEGETABLES IN THE BORDER

There are several reasons why many gardeners reject the idea of devoting a plot entirely to vegetables. One argument is that there is too much work involved, although the bed system (page 150) makes vegetable growing much easier. Others argue that they cannot possibly use all the cabbages, lettuce, sprouts, etc from the plot. Some people feel that the garden should be solely for ornamental plants.

This final point should not be an argument for growing no vegetables at all. There are numerous vegetables which are distinctly ornamental and can be used as such as occasional specimens among flowers, shrubs, bulbs, roses and so on.

You will find examples in this book. Runner beans can be grown as climbing annuals at the back of the border — there are red-, pink- and white-flowered varieties and also the bi-coloured Painted Lady. The pods have little visual appeal but the yellow- and purple-podded varieties of French bean are decorative. For eye-catching leaves there is leaf beet, such as Rainbow Chard. If red leaves or stalks appeal to you there are beetroot, Lollo Rossa lettuce and red varieties of celery and Brussels sprouts. Among the herbs there are eye-catchers such as purple sage and yellow marjoram — fruiting vegetables include capsicum, globe artichoke and cherry-type tomatoes.

THE POTAGER

'Potager' is the French word for kitchen garden, but in this country it has acquired a more specialised meaning. It describes a plot in which vegetables, herbs and fruit are grown and where the ornamental aspect is just as important as the practical and productive one. To heighten this ornamental aspect a variety of flowers, bulbs, roses or shrubs is often included, but it is not the same as the mixed border described above. There the vegetables are the poor relations — in the potager they are the main feature.

There are other differences. In the potager the arrangement of the plants is formal and they are grown in a group of beds — these beds form a geometric pattern and are often enclosed by dwarf hedging. The pathways are made of paving slabs or gravel, and archways draped with roses or vines can be constructed along the paths.

It is usual for some if not all of the vegetables and herbs to be ornamental ones — see Vegetables in the Border above. Apart from these plants quite ordinary types can look attractive in the right setting — there are the ferny leaves of carrots and the yellow flowers of courgettes. Use flowers, shrubs etc with care — good potager subjects include climbers for arches and walls, bright patches of flowers or bulbs, dwarf edging shrubs and annuals for cutting, but do not create large flower beds or borders in the potager.

THE BED SYSTEM

The basic principle is to create a series of rectangular beds which are divided by permanent paths. These paths are covered with gravel or bark chippings and the beds must be narrow enough so that all the plants can be reached from the path. Construct the beds so that they run North-South if possible. Organic matter is added to the soil and it should be left to settle for at least a couple of weeks before sowing or planting. The yearly round begins in autumn or early winter when a layer of organic matter such as rotted manure or garden compost is worked into the surface with a fork. Digging is not necessary as you have not trodden down the surface by walking on it.

Choose your vegetables from the A–Z guide on pages 7–107. As a general rule it is a good idea to choose dwarf and early-maturing types — yield per individual plant is of course less than you would expect by the traditional long row method, but surprisingly the yield per sq.m of cultivated land is often higher. On page 151 is a list of easy-to-grow vegetables which are ideal for the bed system — note that the plants are grown at the same distance from each other in both directions. This space is quite close so that the leaves of adjacent plants touch when they are mature.

Care is usually a simple job. There are no muddy walkways between the plants and the closeness of the vegetables smothers most weeds.

FLAT BEDS

The flat bed is the easiest type to create but you do need free-draining soil. Use the dimensions given for raised beds in the drawing below. Turn over the soil and work in a 3 cm (1 in.) layer of organic matter.

RAISED BEDS

3 m (10 ft) maximum

60 cm–1 m (2–4 ft)

1 m (4 ft)

45 cm (1½ ft)

Pathway covered with gravel or coarse bark chippings. Put black plastic sheeting underneath to prevent weed growth

The raised bed is the type to create if drainage is poor and the ground gets waterlogged in winter. You will have to build retaining walls — see the drawing above. Railway sleepers, bricks or blocks can be used but 3 cm (1 in.) thick pressure-treated wooden planks attached to 5 cm (2 in.) square corner posts are the usual choice. The raised bed should be at least 10 cm (4 in.) high — fork over the bottom and then fill with a mixture of 2 parts topsoil and 1 part organic matter.

Easy Vegetables for the Bed System

NAME	SOW	DEPTH	PLANT	DISTANCE BETWEEN PLANTS	HARVEST	TIME TAKEN (weeks)
BEAN, BROAD	February –April	5 cm (2 in.)	—	15 cm (6 in.)	July –August	16S ➤ H
	Begin picking when pods are 8 cm (3 in.) long — cook whole					
BEAN, FRENCH	May –June	5 cm (2 in.)	—	15 cm (6 in.)	July –September	10S ➤ H
	Pencil-podded or Continental varieties (e.g Sprite) are now popular					
BEETROOT	April –June	3 cm (1 in.)	—	8 cm (3 in.)	June –October	11S ➤ H
	Grow a globe variety — harvest when no larger than a tennis ball					
CALABRESE	April –May	1 cm (½ in.)	June –July	40 cm (16 in.)	August –September	15S ➤ H
	De Cicco is a quick-growing, cut-and-come-again variety					
CARROT	March –July	1 cm (½ in.)	—	10 cm (4 in.)	July –October	14S ➤ H
	Pick a quick-maturing short-rooted variety such as Early Nantes					
COURGETTE	May –June	3 cm (1 in.)	—	45 cm (18 in.)	July –September	10S ➤ H
	Cut when 8–10 cm (3–4 in.) long. Zucchini is the popular choice					
KALE	May	1 cm (½ in.)	July	40 cm (16 in.)	December	30S ➤ H
	Pentland Brig is the variety to grow. Pick young leaves in winter					
LETTUCE	March –July	1 cm (½ in.)	—	20 cm (8 in.)	June –October	12S ➤ H
	Grow a miniature e.g Tom Thumb or Little Gem or a loose-leaf variety (e.g Salad Bowl)					
ONION	—	Tip showing	March –April	8 cm (3 in.)	August	20P ➤ H
	Grow sets rather than seed — harvest 2 weeks after stems topple over					
POTATO	—	15 cm (6 in.)	March –April	30 cm (12 in.)	June –July	13P ➤ H
	Grow an early variety for new potatoes in early summer					
RADISH	March –July	1 cm (½ in.)	—	5 cm (2 in.)	May –September	6S ➤ H
	Nothing is easier to grow. All varieties are suitable					
TOMATO	—	—	June	45 cm (18 in.)	August –September	12P ➤ H
	An easy crop in mild areas, but only if you choose a bush variety					
TURNIP	March –June	1 cm (½ in.)	—	15 cm (6 in.)	May –September	10S ➤ H
	Early varieties (e.g Snowball) are sown in spring and picked at golf-ball size					

KEY

DISTANCE BETWEEN PLANTS

These spacings are the recommended distances between rows and mature plants in the rows. See Chapter 2 for spacings recommended for the traditional plot.

TIME TAKEN (weeks)

S : Sowing
P : Planting
➤ : to
H : Harvest

CHAPTER 8
LOOKING AFTER VEGETABLES

Growing vegetables successfully takes time, effort and skill. The skill factor relates to doing the right thing at the right time, and the importance of proper timing cannot be exaggerated. Consider one of the simplest crops — the humble radish. You will, of course, thin the seedlings but if you don't do it early enough then the crop will suffer. Some weeks later you pull up the plants for the kitchen, but if you wait too long then the roots will be woody and hollow. With less robust crops correct timing of cultural operations is even more important.

THINNING

Germination may be inhibited if the surface forms a crust-like cap due to heavy rain followed by drying winds. If this happens water gently to keep the surface soft until germination has taken place.

Despite the often-repeated recommendation to sow thinly you will usually find that the emerged seedlings are too close together. Thinning is necessary, and this is a job to be tackled as soon as the plants are large enough to handle. The soil should be moist — water if necessary. Hold down the soil around the unwanted seedling with one hand and pull it up with the other. If the seedlings are too close together to allow this technique, merely nip off the top growth of the unwanted ones.

After thinning, firm the soil around the remaining seedlings and water gently. This thinning is often done in stages before the final spacing is reached.

TRANSPLANTING

Transplanting involves moving seedlings to their permanent quarters. These transplants may have been raised in a seed bed in the garden, bought from a reliable supplier or grown indoors in pots or trays of compost. It is a temptation to lift thinnings in an overcrowded row of seedlings in the garden and plant them elsewhere, but you must remember that transplanting is not suitable for all vegetables. It is firmly recommended for most brassicas (see page 27), acceptable for some popular crops such as peas and beans and definitely not recommended for many others such as lettuce and root crops.

Water both the seedlings and the site where they are to be planted on the day before transplanting. Use a trowel (or a dibber for brassicas) to set the plants at the depth they were in the seed bed or pot. Firm the soil around the plants and water in to settle the roots.

Transplanting is a critical time in the plant's life. Cold, wet soil can be fatal and so can late frosts for half-hardy vegetables. Water if there is a dry spell after planting.

WEEDING

Weeds are a threat and must be kept at bay. They compete for space, food, water, etc and can harbour pests and diseases. There are a number of tasks you will have to carry out. The first one begins before the crop is sown — at digging time remove all the roots of perennial weeds you can find and bury small annual weeds by completely inverting each spadeful of soil. If the plot has been neglected and is a sea of grass and other weeds then you have a problem on your hands. The best plan is to spray with glyphosate before preparing the bed.

However thoroughly you remove weeds before sowing or planting, additional weeds will appear between the plants. Hoeing is the basic technique to keep the problem under control — it must be carried out at regular intervals in order to keep annual weeds in constant check and to starve out the underground parts of perennial ones. Hoeing can do more harm than good in careless hands — keep away from the stems and do not go deeper than 3 cm (1 in.) below the surface.

Weedkillers have no place in the vegetable garden, but mulching (see page 158) does have a role to play in the battle against weeds. A 3 cm (1 in.) layer of a compost or manure mulch will suppress the germination of annual weeds. Plastic sheeting can be used to stop annual and perennial weeds growing along the paths between rows.

FEEDING

Manure or fertilizer — the age-old argument. Actually there is nothing to argue about; both are vital and neither can be properly replaced by the other. The role of bulky organic matter is to make the *soil* good enough to support a vigorous and healthy crop. The role of fertilizer is to provide the *plants* with enough nutrient to ensure that they reach their full potential.

There are a number of vital nutrients — nitrogen for leaf growth and phosphorus for root development. Potash is required for strengthening disease resistance and for improving the quality and size of fruit. This group is required in relatively large amounts and compound fertilizers contain all three. You will find a statement of the nutrient content on the package. Do follow the instructions carefully — especially the dosage recommendations. Applying double the amount may result in scorch rather than the production of a larger crop.

One of the most important uses for compound fertilizers is to provide a **base dressing** just before sowing or planting. A granular or powder formulation is used. Growmore and fish, blood and bone are favourites.

Crops which take some time to mature will need one or more **top dressings** during the growing season. These can be in powder or granular form, but you must take great care to keep such dressings off the leaves. It is better to use a liquid fertilizer which is diluted and then applied through a watering can. Liquid feeding is the most popular method for container-grown vegetables. The most widely-used type is tomato fertilizer — check that magnesium is present.

WATERING

A prolonged dry spell can result in a small crop or even no crop at all. Heavy rain after drought causes the splitting of tomatoes and roots. Unfortunately, watering is usually dealt with very briefly in most handbooks on vegetable growing. The reason is simple — until the series of summer droughts in recent years many gardeners were able to succeed without watering their kitchen garden apart from sprinkling around transplants.

The first step is to incorporate adequate organic matter into the soil — this increases the water-holding capacity. Next the top 20 cm (8 in.) of soil should be thoroughly and evenly moist but not waterlogged at sowing or planting time. Finally, put down a mulch (see page 154) in late spring.

You will have done all you can to ensure a good moisture reservoir in your soil — the rest is up to the weather. If there is a prolonged dry spell then water will be necessary, especially for tomatoes, cucumbers, marrows, beans, peas, celery and onions.

The rule is to water the soil gently and thoroughly every 7 days when the weather is dry during the critical period. This is between flowering and full pod development for peas and beans, and from seedling to maturity for leaf crops. Apply 10 litres per sq. m (2 gallons per sq. yard) when **overall watering**, and try to water in the morning rather than at midday or in the evening. Remember to water slowly and close to the base of the plants. A watering can is often used but you really do need a hosepipe if watering is not to be a prolonged chore. One of the most effective methods of watering is to use lay-flat perforated tubing or a leaky-pipe watering system between the rows. Simple ... but expensive. Where there is a limited number of large plants to deal with, you would do better to use a technique known as **point watering**. This involves inserting an empty plant pot or creating a depression in the soil around each stem. Water is then poured into the pot or depression.

Keeping the compost in a growing bag properly moist is a different technique to watering the garden. Follow the maker's instructions carefully.

MULCHING

Mulching is an in-season method of manuring. A 3 cm (1 in.) layer of well-rotted compost or leaf mould is spread between the young plants once they are established in spring. Cultivate and water the surface to make sure that it is moist, weed-free and friable before application.

The mulch will reduce water loss, increase nutrient content, improve soil structure and suppress annual weeds.

SPRAYING

Once there was a wide selection of both 'green' and synthetic chemicals to kill or ward off pests and diseases. The number of these pesticides has greatly reduced in recent years. Even some age-old favourites such as derris and sulphur are no longer available. So do read Chapter 9 — these days we have to rely more on good cultural practice and less on spraying in the war against pests.

PROTECTED CROPPING

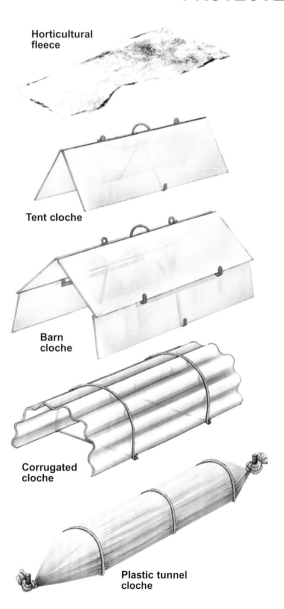

Horticultural fleece

Tent cloche

Barn cloche

Corrugated cloche

Plastic tunnel cloche

The introduction of horticultural fleece has been a great help in the vegetable garden. Draped over small plants in spring it will provide protection against flying pests and frosty weather. The edges must be buried or pegged down, and it must be removed once the warm weather arrives.

Glass or solid plastic sheeting provides better frost protection than fleece. Both the greenhouse and the cold frame are ideal for raising half-hardy seedlings to the planting-out stage, and for giving the hardy types an early start. Neither, of course, has a role to play in the open garden — here we must rely on cloches for protected cropping. Under cloches the sowing or planting of many vegetables can take place weeks earlier than on unprotected ground and that means early harvesting. Half-hardy crops such as aubergines and capsicums can be grown successfully in unfavourable areas and leafy vegetables in winter are kept warm despite the rain and frosts.

A few rules to help you choose wisely — match the height to the expected size of the plants, as leaves should not touch the sides. Tent cloches for small plants, barn cloches for larger ones. Choose plastic for lightness, safety and cheapness — choose glass for clarity, permanence, maximum heat retention and resistance to blowing over. The corrugated PVC cloche is an excellent all-purpose cloche but if you wish to cover large areas cheaply the answer is the plastic tunnel cloche made from wire hoops and polythene sheeting.

With all cloches some ventilation must be provided — increase the amount as temperatures rise. Provide ventilation by leaving gaps between cloches, not by leaving the ends open. There is no need to remove the cloches before watering — the water will run down the sides and into the soil. The time will come when the weather is mild enough for the cloches to be removed — increase ventilation for a few days to harden off the plants before removing their protection.

HARVESTING

Some of the harvesting stages recommended in this book may seem odd — golf ball-sized turnips and finger-long carrots. Such a miniature stage would be uneconomical for the farmer, but they are the times of peak flavour and tenderness. Not all vegetables need be picked at an early stage — the flavour of Swedes, parsnips, celery etc does not decline with size. With some crops, such as marrows, cucumbers, peas and beans, it is essential to pick regularly as just a few ripe fruits or pods left on the plant can bring cropping to an end.

STORING

Nearly all vegetables can be kept for a few days or even a week or two in the refrigerator, but if we take growing seriously then there will be times when long-term storage will be necessary. With beans there is always a sudden glut, and it is far better to pick them at the tender stage for storage rather than trying to extend the harvest period to the time when they will be tough and stringy. Maincrops of roots are generally lifted in autumn for storage indoors as layers between sand (beetroots, carrots etc) or in sacks (potatoes) in a frost-free shed or garage. It is possible to let the vegetable plot act as the vegetable store for some roots — Swedes, parsnips and turnips can be lifted as required.

In the pre-refrigeration era storage methods had to be devised so that a winter supply of vegetables could be provided. Beans and peas were dried and then shelled. Onions and cabbages were hung up in bags or laid out on open trays. Runner beans were salted; onions and beetroots were pickled in vinegar.

Long-term storage, however, has been completely transformed by the advent of the home freezer. This is the ideal storage method for so many vegetables, including the leafy ones which cannot be kept satisfactorily by any other method.

The routine is to blanch, cool, drain and then freeze. A word about blanching. For the various vegetables described in this book which are recommended for freezing you will find a blanching time of several minutes. This involves immersion in boiling water — 100 gm to 1 litre (¼ lb to 1½ pints) of water. Bring quickly back to the boil and begin timing. When the blanching time is reached immerse the produce immediately into ice-cold water. After blanching, drain thoroughly and freeze. Use freezer-grade plastic bags, boxes and other containers, and as much air as possible should be excluded before sealing.

GETTING THE MOST FROM YOUR PLOT

SUCCESSIONAL SOWING

Several vegetables, such as lettuce and radish, cannot be stored for later use. To avoid gluts and then famines it is necessary to sow short rows every few weeks. A boon for the gardeners who are not willing to do this are the 'mixed seed' packets offered by many suppliers. The mixture of early- and late-maturing varieties gives a long harvesting period from a single sowing.

CATCH CROPPING

Purple-sprouting broccoli will have come to the end in April or early May — early peas will be finished by late June or July. Catch cropping is the answer to summer-long bare ground. Fork over the area and level the surface with a rake. Sow a quick-maturing crop such as spring onions, radish, dwarf lettuce, beetroot, turnips or French beans. The crop will be harvested before the time for autumn digging and the rotational plan will not be disturbed.

INTERSOWING

Intersowing is a useful dual-purpose technique which involves mixing the seed of a compact and quick-growing crop such as radish with a slow-to-mature crop such as parsnips or parsley. The radish or lettuce seedlings emerge quickly and mark out the row — an important advantage at hoeing time. Thin out as normal. The radish or lettuce will be ready long before the parsnips have developed to the stage of needing the space occupied by the quick-growing marker plants.

INTERCROPPING

A neater method than intersowing of making the maximum use of land used for a slow-growing crop. Between adjacent rows of notorious slow developers such as Brussels sprouts, leeks, parsnips etc is sown a row of a crop which will be harvested in summer before the prime crop needs the space. Popular intercroppers are radish, early peas, early carrots, spinach and dwarf lettuce. Make sure that the intercropping vegetable doesn't make a nuisance of itself by making the space between the rows too narrow to allow easy passage — widen the recommended row spacings of the main crop if necessary.

CHAPTER 9
VEGETABLE TROUBLES

It is something we all hate to see — vegetables we have so carefully tended suddenly attacked or destroyed by insects or other small creatures. Diseases, too, can cause havoc. Not all vegetable troubles are caused by pests and diseases — split tomatoes and blown sprouts are cultural disorders. The purpose of this chapter is to tell you how to avoid troubles and also to help you identify and control where possible the pests, diseases and disorders which attack a wide range of plants. Specific problems of individual vegetables are dealt with in Chapter 2.

There is a vast array of enemies which can attack your plants, but it is not the intention of this book to frighten you. No matter how long you garden you will never see all of these troubles. The role of these pages is to take away the worry of an unidentified problem, and to provide you with the information to help you deal with the trouble.

Prevent trouble before it starts

● **Choose wisely.** Read about the crop before you buy — don't rely solely on the seed packet. Make sure that the variety is suitable for the chosen sowing date and don't leave your purchase to the last minute — many select varieties sell out early. Sometimes you will need to buy seedlings instead of seeds for transplanting into the plot. Choose carefully — the plants should be sturdy, free from disease and discoloration and there should be a good root system. Here you must leave it to the last minute because there should be as little delay as possible between buying and planting.

● **Prepare the ground properly.** Good drainage is vital — a plant in waterlogged soil is likely to succumb to root-rotting organisms. Follow the rules for the correct way to manure, feed and lime the soil — remember that vegetables vary widely in their soil needs. The time for digging is autumn or early winter if you plan to sow in spring.

● **Rotate your crops.** Soil troubles and nutrient deficiencies can build up if you grow the same crop year after year on the same site. Crop rotation is necessary for successful vegetable production — see the rules on page 4.

● **Avoid overcrowding.** Sow seed thinly. Thin the seedlings as soon after germination as practical — overcrowding leads to crippled plants and high disease risk. Do not leave thinnings on the plot — put them on the compost heap or burn if instructed to do so.

● **Get rid of weeds and rubbish.** Weeds rob the plants of water, food, space and light. Rubbish, like weeds, can be a breeding ground for pests and diseases.

● **Get rid of badly infected plants.** Do not leave sources of infection in the garden. Remove and destroy incurable plants when this book tells you to do so.

● **Feed and water correctly.** Some plant troubles are due to incorrect feeding and soil moisture problems. Use a balanced fertilizer containing nitrogen, phosphates and potash — follow the instructions. Never let the roots get dry but daily sprinklings instead of a good soaking may do more harm than good.

Deal with trouble as soon as you can

● **Remember that prevention is now more important than it used to be.** At the end of the last century there was a wide range of pesticides in the shops. There were insecticides for soil- and many above-ground pests and there were fungicides for blights, mildews etc. Some of these were systemic products, which went inside the plant to protect it. But most of these sprays have gone — phrases like 'chemical control is no longer available' appear quite regularly in the Troubles pages in Chapter 2. For this reason the cultural methods to prevent problems are now very important.

● **Spray when necessary.** Inspect the plants regularly and at the first sign of trouble look up the cause in the appropriate section of this book. Once you have put a name to the problem, act quickly — some pests and diseases can be checked quite easily if treated promptly, but may be difficult or impossible to control if left to get out of hand.

There are a few simple rules to ensure effective, safe and economical pest control. Read the label carefully and make sure that the product is recommended for the plants you wish to spray. Follow the instructions.

Try to pick a day when the weather is neither sunny nor windy and apply a fine forceful spray until both sides of the leaves are covered and the liquid has just started to run off. After spraying, wash out equipment and wash hands and face. Store packs in a safe place and do not keep unlabelled or illegible bottles or boxes. Never decant pesticides into old lemonade bottles etc.

Correct timing is important. Insecticides are normally applied at the first sign of attack. Systemic products go inside the sap stream and protect parts not reached by the spray. Fungicides usually work as protectants and so they need to be applied before trouble appears.

Some problems (red spider mite, whitefly, diseases, etc) need repeated spraying. Once again follow the instructions on the label. Finally, choose a product with a suitable harvesting interval — during the picking season choose a chemical with a 0–2 day interval between spraying and gathering.

GENERAL PESTS & DISEASES

APHID

The weakening effect of greenfly and blackfly on leaves and shoots is obvious. There are, however, other damaging results. Sticky honeydew is deposited, and the sooty moulds which grow on it are unsightly and block the leaf pores. Even worse is the danger of virus infection, as aphids are the prime carriers. For these reasons aphids should be tackled quickly. Spray with thiacloprid or insecticidal soap. Read the label for crop restrictions.

CATS

Cats often choose seed beds for toilet purposes, and usually avoid their own gardens. This is a difficult problem — it is worth trying a cat repellent dust or spray where cats are a nuisance.

EARWIG

The leaves of beetroots, parsnips and carrots may be skeletonized by this pest. Spray with pyrethrins when they are first noticed.

BIRDS

Birds are a joy in the garden and most of them do no harm. A few species, however, are a serious nuisance to seeds, seedlings and some mature crops, and netting is necessary.

SOIL PESTS
GROUP 1: Controlled by chemicals

There are various ways of tackling slugs — metaldehyde pellets, beer-filled saucers, sharp grit barriers, ferric phosphate baits and so on. Unfortunately, there are no longer any chemicals available for controlling the other soil pests — it is necessary to rely on cultural methods.

SLUGS & SNAILS

YES

Extremely troublesome pests especially in wet weather. Seedlings may be killed; leaves, stems and roots of older plants are damaged. Look for the tell-tale slime trails.

LEATHERJACKET

NO

Dark grey grubs, about 3 cm (1 in.) long. Most active in light soils and wet weather. Stems are attacked, lower leaves devoured. Root crops are tunnelled.

MILLEPEDE

NO

Pink or black grubs which curl up when disturbed. They attack underground parts of plants, often extending areas damaged by other pests. Most troublesome under cool, damp conditions. Not easy to control.

WOODLICE

NO

Hard-coated pests found in greenhouses. Seedlings and young plants are attacked. They hide during the day.

SOIL PESTS
GROUP 2:
Controlled by nematode-based insecticides

These products contain living organisms rather than chemicals. Inside the package there are millions of microscopic nematodes (eelworms) which kill the larvae of several common soil pests. Cabbage root fly, vine weevil, leatherjacket, as well as cutworm and chafer grub are all vulnerable. This non-chemical approach appeals to the environmentally-minded, but it does not work when the temperature falls below 10ºC (50°F) and the shelf-life is quite short.

CUTWORM

Fat grey or brown caterpillars, 3–5 cm (1½–2 in.) long. They live near the surface and eat young plants at ground level. Stems are often severed.

CHAFER GRUB

Large curved grubs, over 3 cm (1 in.) long. They feed throughout the year on roots and are often a serious pest in newly broken-up grassland.

DAMPING OFF

Germinating seedlings can be attacked by the damping off fungi, withering and blackening at the base before toppling over. Indoors use sterilized compost, sow thinly, water carefully, ventilate properly and provide adequate light. Outdoors avoid sowing in cold wet soil, sow thinly and do not overwater. If the disease does occur remove the affected seedlings immediately and water remainder with Cheshunt Compound.

GENERAL DISORDERS

Some vegetable troubles attack a single or small group of crops — examples are potato blight, carrot fly and pea moth. Other problems can attack a wide range of plants and these are the general disorders (described on this page) and general pests and diseases (see page 157).

WIND

Wind is often ignored as a danger, yet a cold east wind in spring can kill in the same way as frost. More frequently the effect is the browning of leaf margins. Another damaging effect is wind rock, which can lead to rotting of the roots.

FROST

A severe late frost will kill half-hardy vegetables. The shoots of asparagus and potatoes are blackened, but healthy shoots appear after the frosts have passed. The general symptoms of moderate damage are yellow patches or marginal browning of the leaves. The basic rule is to avoid sowing or planting before the recommended time unless you can provide protection. If your garden is on a sloping site, open part of the lower boundary to air movement so as to prevent the creation of a 'frost pocket'.

TOO LITTLE WATER

The first sign is a dull leaf colour, and this is followed by wilting of the foliage. Discoloration becomes more pronounced and growth is checked. Lettuces become leathery, roots turn woody and some plants run to seed. Flowers and young fruit may drop off. If water shortage continues, leaves turn brown and fall, and the plant dies. Avoid trouble by incorporating organic matter, by watering thoroughly and by mulching.

TOO MUCH WATER

Waterlogging affects the plant in two ways. Root development is crippled by the shortage of air in the soil. The root system becomes shallow, and also ineffective as the root hairs die. Leaves often turn pale and growth is stunted. The second serious effect is the stimulation of root-rotting diseases. Good drainage is therefore essential, and this calls for thorough autumn digging. Incorporate plenty of organic matter into heavy soil — the correct timing for humus addition depends on the crop being grown.

HEAVY RAIN FOLLOWING DROUGHT

The outer skin of many vegetables hardens under drought conditions, and when heavy rain or watering takes place the sudden increase in growth stretches and then splits the skin. This results in the splitting of tomatoes, potatoes and roots. Avoid by watering before the soil dries out.

TOO LITTLE PLANT FOOD

The major plant foods are nitrogen, phosphates and potash, and a vigorous crop acts as a heavy drain on the soil's resources. Nitrogen shortage leads to stunted growth, pale leaves and occasional red discoloration. Potash shortage leads to poor disease resistance, marginal leaf scorch, and produce with poor cooking and keeping qualities. Before sowing or planting apply a complete fertilizer, such as Grow-more fertilizer, containing all the major nutrients.

Apply one or more dressings to the growing plants. Backward vegetables are helped by spraying dilute liquid fertilizer over the leaves.

SHADE

In a small garden deep shade may be the major problem. Straggling soft growth is produced and the leaves tend to be small. Such plants are prone to attack by pests and diseases. Grow leaf and root types rather than fruit and pod vegetables.

TRACE ELEMENT SHORTAGE

Vegetables often show deficiency symptoms such as yellowing between the veins and leaf scorch. The most important trace elements are magnesium, manganese, iron, molybdenum and boron. Make sure the soil is well supplied with compost or manure. If your soil is known to have a trace element deficiency problem, undoubtedly the best answer is to water the ground early in the season with a sequestered trace element product which will supply the minor nutrients needed by the plants.

TOO LITTLE ORGANIC MATTER

The soil must be in good heart and this calls for liberal amounts of organic matter. Not all materials are suitable; peat may increase aeration and water retention but the need is for an active source of humus. Good garden compost and well-rotted manure are ideal. Timing is all-important — look up individual crops in this book for details.

CHAPTER 10
VEGETABLE & HERB INDEX

Acknowledgements

Over the years many people have helped in the production of the various editions of the Vegetable & Herb Expert, and their invaluable contribution is once again acknowledged here.

Some of these individuals and organisations have helped once again in this latest edition. Tyrone and Linda McGlinchey (Garden World Images) have used their photographic skill and large collection to supply many of the photographs. My long-suffering PA Gill Jackson has once again been a tower of strength. The repro skills of Ian Harris (Spot-On) and the support of the Transworld team led by Larry Finlay have once again been invaluable.

Many new vegetables are described and illustrated in this latest edition, and thanks are due to Tracy Collacott (Mr Fothergill's), Marilyn Keen (Thompson & Morgan), photographs supplied by Photoshot, Pam Richardson and Edyta Majcher (Marshalls) and Francijn Suermondt (Suttons Seeds). A special word of thanks goes to Tony Ward, Tracy Palmer and Liz Humpoletz of Kings Seeds for their information and photographs.

Authors need many things to produce a series like the Experts — information, artwork, photographic images and so on, but they also need encouragement and belief in their work. Here I owe a debt of gratitude to Tom Weldon (CEO Penguin Random House UK).